Class, Gender and Migration

Using a gender-sensitive political economy approach, this book analyzes the emergence of new migration patterns between Central Mexico and the East Coast of the United States in the last decades of the twentieth century, and return migration during and after the global economic crisis of 2007.

Based on ethnographic research carried out over a decade, details of the lives of women and men from two rural communities reveal how neoliberal economic restructuring led to the deterioration of livelihoods starting in the 1980s. Similar restructuring processes in the United States opened up opportunities for Mexican workers to labor in US industries that relied heavily on undocumented workers to sustain their profits and grow. When the Great Recession hit, in the context of increasingly restrictive immigration policies, some immigrants were more likely to return to Mexico than others. This longitudinal study demonstrates how the interconnections among class and gender are key to understanding who stayed and who returned to Mexico during and after the global economic crisis. Through these case studies, the authors comment more widely on how neoliberalism has affected the livelihoods and aspirations of the working classes.

This book will be of key interest to scholars, students and practitioners in migration studies, gender studies/politics, and more broadly to international relations, anthropology, development studies, and human geography.

María Eugenia D'Aubeterre Buznego is Professor of Anthropology in the Social Science and Humanities Institute of the Benemérita Universidad Autónoma de Puebla, Mexico.

Alison Elizabeth Lee is Associate Professor in the Department of Anthropology at the Universidad de las Américas Puebla, Mexico.

María Leticia Rivermar Pérez is Professor of Anthropology in the Social Science and Humanities Institute of the Benemérita Universidad Autónoma de Puebla, Mexico.

Gender in a Global/Local World

Series Editors: Jane Parpart, *University of Massachusetts Boston, USA,*
Marianne Marchand, *Universidad de las Américas Puebla, Mexico, and*
Rirhandu Mageza-Barthel, *University of Kassel, Germany.*

Gender in a Global/Local World critically explores the uneven and often contradictory ways in which global processes and local identities come together. Much has been and is being written about globalization and responses to it but rarely from a critical, historical, gendered perspective. Yet, these processes are profoundly gendered albeit in different ways in particular contexts and times. The changes in social, cultural, economic and political institutions and practices alter the conditions under which women and men make and remake their lives. New spaces have been created – economic, political, social – and previously silent voices are being heard. North-South dichotomies are being undermined as increasing numbers of people and communities are exposed to international processes through migration, travel, and communication, even as marginalization and poverty intensify for many in all parts of the world. The series features monographs and collections which explore the tensions in a 'global/local world', and includes contributions from all disciplines in recognition that no single approach can capture these complex processes.

Recent titles in the series include:

Mobilizing Transnational Gender Politics in Post-Genocide Rwanda
Rirhandu Mageza-Barthel

Women, Gender, Remittances and Development in the Global South
Edited by Ton van Naerssen, Lothar Smith, Tine Davids and Marianne H. Marchand

Gender Transitions Along Borders
Marlene Solís

Rethinking Silence, Voice and Agency in Contested Gendered Terrains
Beyond the Binary
Edited by Jane L. Parpart and Swati Parashar

Gender and Island Communities
Edited by Firouz Gaini and Helene Pristed Nielsen

Class, Gender and Migration
Return Flows between Mexico and the United States in Times of Crisis
María Eugenia D'Aubeterre Buznego, Alison Elizabeth Lee and María Leticia Rivermar Pérez

Post-Apartheid Same-Sex Sexualities
Restless Identities in Literary and Visual Culture
Andy Carolin

For more information about this series, please visit: https://www.routledge.com/Gender-in-a-GlobalLocal-World/book-series/GENDERLOCAL

Class, Gender and Migration
Return Flows between Mexico and the United States in Times of Crisis

María Eugenia D'Aubeterre Buznego,
Alison Elizabeth Lee and
María Leticia Rivermar Pérez

LONDON AND NEW YORK

First published 2020
by Routledge
2 Park Square, Milton Park, Abingdon, Oxon OX14 4RN

and by Routledge
52 Vanderbilt Avenue, New York, NY 10017

Routledge is an imprint of the Taylor & Francis Group, an informa business

© 2020 María Eugenia D'Aubeterre Buznego, Alison Elizabeth Lee and María Leticia Rivermar Pérez

The right of María Eugenia D'Aubeterre Buznego, Alison Elizabeth Lee and María Leticia Rivermar Pérez to be identified as authors of this work has been asserted by them in accordance with sections 77 and 78 of the Copyright, Designs and Patents Act 1988.

All rights reserved. No part of this book may be reprinted or reproduced or utilized in any form or by any electronic, mechanical, or other means, now known or hereafter invented, including photocopying and recording, or in any information storage or retrieval system, without permission in writing from the publishers.

Trademark notice: Product or corporate names may be trademarks or registered trademarks, and are used only for identification and explanation without intent to infringe.

British Library Cataloguing-in-Publication Data
A catalogue record for this book is available from the British Library

Library of Congress Cataloging-in-Publication Data

A catalog record has been requested for this book

ISBN: 978-1-138-31894-6 (hbk)
ISBN: 978-0-367-52098-4 (pbk)
ISBN: 978-0-429-45419-6 (ebk)

DOI: 10.4324/9780429454196

Typeset in Times New Roman

For Pahuatecos/as and Zapotitecos/as here and there
For Enrique, who waited for Maru each night
For Alison's family, Ciro, Alexa, Annika and Mom
For Vale, Lety's daughter

Contents

List of figures		viii
List of tables		ix
Acknowledgments		x
1	Understanding accelerated and return migration in Central Mexico: migration, class and gender	1
2	Rural Central Mexico and the East Coast of the United States: articulating surplus labor and restructured economies	25
3	Disarticulation of agriculture, transition to a service economy in the Sierra Norte of Puebla and accelerated migration to the *Nuevo* New South	60
4	"I was motivated to do everything": undocumented "entrepreneurs of the self" in New York	84
5	Deceleration of migration and the selectivity of return migration in the Northern Sierra of Puebla	108
6	"In Zapotitlán, we won't have to pay for so many things": the Great Recession, return migration and social reproduction	132
7	Economic crisis and the social reproduction of Mexican transnational working classes	156
	Index	172

Figures

2.1	Map of Puebla	28
2.2	First international migration: Pahuatlán and Zapotitlán	47
2.3	Zapotitlán: first international migration by gender	47
2.4	Pahuatlán: first international migration by gender	48
2.5	Return migration: Pahuatlán and Zapotitlán	50

Tables

2.1 Pahuatlán: economically active population by sector 31
2.2 Zapotitlán: economically active population by sector 34
2.3 Migration profile 49

Acknowledgments

We thank the Pahuatecos/as and Zapotitecos/as who graciously received us in Mexico and the United States, welcoming us into their homes and sharing their experiences with us. Without their trust, good humor and faith in us, we would not have been able to complete this project. We would also like to acknowledge Pahuatlán and Zapotitlán's municipal authorities for providing official permission to conduct research.

We are especially thankful to Leigh Binford, Professor Emeritus of the City University of New York, for developing the research protocol and securing funding (August 2010 to March 2014) from the Mexican National Science and Technology Council (CONACYT) for the project that forms the basis of this book (CV-22008-01-001022222). Leigh left Puebla in 2010 and invited María Eugenia to assume the role of principal investigator of the project. She, in turn, invited María Leticia and Alison to collaborate. Leigh gave generously of his time during the duration of the project. He provided an initial statistical analysis, wrote two chapters for edited volumes published in Spanish (one with Nancy Churchill as co-author), and commented on drafts of the majority of the chapters contained in this volume. We are grateful for his guidance and entrusting us to work with and build off of his initial ideas.

There are a number of research assistants who helped during various phases of the project. We especially thank Christian Pacheco, Antonio Morfin, Mario Macias, Karla Buenrostro, Elías Galindo, Desiree Otero, Luis Fernando Gutiérrez, Armando Carrera, Diana Villegas, Rocío Osorno, Montserrat Pérez, Selene Rosales, Andrea Leal, and Emanuel Huerta for their help. Thanks to José Luis Aranda for assistance with quantitative analysis, to Aimée Valckx Gutiérrez for translating two chapters and Nereo Zamitiz for help with the map and figures.

We are grateful for the series editors, Jane Parpart, Rirhandu Mageza-Barthel and, in particular, Marianne Marchand, who provided invaluable encouragement and guidance throughout the project. We thank our publisher at Routledge, Andrew Taylor, and editorial assistants Sophie Iddamalgoda and Jessica Holmes for their attention to the manuscript.

Alison would like to give special thanks to Cuca, Guille, Toño, Angelica, Julio, Pedro, Eulogio, Rosa, Ángeles, Guille, Sofia, Lorenza, Eulogia, Judith, Gladys and their partners and children for providing unwavering support throughout the more than 15 years of working in Zapotitlán. Nothing would have been possible without your help. There are dozens more people who helped in big and small ways. Thank you to all of you.

Alison acknowledges support from the Universidad de las Américas Puebla (UDLAP) for a course release during various semesters for research and writing and a semester sabbatical in Spring 2019 to complete the manuscript. A special thanks to Ana Aguirre, Enrique Ajuria, Guy Emerson, Tim Knab, and Marianne Marchand for their collegiality, mentorship and humor. An UDLAP-Cambridge University mobility grant allowed Alison to be a visiting researcher at the Centre for Latin American Studies at Cambridge in 2019. Thanks to Sarah Radcliffe, Pedro Mendes and Felipe Hernández for their warm welcome, kindness and conversation. Mia Gray and her family graciously hosted Alison in their home during the stay.

Alison's research has been deeply shaped by countless exchanges with mentors, colleagues and friends. A heartfelt thanks is due to the members of her doctoral committee, Tom Patterson, the late Michael Kearney and Carlos Vélez-Ibáñez. Their exemplary scholarship, kind mentorship and constant encouragement made a lasting impression. Arturo Gómez-Pompa provided guidance, support for fieldwork and introductions to researchers in Mexico. Andrea Kaus gave good advice and helped navigate the ups and downs of graduate school. Patricia Dávila Aranda and Rafael Lira Saade kindly invited Alison to work as a volunteer research assistant on an ethnobotanical project in Zapotitlán in the late 1990s. Thanks to Martin, Memo, Claudia, Vicente and the other student research assistants for their patience and introduction to Zapotitlán and fieldwork.

A number of scholars have provided Alison with important insights, guidance and advice over the years. Their generosity is much appreciated: Mike Agar, Wendy Ashmore, Leigh Binford, Nancy Churchill, Maria Cruz-Torres, Tine Davids, Jill De Zapien, Christine Gailey, Alyshia Galvez, Carrie Furman Glover, Josiah Heyman, Harlan Koff, Lisa Koops, Ricardo Macip, Carmen Maganda, Daniel Martinez, Konane Martinez, Carole Nagengast, Cecilia Rosales, Samantha Sabo, Jeremy Slack, Travis Stanton, Gaku Tsuda, Alayne Unterberger, Scott Whiteford and Kristin Yarris.

Harlan Koff, at the University of Luxembourg, and Tine Davids, at Radboud University, graciously invited Alison to present an earlier draft of Chapter 6 to students and colleagues who provided insightful comments. Scott Whiteford, Jill De Zapien and Cecilia Rosales reached out and introduced Alison to Jeremy Slack, Daniel Martinez and Samantha Sabo who shared generously of their knowledge about the violence on the US–Mexico border and were excellent co-authors. Jeaqueline Flores, Mario Macias and Kristin Yarris graciously read drafts of several chapters of the book and provided helpful feedback; Lisa Koops provided constant guidance and encouragement during the writing process; Ilana Dzuba and Antonia Kirkland offered friendship during fieldwork in New York and beyond.

Initial fieldwork in Zapotitlán and New York City was conducted as part of Alison's dissertation (2003–2005) and forms the basis for Chapter 4. She thanks

Alba Guevara, Laura Bautista, Raquel Carrillo, Judith Peralta, Arely Hidalgo and Celina Barragan, students from Zapotitlán, who assisted with the application of a survey. Alison acknowledges support from the Fulbright-Hays Dissertation Research Abroad Program, the National Science Foundation, the University of California Institute for Mexico and the United States (UCMEXUS) and the University of California Office of the President Pacific Rim Research Program. Initial analysis of this data was completed while Alison was a visiting fellow at the Center for US-Mexican Studies (USMEX) and the Center for Comparative Immigration Studies at the University of California, San Diego, during the 2005–2006 academic year.

María Eugenia D'Aubeterre Buznego and María Leticia Rivermar Pérez are grateful for the support of Drs. Agustín Grajales Porras and Francisco Manuel Vélez Pliego, successive directors (2007–2019) of the Social Science and Humanities Institute (ICSyH) of the Benemérita Universidad Autónoma de Puebla (BUAP), María Eugenia's and Leticia's academic affiliation. The Vice rector of Research and Graduate Studies provided funds for fieldwork in Pahuatlán for six years. María Eugenia and Leticia are grateful for the funds provided by the Program of Professional Development from the Secretary of Public Education that allowed them to conduct fieldwork in Durham in 2013 and 2014. ICSyH graciously gave permission to use sections of three edited volumes in this book.

Dr. Regina Cortina, of New York University, inspired María Eugenia and Leticia's first incursions into Pahuatecan migration to North Carolina in 2007. At this time, Dr. Cortina directed a project at the University of Chapel Hill studying the presence of indigenous children from the Sierra Norte of Puebla in elementary schools in Durham. She put María Eugenia and Leticia in contact with Dr. Emilio Parrado of the University of Pennsylvania, who was directing a project at Duke University examining reproductive and sexual health among Mexican immigrants residing in North Carolina. María Eugenia and Leticia conducted in-depth interviews for this project with men and women who had returned to Pahuatlán from North Carolina. The honoraria they received from this collaborative effort allowed them to continue fieldwork and establish the contacts with return migrants and their families. This initial research resulted in the publication of *Migraciones en la huasteca poblana. Actores y procesos* (*Migrations in the Huasteca Poblana: Actors and Processes*) published by the BUAP and ICSyH in 2011. María Eugenia and Leticia thank Dr. Hernán Salas, of the Institute of Anthropological Research (IIA) of the Universidad Autónoma de México (UNAM) for organizing the book's presentation at the IIA's Book Fair. The book was presented by Drs. Ana Bella Pérez, Martha Patricia Castañeda and Antonio Fuentes.

María Eugenia and Leticia thank Dr. Elaine Levine, of the Center for the Research of North America at the UNAM, for her review of the book *¿Todos vuelven? Migración acelerada, crisis de la economía estadounidense y retorno en cuatro localidades del estado de Puebla, México* (*Everyone Returns? Accelerated Migration, United States Economic Crisis and Return in Four Towns in* *the State of Puebla*), published by the ICSyH, BUAP and UDLAP in 2014. Dr. Francisco Vélez, of the ICSyH, and Sergio Cortés, of the Department of Economics in the BUAP, presented the book in an academic forum in the ICSyH.

A group of Pahuatecos/as deserve special mention. The late Doña Inocencia Aparicio, her son Rafael Lechuga, Don Enrique Franco, the late Don Raúl López and Doña Claudia Barreda with whom María Eugenia and Leticia shared pleasant visits and long conversations about Pahuatlán in the 1940s, 50s and 60s. They helped identify important milestones in the region's recent history, especially with respect to the Bracero Program, a little-studied topic in this area. We owe them an enormous debt. Gabriela Soto and Erika Vázquez were María Eugenia and Leticia's gatekeepers, opening the doors to a cohort of young return migrants from North Carolina and others who did not migrate yet lived through the profound transformations that unfolded in Pahuatlán due to the accelerated migration to the United States in recent decades. San Pablito Pahuatlán attracted our attention because accelerated migration began in this town in the 1980s. There, the hospitality, warmth and assistance of the Santos brothers and their families, along with Amalia Santos and her mother, the late Doña Vicky, provided contacts on the other side of the border. Lucero Vargas connected us with his daughters, Lucero and Artemisa, residents of Durham, who were key in constructing a network that provided María Eugenia and Leticia with support during fieldwork in that city in the Southeastern United States.

1 Understanding accelerated and return migration in Central Mexico
Migration, class and gender

Right now, there is no difference. With the crisis, we are living the same situation, because there is no work here, in Mexico. It is the same there, no work. There is another disadvantage, in a sentimental sense, in an emotional sense, because when you are there, you are thinking, how is my family? Have the children eaten? Is my wife O.K.?

(Marco Antonio, Pahuatlán)

I want to start a business. I have it in mind. But, like I told you, these are moments of crisis. The only thing left to think about is how to make it through the day.

(Ernesto, Zapotitlán Salinas, Puebla[1])

Beginning in 2008, the United States fell into its worst financial crisis since the 1930s. The rapid rise in Mexican migration to the US over the previous decades appeared poised to reverse. Some speculated that the Great Recession would force millions of Mexicans back to their country of origin, a remarkable change for one of the largest economic migration flows in the world. Growing anti-immigrant hostility during and after the crisis along with the soaring numbers of deportations of Mexicans and the exile of their US-born children to Mexico added hundreds of thousands to return flows. By the early 2010s, census data indicated that migration between the two countries had reached net zero and perhaps below: flows leaving Mexico for the US were equal or smaller to those returning to Mexico (Gonzalez-Barrera, 2015; Passel, Cohn, & Gonzalez-Barrera, 2012).

Although the "massive" exodus of Mexicans fleeing the recession never materialized, migratory patterns changed significantly. Some argued that a permanent decline in the need for immigrant labor resulting from the economic crises stemmed flows to the US (Levine, 2015; Villarreal, 2014). The increasing risks to crossing the militarized border may have also deterred some migrants from attempting to cross into the United States (Lee, 2018). Further, households felt the economic impacts of the recession. After a decade of robust growth, remittances fell significantly, recovering to their pre-recession levels in 2016,

DOI: 10.4324/9780429454196-1

years after the official end of the crisis (BBVA Bancomer & CONAPO, 2018, p. 126).

This book examines the causes, dynamics and impacts of changing migration flows on Mexico and the United States. However, instead of focusing on migration and return as objects of study in and of themselves, our ethnographically and historically grounded research compels us to view them as symptoms of deeper structural changes on both sides of the US-Mexican border. We step back from the singular shock of the Great Recession and cast our gaze over the last several decades of the twentieth century to analyze several waves of economic and social restructuring that transformed livelihood conditions in Mexico and led to the expulsion of labor from rural localities. Similar processes in the United States remade accumulation regimes on the East Coast now sustained by new waves of immigrant labor from Mexico and Central America.

Through close examination and contextualization of the lives of rural women and men from Central Mexico, we situate the return flow of migrants in a broader historical process of the supply of Mexican labor to US labor markets sustaining the accumulation of capital in different regions for more than 100 years. We explore the process of class formation among rural migrants who insert into labor markets in the US East Coast, exploring the construction of subjectivities shaped by class, gender and US immigration status. From this perspective, migration and return appear as defining features of a new global proletariat.

Our research focuses on return migration in Pahuatlán de Valle and Zapotitlán Salinas in the Mexican state of Puebla located, respectively, in the Northern Sierra and in the southeastern region of the state (see map, Figure 2.1). Based on our long-term ethnographic and survey research in the two towns, we examine the emergence and acceleration of migration followed by the contention of northward flows and increasing returns. We share Bourgois and Schonberg's vision (2009, p. 318) of the importance of focusing on long-term processes through ethnography with the intent to understand "… the way structural forces operate at the individual everyday level." Gavin Smith argues that our task as ethnographers involves interpreting people's self-understanding "in a particular historical setting, so that characterizing those settings in quite rigorous terms becomes an important component of our work" (1999, p. 9). Using a framework he calls "historical realism," Smith challenges ethnographers to "find means of investing interpretative methods with ways of comprehending power and the situatedness of cultural perception." This perspective also "calls for the need to embed social practices and relationships in the historical shaping of institutions …" (1999, p. 11). Inspired by these perspectives, in our fieldwork we follow families' trajectories and transitions, including the families of returned migrants, those that never migrated to the US as well as those who remained in the US.

The book addresses the following three objectives:

1. Analyze the disarticulation of the conditions of reproduction of rural populations in Central Mexico and the insertion of recent undocumented migration

flows that manifested a heterogeneous demographic profile in terms of gender and age.
2. Document how gender and class articulate to shape emergent migration flows from Puebla to the United States that began in the late 1980s and accelerated in the 1990s in the context of neoliberal deregulation and the articulation of the economies of both countries through free trade agreements and the supply of cheap labor.
3. Identify how gender and class articulate in conflicts and negotiations related to migrants' returns and reinsertion in Mexico in the context of prolonged stay in the US and limited circulation between the two countries due to the US economic and financial crisis, border militarization and heightened interior enforcement.

Accelerated migration as a symptom of restructuring of both the Mexican and US economies

Although Mexican migration to the United States began in the late nineteenth century, migration flows originating in the Central Mexican state of Puebla date only to the mid-twentieth century (Rivera Sánchez, 2004; Smith, 2006). In Pahuatlán, for example, a few dozen men participated in the Bracero Program (1942–1964), a guest worker program supplying the United States with male agricultural laborers during and after World War II. However, there was no continuity between these men's experiences and the massive, undocumented flow of the last 30 years, which is the focus of this book. In Zapotitlán, international migration emerged in the 1980s. Once the flows from these two towns began in the 1980s, they expanded rapidly, incorporating wide swaths of the local population in a short period. Following Binford (2003) we refer to this pattern as accelerated migration, whereby a significant proportion of the adult population (about 30 percent) acquired international migration experience within two decades, from the 1980s to the early 2000s. A symptom of the economic restructuring of both the Mexican and US economies (Binford, 2004), accelerated migration characterized the migration flows of perhaps hundreds of towns in Central Mexico. In contrast, in Western Mexico, the traditional sending area of migrants to the United States since the nineteenth century, the growth of migration flows occurred at a much slower pace (Massey, Goldring, & Durand, 1994).[2]

Restructuring and massive, accelerated flows contributed to the unprecedented growth of Mexican migration to the US in the last third of the twentieth century (Massey, Durand, & Malone, 2002; Zúñiga & Hernández-León, 2005). From 1990 to 2000, the migrant flow increased ten times in comparison with previous decades (Arroyo-Alejandre, Berumen-Sandoval, & Rodríguez-Álvarez, 2010; BBVA Bancomer & CONAPO, 2014). The number of children born in the US from Mexican-origin families equaled the number of new immigrants from Mexico: 4.7 million. From 2000 to 2010, the number of children born in the US from Mexican-origin parents reached 7.2 million, surpassing the 4.2 million new immigrants (Pew Hispanic Center, 2011). This changing socio-demographic profile of migrants was the result of the overlap of three patterns of mobility: the continuing migration of unaccompanied men, the growing number of families moving together and, finally, unaccompanied, single women who migrated to the United States and started families there.

The vast majority of Pahuatecos/as and Zapotitecos/as incorporated into these massive flows to the United States at the end of the twentieth century. They, along with millions of other Mexican migrants, arrived to the United States after the passage of the Immigration Reform and Control Act (IRCA) of 1986, an amnesty that legalized 2.3 million Mexicans who had worked and resided continuously in the country since 1982.[3] Without legal status, this workforce labored and lived in the shadows (Chavez, 1992); their condition of deportability (De Genova, 2002) cheapened their labor-power. Their "illegality," disposability and vulnerability shaped their labor market insertion and their minimal conditions of social reproduction.

Accelerated migration was sustained by the relatively porous border that prevailed until the mid-2000s, although thousands of people lost their lives in the extreme conditions of the border region (Cornelius, 2001). Up until the mid-2000s, migrants apprehended by the border patrol were deported back to the border area in Mexico and re-attempted clandestine crossings until they successfully crossed and reached their destination in the US interior (Espenshade, 1994). In this process, which Heyman termed "the voluntary-departure complex," the US appeared to be making an impressive number of arrests, protecting the country from illegal "aliens" while continuing to import Mexican labor on a large scale (Heyman, 1995). The porosity also allowed for circular migration at intervals of several years among undocumented adults and children.

After accelerated migration: conceptualizing return

After the mid-2000s, accelerated migration came to an end, a consequence of the financial crisis, and, to a lesser extent, the growing criminalization of immigration. As return migration to Mexico increased, scholars—ourselves included—grappled with conceptualizing return. Neoclassical or social network theories developed to explain the growth of migration flows in a context of migrant circularity could not be applied in reverse. They were no longer useful in the political economic context that presented itself in the first decades of the twenty-first century (Sandoval & Zúñiga, 2016). Our historical-structural framework to migration and return migration takes as a starting point the idea that short-cycle migration in Puebla develops within the context of the configuration of an economic block—the North American Free Trade Agreement (NAFTA)—that required the development of a labor force that corresponded to new forms of accumulation in the hemisphere. The changes in accumulation regimes, detailed in Chapter 2, created mobility patterns between Mexico and the United States that selected for particular individuals in Mexico. In the context of the economic crisis and slow recovery, return migration was also selective. In order to understand selectivity, the conditions of social reproduction on both sides of the border form a central part of our analysis.

Social reproduction refers to the "social capacities" of sustaining biological processes of life and meaningful social connections that are essential to households and broader communities (Fraser, 2016). Most often performed by women, social reproductive labor unfolds in the domestic and family sphere—often as unpaid labor—and also in the state, market and community (Bhattacharya, 2017; Glenn, 2004; Kofman & Raghuram, 2015). Capital accumulation requires social reproduction; however, "capitalism's orientation to unlimited accumulation tends to destabilize the very processes of social reproduction on which it relies" (Fraser, 2016, p. 100). As we will see, the tensions and conflicts that traverse migrants' lives are manifestations of the destabilization of social reproduction.

This historical-structural-social reproductive approach to the short migration cycle that developed in Puebla departs from the dominant theoretical perspectives on migration and return. To review these theories in depth is beyond the scope of this chapter. We refer readers to overviews written by others (Cassarino, 2004; Sandoval & Zúñiga, 2016). A central idea in our reflection is that return migration is configured by the cycle of reproduction of capital and the restrictive immigration policies adopted by receiving states when foreign workers become temporarily superfluous in the context of economic contraction in destination countries or when capital abandons "old" sites installing itself in "new" sites looking to increase profits. With Wolf (1982), we claim that, in its process of re-creation, capital differentiates classes from one another. Within this continuous movement of the genesis of new sources of the production of surplus and of renewed recession, not only are property owners differentiated and made to compete for slots among the "winners" and "losers," the labor force also passes from full employment to underemployment to unemployed. By studying the cycles of migration-return we observe the formation and reconfiguration of these working classes and gender relations.

Our analysis considers the specific circumstances of migration flows, destinations and processes of accumulation in distinct regions. It distinguishes different modalities of displacement and focuses on the household demographic cycle, considering its composition and the migratory status of its members, among other intervening factors in what we could call "the selectivity of staying-returning." Structural aspects linked to production are just as important to take into account as those aspects related to the reproduction of life conditions of workers and their families.

This theoretical positioning moves us away from neoclassical perspectives that champion the individual, rational decision maker and social network theories that place a heavy burden on the dynamics of personal relationships to explain population movements. It also distances us from transnational scholarship that attempts to overcome the distinction between migration and return by highlighting the fluidity of mobility and the adaptation capacity of "actors."

Transnationalism often celebrates the "cultural versatility" and the "bifocality" of lives constructed in a community that goes beyond the geopolitical borders of a single nation-state, rejecting the fixity of categories such as "here" and "there" (Basch, Glick Schiller, & Szanton-Blanc, 1994; Vertovec, 2004).

A fair amount of research on return migration has attempted to explain how it relates to development in origin countries (for example, Cassarino, 2004). Scholars highlight how migrants' human and social capital as well as remittances spur development. The emphasis on how migrants will be agents of development in origin countries places a terrible burden on individuals who assumed the costs of migration to look for better opportunities, often in destination countries systematically discriminating against them and deporting them "home."[4] Comparing return of Mexican migrants between 2000 and 2010, Gandini, Lozano-Ascencio, and Gaspar (2015) warned that the more recent return flows are predominantly made up of men of productive and reproductive age who are looking to reinsert in the labor market. Their plans are frustrated as they confront the deterioration of economic conditions in Mexico with respect to the previous decade. We agree with scholars such as Canterbury (2012) and Delgado Wise, Márquez Covarrubias, and Rodríguez Ramírez (2009) that this somber panorama challenges studies celebrating migrants as agents of change through the transfer of their social and human capital. These perspectives hide deep structural causes of migration and the contributions immigrants make to the growth of the economy in destination countries. At the same time, they mask the human and material costs that migration represents for sending countries (Delgado Wise et al., 2009).

We decenter this developmentalist perspective by drawing on literature that poses the possibility of classes permanently excluded from the capitalist system and permanently surplus to capital (Li, 2009; Smith, 2011). Most research on return does not take into account geographic, economic and social factors that permit the successful transfer of human and social capital. Some recent studies consider the obstacles, the lack of local opportunities, the precarity of employment, the administrative traps to enroll children in education and health systems that returnees and their families face, especially children born in the United States or taken there at young ages (Mestries, 2013; Zúñiga & Hamann, 2015). These difficulties multiply in the cases of individuals forcibly returned through deportation, a process of dispossession that fractures families through its chaotic and disorienting effects (Boehm, 2016; see also Caldwell, 2019).

Research about return tends not to be longitudinal nor does it consider the intersection of class and gender. It lends little attention to the changes in the conditions of reproduction of workers' households (see Boehm, 2012, 2016; Rothstein, 2016 for important exceptions). We assume that return is only one milestone in the migratory cycle and does not necessarily mark the end of a cycle, although the migratory flows that we analyzed lost circularity and migrants' prolonged stays in the United States tended toward settlement. Along with Pascual de Sans (1983, p. 72), we agree that return is not a triumphal moment, or a return to an original state. Rather, we conceive migration-return within the framework of the production of surplus populations, an expression of the processes of proletarization, semi-proletarization and deproletarization (Cook & Binford, 1990) and disposability (Wright, 2006), linked to a new model of accumulation. That is, impoverished subsistence producers are not drawn into waged work to then forever leave behind their subsistence production. There is no unilinear trajectory for the world's surplus populations. Rather, they may be drawn into temporary, seasonal or part-time work and expelled in continuous yet uncertain cycles of varying duration and undetermined frequency (Li, 2009).

The analysis moves beyond methodological nationalism (Glick Schiller, Basch, & Blanc-Szanton, 1992) to consider transnational class formation, a unit of analysis more suitable to the mobile working classes that we examine. We seek to understand how these classes are essential to the reproduction of capitalism in the neoliberal era (Canterbury, 2012). We position ourselves alongside other historical-structural approaches to migration. Instead of the agency of actors, we show the limited parameters within which subjects can act. While this may be viewed as "pessimistic," our long-term ethnographic research suggests the need to consider seriously and systematically the precarious position of rural Poblanos after almost four decades of neoliberal capitalism.

New global migratory order and new formations of class and gender

A new global migratory order (Kofman & Raghuram, 2015) emerged alongside the transformation from Fordist to flexible accumulation (Harvey, 1989; Oso & Ribas-Mateos, 2013). This transition was bound to multiple, old and new forms of dispossession and expropriation on a global scale and carried out to a rhythm without precedent (Fraser, 2016). This process entailed reconfigured stratifications and a reclassification of populations, giving rise to new class inequalities and racial, ethnic and gender hierarchies.

Historically, capital has resolved its demand for the workforce locally. Over the last few decades, capital resolved this problem through the ever-intensifying process of decentralizing and disarticulating production chains and relocating its operations in different places across the globe. In the first instance, without leaving "home," capital goes without some workers and incorporates others in the space of production as well as in the different sites of reproduction. In this way, for example, some categories of men are replaced with certain categories of women, adults are replaced by youth, some racial minorities are replaced by others (Glenn, 2004). The availability of unwaged work, in "undeveloped" countries as well as in the metropole, allows capital to abandon those production areas where the workforce has become too expensive and undermine the power that workers had previously gained through struggle. When capital cannot escape to the "Third World," it has opened its doors to women, minorities and youth in the metropoles or immigrants from the "Third World" (Federici, 2018, p. 39).

The background to this incessant replacement is the proliferation of relative surplus populations (Smith, 2018). Diverse forms of violence in different scales usually precede this proliferation: military interventions, expulsions, natural resource destruction and climate emergencies in regions with deficient infrastructure that convert into "natural" disasters given the carelessness of neglectful governments. Further, structural adjustment policies intervene in the production of these populations to impoverish elderly dependents and the women charged with their care who also play a central role in the reproduction of the fit. In brief, we are talking about the disarticulations of the conditions that make life possible, processes of expropriation that occur in migrants' origin and destination countries. In multiple zones of the planet, deindustrialization and relocalization of capital translated into the destruction of hundreds of thousands of formal jobs and the proliferation of jobs that require maximum flexibility, a distinctive characteristic of the new global proletariat.

In this way, capital decentralized and relocated, making alliances with national governments, accommodating locals and elites eager for investments to strengthen, relaunch and revalue their businesses. Capital takes advantage of cheap, abundant labor and the promising zones of comparative advantages that offer commodities, water, landscapes and exoticized bodies used in tourist and sex industries (Pini & Leach, 2011). Globalization and the accompanying hypermobility of capital always require the state's support (Jean Comaroff & Comaroff, 2001) through fiscal exemptions, work visas, economic treaties, etc. and, in current times, through supra-state actors that administer and classify populations and the promotion or the contention of the mobility of global workers (Kofman, 2014).

The selective absorption of certain segments of the population, whether definitive, cyclical or temporary (Li, 2009; Narotzky & Smith, 2006), modifies material and cultural forms of daily life and work (Carbonella & Kasmir, 2015). These transformations change the social relations of production and reproduction crystalized in the pre-existing formations of class, gender and race in one or another pole of these migratory circuits and stations. In the new global migratory regime, upon the destruction or reshaping of pre-existing relationships, who migrates, how and to where has been redefined. New circuits, legislation, agreements formulated in different scales of governance—local, regional, national, global—emerge. Institutions specialized in the subject and the management of recurrent conflicts (i.e., security, terrorism, xenophobia, humanitarian crises) appear to administer and regulate the mobility of populations, not without contradictions and unexpected effects. The borders and distinctions that separate the regularized and the irregular, residents and temporary residents, asylum seekers, refugees and the deported tend to be tenuous and unstable (Kofman & Raghuram, 2015; Mezzadra & Neilson, 2013). Class and gender are fundamental theoretical coordinates for the understanding of the migration-return cycle of Central Mexico analyzed in this book. In the following sections, we will review the articulations among class, gender and migration.

Class

Despite a general tendency toward the abandonment of class as an analytical category in the social sciences, our analysis relies on a renewed notion of class, refashioned from lively debates about the need to conceptualize growing economic and social inequalities. Class "[…] is not just the bundle of contractual relations between capitalist employers and employees in a particular place, or the distributional inequalities between people […]." (Kalb, 2015, p. 14). Following Kalb, we adopt a vision of class "[…] to perceive and make sense of the interlocking exploitative, extractive, uneven and constantly transformative relational antagonisms that fire up and refuel the variable engines of global capitalism" (Kalb, 2015, p. 14). Instead of a self-contained, subaltern group, with a secure financial base and group consciousness, we use the idea of class to analyze diffuse and disorganized sociocultural formations shaped by multiple forms of dispossession.

The virtual absence of class in the study of contemporary migrations is in line with the changing socio-demographic of the labor force given the nature of the increasingly global division of labor. The diversity of the labor force seemingly justifies the growing scholarly emphasis in the dimensions of gender, sexuality, race and ethnicity (Archer, 2013). However, class hides in the folds of the costumes of a carnivalesque parade of identities, sexual preferences and artistic manifestations; traditions that inundate the "de-classed" post-industrial, global cities of the world (Carbonella & Kasmir, 2014). The academy did not escape this fascination, and, in excess, declared the disappearance of class and its replacement by "consumers," as Sennett observed (2000). Further, as a result of the changes in employment and technology, class was not considered a relevant identity nor a political category (Pini & Leach, 2011, p. 4).

Historical analysis, however, reveals the diverse subjects constituting the proletariat since its emergence. Smith (2002), for example, reflects on the exceptional figure of the nineteenth-century Manchester worker. Confronting this selective narrative that dominated social theory, Smith discusses the overwhelming diversity of subjects that lived straddling the condition between waged and unwaged workers: men, women and children hidden in factories, workshops and small-scale commerce, often paid in kind with the waste from the production line or the fields. The "male breadwinner" is not the only one who has supplied the kitchen table of the working class. Diffuse profiles of class are a generalized condition of contemporary life. With respect to this idea, van der Linden (2014, pp. 73, 75) alludes to the process of formation of a "multiform" proletariat in diverse regions of the planet, which he refers to as "the extended or subaltern working class" (van der Linden, 2014, p. 78).

We follow the suggestive proposal of Wolf (1982) to study these new classes of global workers as situated within relations of connection and mutual constitution, with the intent to make visible relations that are completely absorbed by capital—salaried workers—and others, more elusive and hidden—laborers outside of the salary relationship. The adscription of one or another exploitative relationship dominated or not by the salary form is frequently part of the class experience of these workers and can differ from one generation to another. These situations call for historical ethnography (Carbonella & Kasmir, 2014; Narotzky & Smith, 2006). Class has been defined by the relationship between owners of the means of production and non-owners, with the latter obligated to sell their labor-power to sustain the former who generate wealth from the appropriation of labor-power (Kalb, 2015, p. 1). However, when we discuss class, we are not referring to a homogeneous subject, nor one always bound to a shared political project and a class identity configured opposite capital. The current moment of capitalist restructuring and dispossession is producing a range of new labor relations.

The malleability of class is a historical project (Thompson, 1963). Instability and disorganization characterize the new working classes of post-Fordism (Carbonella & Kasmir, 2015, p. 49) that feed the migratory circuits studied in this book. These clarifications are extremely pertinent if we consider that the migrant subject is not a worker interpellated by his or her position opposite capital, but rather for his or her illegibility as a subject stripped of citizenship, situated in a gray zone, and saturated with the neoliberal mantra of self-making and remaking through individual solutions. The contradictory narratives of these experiences among immigrant workers appear throughout the book.

While in destination countries immigrants occupy the lowest positions in the hierarchy and labor in undesirable jobs (Amorós, 2008; Sassen, 2003), in origin countries these same immigrants can convert themselves into property owners and experience ascending class mobility that manifests in consumption underpinning distinctions and distorted class identities. Referring to this ambivalence, Kofman and Raghuram (2015), among others, emphasize that class continues to be key to understanding migration because flows are stratified in diverse ways. Class must be understood not only through work as exploitation, but also in its multidimensional character as it articulates with structures such as gender, sexuality, race and ethnicity. The idea of the "contradictory mobility of class," adopted by these scholars, is a useful analytical tool in the understanding of the configuration of subjectivities forged in the heat of the instability of life and work conditions of unauthorized immigrant workers who incorporated in the 1990s into the accelerated migratory flows from Central Mexico documented in this text.

The subjectivity of these workers forms through contradictions. On one side, the constant fear of deportation and uncertainty that surrounds their lives intervenes in this process. On the other hand, the imperative of hyper-mobility in the desire to "make one's self" also plays a role. In this sense, Catarino and Morokvasic cited in Oso and Ribas-Mateos (2013, p. 8) argue that

> ... migrants are more anxious to 'settle in mobility' than to settle in the receiving country. Mobility therefore becomes an alternative to migration; migrants attempt to remain mobile in order to guarantee the standard of living in their country of origin.

However, this longed-for hyper-mobility is an asset distributed unequally according to class, gender and race. Further, as we alluded to earlier, the rigidity of borders that criminalize unskilled, undocumented workers cheapening their labor-power restrict hyper-mobility and circulation.

Accumulation and reclassification of the population are processes that, historically, have gone hand in hand (Federici, 2006). We can understand the segmentation of class to be "... a result of this reclassification of waged and unwaged work, thereby simultaneously intensifying gender, ethnic and racial hierarchies" (Carbonella & Kasmir, 2015, p. 47). In sum, it is pertinent to resume the project of African American feminists to dismantle "[...] the singularity that some have too often attributed to "the proletariat" privileged White, male, industrial workers and their political institutions at the expense of a wider, heterogeneous social formation" (Carbonella & Kasmir, 2015, p. 50).

Under Fordism, the term "migrant" became synonymous with male worker on account of the numerical superiority of men in Mexican migration flows, an imbalance shaped by the demand for workers in laying railroad tracks, agro-industry and construction; that is, "men's work" (Hondagneu-Sotelo & Cranford, 2006). In the case of Mexican migration to the United States, in many towns the term *bracero* (arms) refers to migrants, an appropriation dating to the Bracero Program (1942–1964).

In spite of women's increased participation in migrant flows in the last several decades, a phenomenon that corresponds to the transition toward flexible accumulation, it is important to identify an androcentric bias manifest in the unsurpassed difficulty to understand women as part of the working class. It is assumed that men are salaried workers, that is, economic subjects. However, until the 1980s, female migrants appeared represented in the figure of wives reunified with their families and caretakers of the home (Hondagneu-Sotelo, 2001; Oso & Ribas-Mateos, 2013). This representation relegated female immigrants to the familiar sphere of reproduction, ignoring their experiences of class by hiding the fact that they also generated income from their work in domestic spaces although not necessarily in exchange for a salary (Leach, 1996). "In much leftist analysis women are assumed to be without class, as these theorists often remain unable to see the category 'working class' unless it is marked white and male" (Bettie, 2003, p. 33). Bettie alludes to the hyper-masculinization of the category of class, on the one hand, and, on the other, the hyper-feminization of the category of gender. This gender-blind imaginary of class is a consequence not only of the failure of social theory to conceptualize women as class subjects, but also discourse that exaggerates maternity and the care of others as primordial aspects of women's identities.

Gender

The configuration of emergent migratory profiles and patterns shaped by gender provoked the attention of feminists beginning in the 1970s with the desire to confront the persistent absence of women in the census registers, the androcentric biases that prevailed in this area of study and normative assumptions (Hondagneu-Sotelo & Cranford, 2006; Kofman & Raghuram, 2015; Verschuur, 2013). To this end, they developed innovative approaches to the issue based in critical feminist theory that explored the power relations articulated to the expansion of capitalism in its neoliberal phase after 1989 (Nagar et al., in Silvey, 2004, p. 1).

In the 1980s, in the context of the post-structural turn and the interest in identity, the female migrant subject of the Global South that deserved recognition based on her differences emerged. Bastia (2014, p. 240), following Fraser (2007), argues that in the "Post-socialist era" the struggles for equal redistribution were subordinated to the struggles for cultural recognition. Accordingly, in the 1990s, impregnated by neoliberal multiculturalism and the hegemony of difference opposite inequality, the articulation between gender and class in migration studies was blurred. Structural feminist theories conceptualized gender not only as a characteristic of individuals, but also of collectives, institutions and structures. Some scholars believe that the most promising structural theories are those that include agency and micro-level processes as well as the structural hierarchies that are the focus of their analysis. That is, they are interested in recognition without underestimating redistribution (Fraser, 2007). These frameworks make it possible to understand gender as an individual status that shapes lived experience and as a characteristic of social institutions that are themselves gendered. Key institutions such as labor markets are gendered, continually reified, and transformed through the micro-social interactions among gendered individuals (Nawyn, Reosti, & Gjokaj, 2009, p. 175). From this position, it is possible to think of gender as a dimension that shapes migratory processes.

Even at the end of the 1970s, women were not considered active agents in migration contexts; they were considered dependents, especially as recipients and administrators of remittances sent by men that circulated between one country and another. It was a given that these resources would act as a lever for development of origin countries and migrant sending communities, and that women would play a fundamental role in the administration of these assets. Analyzing the changing definitions of the field, Hondagneu-Sotelo (2011) maintains that, since the 1990s, research shifted from "the study of female migrants" to the analysis of "migration as a gendered process." That is, she postulates that gender is a constitutive element of migration. This perspective transcends the limited analysis of gender at the individual level of difference between women and men and the statistical register of the unequal participation in migratory flows, to understand how gender shapes a variety of practices, identities and institutions implicated in migration. Along these lines, Nawyn et al. (2009, p. 175) analyze the function of four gendered institutions and processes that precipitate migration: (1) global labor markets; (2) family and care work; (3) social networks; and (4) violence.

Conceiving gender as a structure permits the recognition of its manifestation in the global restructuring of work, in the selectivity of migratory flows (asylum policies, family reunification, recruiting temporary workers, special visa programs, classification of migrant populations, etc.) and in the configuration of "men's" and "women's" labor markets (Archer, 2013; Hondagneu-Sotelo, 2011; Kofman & Raghuram, 2015). Gender also shapes corresponding migratory patterns and "gender regimes" (Connell, 1987) that develop in origin and destination places, giving way to flexible and transitory domestic arrangements throughout the household demographic cycle (Arias & Mummert, 1987; Cravey, 2003). In recent years, the contributions of feminist geographers (Cravey, 2003; Nawyn et al., 2009; Smith & Winders, 2007; Wright, 2006) emphasize space and highlight the importance of considering the contemporary mobility of women articulated in different scales (global, national, regional, communal, familiar) with a historical dimension. These perspectives overcome the tendency of localism and the ethnographic present of anthropology in the study of those "at the margins" allowing for an analysis that transcends national space and takes into account global processes. In sum, we agree with Nawyn et al. (2009, pp. 175–176) that the integration of gender into the analysis of international migration has been slow. It began with the idea of gender as an individual attribute, a static category determined at birth. Many approaches incorporated gender in the analysis of migration to simply complete the operation "add women and stir" and obtain a new result, reducing the empirical analysis of gender to the individual level of difference. Moreover, the authors conclude that research has paid less attention to how gender shapes the decision to migrate and the opportunities to migrate.

In the horizon of a globalizing, neoliberal and financialized capitalism (Fraser, 2014), of the privatization of wellbeing and the proliferation of the service sector, the number of women who incorporated into internal and international migratory flows increased in absolute and relative terms. Their mobility linked the Global South and the Global North, heterogeneous regions with significant economic, social and cultural differences. The term "feminization of migration" refers to this tendency. Some scholars (Kofman & Raghuram, 2015; Oso & Ribas-Mateos, 2013; Sassen, 2002) point out that, instead of a drastic increase in female migrants across the world, the term refers to their greater visibility in official reports and academic research.[5] It also alludes to the feminization of work (Amorós, 2008; Cobo, 2005), where women are removable and replaceable pieces in the chains of production that can be assembled, disassembled and relocated with greater ease. We agree with Verschuur (2013, p. 150) that although migration has increased among men and women, the "feminization of migration" refers to the process of women migrating as independent workers.

> The focus has thus shifted from being on women as only mothers, to women as mainly 'workers,' to now being on women as subjects, where productive and reproductive activities and the social relations they need to carry them out are intertwined. Links are made between the new international division of labour in the global capitalist system, the cultural agency of the subjects and their concrete social struggles.
>
> (Verschuur, 2013, p. 150)

Various processes lie behind the massive incorporation of women in deregulated labor markets (Ehrenreich & Hochschild, 2003; Marchand & Runyan, 2011). These include the reduction of state investment, the privatization of the provision of care, and the lowering of the cost of production by way of the cheapening of living labor through the adoption of subcontracting, part-time and other redesigned forms of super-exploitation. Further, a host of skills historically constructed as "feminine" under the patriarchal regimen of the sexual division of labor, have become standard requisites for workers in a number of occupations. In the context of service sector expansion, linguistic, affective and interpersonal skills, demanded especially from women, have become particularly relevant (Mezzadra & Neilson, 2013, p. 104). The prejudices concerning the marginal contribution of women to the national and domestic economies, the complementariness of their salaries and their erratic and transitory insertion in work underlie these processes (Castañeda & Zavella, 2007; Kofman, 2014; Lee-Treweek, 2012; Pessar, 2005). Ethnographic research focusing on the households of these new global workers challenge these prejudices. Our analysis unfolds in that direction.

Ethnographic research in Mexico and the United States

This ethnographic, longitudinal study draws on participant observation, interviews and surveys conducted during numerous fieldwork seasons in rural Puebla and in the United States. Long-term engagement with Pahuatecos/as and Zapotitecos/as allowed us to forge enduring relationships with men, women and children who invited us into their homes on both sides of the border to share their experiences. Our multi-sited, transnational research allowed us to situate these experiences in broader economic and political transformations that were dramatically changing life circumstances for people in Mexico and the United States (Marcus, 1995). Qualitative work allowed us to unveil the tensions and inequalities that underlie the formation of this new class of precarious workers, both in relation to capital, as well as outside the production process itself, taking into account the intersection of this process to social reproduction. Our strategy allowed us to follow the course of our subjects' movement across borders, not only in a single direction in terms of migration-settlement from South to North, but also the instability and contingency of migrants' "illegal" insertion.

While the book draws primarily on research conducted since 2010, we had extensive research experience in Pahuatlán and Zapotitlán before the economic crisis. This allowed us to identify patterns of change over time in mobility and the meaning and experience of migration for a region that became highly dependent upon transnational migration beginning in the 1990s. For example, Lee conducted fieldwork in Zapotitlán for 20 consecutive months from January 2003 to August 2004 and in New York City from September 2004 to February 2005 as part of her doctoral thesis research. In the village, she lived with two families whose male head of household was in the United States at the time of the research, participating in special events such as religious rituals, school presentations, civic ceremonies and birthday parties as well as mundane, routine activities such as meal preparation, taking children to school and food and clothing shopping. She conducted interviews mostly in people's homes. In New York, she talked with people at the restaurants where they worked (usually during the lull between lunch and dinner) and conducted interviews in migrants' apartments or in restaurants and delis.

From 2007 to 2010, D'Aubeterre and Rivermar conducted an investigation exploring migration and education in Pahuatlán. This project started after Regina Cortina, a researcher at the University of North Carolina Chapel Hill, shared her research with them. She had observed a rapid increase in the number of children from rural and indigenous towns in the municipality of Pahuatlán attending public schools in Durham. In the 2007–2008 school year, D'Aubeterre and Rivermar surveyed students in their final year of middle school and high school in four towns in the municipality: Pahuatlán de Valle (the county seat), Atla and Xolotla (Nahua towns) and San Pablito Pahuatlán (an Otomí town).[6] They conducted focus groups with students, teachers and school administrators to investigate the repercussions of migration in the education trajectories of youth. Their research provided valuable information about household composition, remittances from North Carolina since the 1990s and the migration and occupation of parents in Mexico and the United States. Additionally, it allowed D'Aubeterre and Rivermar to identify the configuration of a migration habitus during three generations, beginning with the Bracero Program (1942–1964).

After the crisis unfolded, D'Aubeterre, Rivermar and Lee initiated fieldwork to collect the data upon which this book is primarily based. We drew on our understanding of regional conditions and reactivated our local contacts to carry out three phases of fieldwork between 2010 and 2014. In the first phase, we applied a modified version of the Mexican Migration Project's (MMP) Ethnosurvey to 135 households in Pahuatlán de Valle (20 percent sample) between August and December 2010 and 170 households (a 25 percent sample) in Zapotitlán in May and June 2011.[7] On account of our long-standing relationships with numerous contacts in the communities, the refusal rate in both villages was less than 5 percent. In fact, conversations often extended well beyond the questions in the survey. Our research team—consisting of our undergraduate and graduate students—made many brief notes in the margins to follow up on later. In both villages, we used a systematic, spatial sampling method, administering the Ethnosurvey to every fourth (Zapotitlán) or fifth (Pahuatlán) house on each housing block (Schensul & LeCompte, 2013, pp. 301–302). The Ethnosurvey provided basic demographic information about each member of the household along with their migration and work histories. The data was coded and analyzed using SPSS software; it forms the basis for the graphs and tables in the book.

In the second phase (February and April 2011 in Pahuatlán; May and June 2011 in Zapotitlán), we identified individuals (27 in Pahuatlán; 29 in Zapotitlán) who returned between 2007 and 2010 from the results of the Ethnosurvey and through participant observation in the communities. With these return migrants we conducted semi-structured interviews in returnees' homes with questions designed to elicit information about employment and work conditions prior to migration, border crossings, working and living conditions in the United States, family relations and remittances, reasons for return and future plans. Interviews lasted about an hour. However, some extended to two hours or more, as interviewees discussed some topics in greater depth than we had initially anticipated.

Finally, in the third phase we identified 16 households in each community to follow for an 18-month period to identify and assess the strategies employed to weather the economic crisis. The households were divided into four categories and four households were assigned to each: (1) households with at least one voluntary return migrant; (2) households with at least one forced return migrant; (3) households with at least one migrant still in the United States; and (4) households with no active migrants in the past five years. Group 4 was a control group, since we believed that households in this group would be the least affected by changes in migration experience due to the economic crisis because they were not dependent upon remittances. We developed the interview schedules, which varied slightly because of the different household situations, based on the responses we received in Phase 2 of the research and other insights we gained as the research project developed and matured. We scheduled six interviews with household members (usually the female and/or male heads of households) at approximately three-month intervals. Inspired by Hirsch's methodology (2003), we believed that revisiting the same households over time would increase rapport and make it easier for household members to discuss sensitive issues with researchers. This was largely the case. Research assistants transcribed digitally recorded interviews, and these were coded using NVivo software.

Although not initially contemplated in the original study design, Mario Macias, a member of the research team, conducted several interviews with Zapotitecos/as in New York during July and August 2014. D'Aubeterre and Rivermar conducted research in Durham among Pahuatecos/as they had originally met in Mexico and their extended family members in October 2013 and May 2014. They interviewed members of 13 households, three of them linked by kinship. Furthermore, they informally interviewed acquaintances of these groups, or people close to them, during casual encounters in shops and family-owned restaurants. This strategy allowed them to collect information about everyday life, work, routines and social environments and to observe consumption practices and visit businesses owned by Pahuatecos, which have flourished in Durham.

Structure of the book

Chapter 2 examines the conditions from which migratory flows to the United States emerged and accelerated in Puebla during the last two decades of the twentieth century. We consider both the impact in rural life of economic restructuring undertaken by the Mexican state beginning in the 1980s and the deindustrialization of the US economy. The analysis captures the articulation, through the supply of cheap and precarious labor, between the state of Puebla, in Central Mexico, and New York City and the Raleigh-Durham corridor in North Carolina. Statistical information from our survey data allows us to compare Zapotitlán Salinas and Pahuatlán de Valle in terms of the emergence and acceleration of migration and staying in the US or returning to Mexico.

In Chapter 3 we examine the connection of two distant and unequal territories through the provision of cheap and undocumented workers from Pahuatlán in the Northern Sierra of Puebla, in the center of Mexico, to North Carolina, in the *Nuevo* New South, during the last four decades.[8] International migration, initiated in the 1980s, spread throughout the municipality. Between 1995 and 2007, we identify a short-cycle accelerated migration that developed in the region and the combination of the traditional model of individual and cyclic mobility of male predominance, a "military model of migration," with a mobility scheme of single women or with dependents, which overlaps with the migration of young couples with or without children. We document the conditions that underlie the production of the mother-worker-undocumented migrant subject, whose experience of mobility between two countries is intertwined with precarious work, overexploitation and gender inequality. We describe and explain the tensions that traverse a type of binational domestic arrangement in which children born in Mexico and North Carolina were raised in the United States, a formation that has grown during the last three decades in the context of the decrease of circular migration.

Through the accounts of women and men situated along different points of the transnational circuit, Chapter 4 traces villagers' experiences with changing political economic regimes in Zapotitlán and New York City. Some Zapotitecos/as responded to the economic crisis in Mexico of the 1980s by migrating to the United States, while others, especially women, increased their participation in waged work, particularly in recently established garment factories that produced for domestic and international markets. As the crisis deepened in the 1990s with the devaluation of the peso, migration accelerated, and many more men and women migrated north to work in New York's expanding service sector. Providing for families' basic needs appeared to be "progress" against the backdrop of worsening conditions of social reproduction in Mexico. As low-waged service workers Zapotitecos/as struggled to meet the basic social reproductive requirements for their families. While the women's labor and migration trajectories demonstrate the ways in which flexibility, precarity and disposability traverse their working lives on both sides of the border, they also show how they have moved through different class positions with respect to the wage relationship. In the final section, the discussion turns to the forms of discipline that traverse gendered, "illegal" subjects laboring as restaurant workers, domestics and garment factory workers. We note how collective class struggle is abandoned and replaced by a repressive individualism in which problems are internalized and can only be resolved by the individual working on him or herself.

18 *Migration, class and gender*

In the following two chapters we discuss migration and return in the aftermath of the Great Recession and increasingly restrictive border policies. Chapter 5 analyzes the containment of an accelerated migratory flow to North Carolina in the preceding and subsequent years of the so-called great crisis, the selectivity of staying-returning and the context in which these men and women went back to the municipality of Pahuatlán, in the center of Mexico. We consider two modalities identified in this municipality: the return of the worker without dependents and the family or joint return migration. We resume the proposals of several feminist authors who analyze the relationship between migration and the crisis in social reproduction, as one of the three elements, along with the crises of ecology and finance, contributing to the contemporary crises of global capitalism. From our perspective, Pahuatecan migrants' return expresses at the macro level the oscillating relationship of surplus populations with the capital, trapped in the sway between full employment, underemployment and unemployment in both sides of the border. At the macro and the micro level, the return entails destabilization and reorganization of reproductive processes in binational households integrated by citizens wielding uneven rights, impeding—or at times facilitating—the mobility of the group, or of some of its members, between both countries.

Chapter 6 explores how the Great Recession and increasingly restrictive immigration policies shaped the selectivity of return to Zapotitlán. Which migrants returned to Zapotitlán and why? Into what social and economic context did return migrants insert? Which migrants re-migrated to the United States and why? How did migrants and others make sense of these changes? The multiple links among productive and social reproductive labor inform migrants' complex decision-making processes about mobility. Gender traverses decisions about mobility because most social reproductive tasks are assigned to women in rural Mexico and among female migrants in the United States. Furthermore, state interventions into social reproduction shaped the quality of life that migrants could expect to enjoy in the United States or Mexico that in turn had an effect on decisions about migration and return. In Mexico, we explore how the state intervened in local development through a tourism project and how these processes played out in Zapotitecos/as' lives. Credit from different types of financial institutions mediated productive and reproductive relations in Zapotitlán, often in the form of microloans to stimulate women's "empowerment." Finally, we analyze how remittances played a role in social reproduction after the Great Recession.

Chapter 7 summarizes our main findings by drawing together the experiences of Pahuatecos/as and Zapotitecos/as through whose lives we can detect broader economic and political transformations. We will also discuss the implications of our research for the study of migration-return, class and gender particularly through the lens of social reproduction. We believe our contributions have not only something to say about the Mexican migrant lives we analyze here, but about the lives of working-class people in many places where a blind faith in so-called "free trade" for four decades has crushed livelihoods and aspirations.

Notes

1. We use pseudonyms for all research participants throughout the book.
2. For an overview of the emergence of migratory flows from Western Mexico see Arias and Mummert, 1987; Bustamante, 1997; Durand, 1994; López Castro and Pardo Galván, 1988. For migratory patterns in southwestern Puebla see Macías and Herrera, 1997; Rivera Sánchez, 2007; Smith, 2006.
3. Although the law criminalized the hiring of undocumented workers, sanctions against employers were rarely enforced. Nor did IRCA reduce the demand for Mexican labor as lawmakers had intended. Instead, migration flows grew rapidly over the next two decades (Gaspar Olvera, 2012; Massey et al., 2002).
4. For a critique of this idea in the European context with failed asylum applicants, forced return and development potential in origin countries, see van Houte and Davids, 2008.
5. For example, Verschuur points out that

    [w]omen and men have always migrated. The circulation of people, even when it is not regulated or officially encouraged—except for very qualified migrants—is widespread. In 2010, the number of women migrants was estimated at 105 million and the number of male migrants was 109 million. Within 20 years, both numbers have increased by 38 per cent. Since 1975, the number of migrants has more than doubled.
    (Verschuur, 2013, p. 149)

6. Nahua and Otomí refer to groups that speak pre-Hispanic indigenous languages.
7. The Mexican Migration Project (MMP) is a binational research program that has tracked migration flows between Mexico and the United States since the 1980s. The MMP's Ethnosurvey is the key instrument used to collect information in hundreds of origin and destination localities in both countries. More information about the Mexican Migration Project and the Ethnosurvey is available at https://mmp.opr.princeton.edu/.
8. *Nuevo* New South refers to the profound transformation of the 11 states that make up the Southern region of the United States stemming from the increased presence of Latino populations from traditional areas of Latino settlement in the US or directly from Mexico and Central America (Furuseth & Smith, 2016; Mohl, 2003).

References

Amorós, C. (2008). Globalización y orden de género. In C. Amorós & A. de Miguel (Eds), *Teoría feminista: de la Ilustración a la globalización. De los debates sobre el género al multiculturalismo* (pp. 301–330). Madrid: Minerva Ediciones.

Archer, S. (2013). Cambios de paradigma en el pensamiento feminista de EU. *Mundo Siglo XXI, 9*(31), 11–26.

Arias, P., & Mummert, G. (1987). Familia, mercados de trabajo y migración en el centro-occidente de México. *Nueva Antropología. Revista de Ciencias Sociales, 32*, 105–128.

Arroyo-Alejandre, J., Berumen-Sandoval, S., & Rodríguez-Álvarez, D. (2010). Nuevas tendencias de largo plazo de la emigración de mexicanos a Estados Unidos y sus remesas. *Papeles de Poblacion, CIEAP/UAEM, 16*(63), 9–48.

Basch, L., Glick Schiller, N., & Szanton-Blanc, C. (1994). *Nations unbound: Transnational projects, postcolonial predicaments and deterritorialized nation-states*. Langhorne, PA: Gordon and Breach Science Publishers.

Bastia, T. (2014). Intersectionality, migration and development. *Progress in Development Studies, 14*(3), 237–248. https://doi.org/10.1177/1464993414521330.

BBVA Bancomer & CONAPO. (2014). *Yearbook of migration and remittances*. Mexico City: BBVA Bancomer and Consejo Nacional de Población.
BBVA Bancomer & CONAPO. (2018). *Yearbook of migration and remittances, Mexico*. Retrieved from www.bbvaresearch.com/wp-content/uploads/2018/09/1809_Anuario MigracionRemesas_2018.pdf.
Bettie, J. (2003). *Women without class: Girls, race, and identity*. Berkeley: University of California Press.
Bhattacharya, T. (2017). How not to skip class: Social reproduction of labor and the global working class. In T. Bhattacharya (Ed.), *Social reproduction theory: Remapping class, recentering oppression* (pp. 68–93). London: Pluto Press.
Binford, L. (2003). Migración acelerada entre Puebla y los Estados Unidos. In E. Masferrer, E. Díaz Brenis, & J. Mondragón Melo (Eds), *Etnografía del Estado de Puebla: Puebla Centro* (pp. 58–67). Ciudad de México: Gobierno del Estado de Puebla, Secretaría de Cultura.
Binford, L. (Ed.). (2004). *La economía política de la migración internacional en Puebla y Veracruz: Siete Estudios de Caso*. Puebla, México: Benemérita Universidad Autónoma de Puebla, Instituto de Ciencias Sociales y Humanidades.
Boehm, D. A. (2012). *Intimate migrations: Gender, family, and illegality among transnational Mexicans*. New York: New York University Press.
Boehm, D. A. (2016). *Returned: Going and coming in an age of deportation*. Oakland: University of California Press.
Bourgois, P., & Schonberg, J. (2009). Righteous dopefiend. *California Series in Public Anthropology*. Berkeley: University of California Press.
Bustamante, J. (1997). *Cruzar la línea. La migración de México a los Estados Unidos*. México City: Fondo de Cultura Económica.
Caldwell, B. C. (2019). *Deported Americans: Life after deportation to Mexico*. Durham: Duke University Press.
Canterbury, D. C. (2012). *Capital accumulation and migration*. Leiden: Koninklijke Brill NV.
Carbonella, A., & Kasmir, S. (2014). Introduction: Toward a global anthropology of labor. In A. Carbonella & S. Kasmir (Eds), *Blood and fire: Toward a global anthropology of labor* (pp. 1–29). New York: Berghahn Books.
Carbonella, A., & Kasmir, S. (2015). Dispossession, disorganization and the anthropology of labor. In J. G. Carrier & D. Kalb (Eds), *Anthropologies of class: Power, practice and inequality* (pp. 41–52). Cambridge: Cambridge University Press.
Cassarino, J. (2004). Theorising return migration: The conceptual approach to return migrants revisited. *International Journal on Multicultural Societies*, 6(2), 253–279.
Castañeda, X., & Zavella, P. (2007). Changing constructions of sexuality and risk: Migrant Mexican women farm workers in California. In D. Segura & P. Zavella (Eds), *Women and migration in the US–Mexico borderlands: A reader* (pp. 249–268). Durham: Duke University Press.
Chavez, L. (1992). *Shadowed lives: Undocumented immigrants in American society*. Ft. Worth, TX: Harcourt Brace Jovanovich College Publishers.
Cobo, R. (2005). Globalización y las nuevas servidumbres de las mujeres. In C. Amorós & A. de Miguel (Eds), *Teoría feminista: de la Ilustración a la Globalización*. Madrid: Minerva Ediciones.
Comaroff, Jean, & Comaroff, J. L. (2001). Millennial capitalism: First thoughts on a second coming. In J. Comaroff & J. L. Comaroff (Eds), *Millennial capitalism and the culture of Neoliberalism* (pp. 1–56). Durham: Duke University Press.

Connell, R. W. (1987). *Gender and power: Society, the person and sexual politics*. Stanford: Stanford University Press.
Cook, S., & Binford, L. (1990). *Obliging need: Rural petty industry in Mexican capitalism*. Austin: University of Texas Press.
Cornelius, W. A. (2001). Death at the border: Efficacy and unintended consequences of US immigration control policy. *Population and Development Review*, *27*(4), 661–685.
Cravey, A. J. (2003). Toque una Ranchera, por favor. *Antipode*, *35*(3), 603–621. https://doi.org/10.1111/1467-8330.00341.
De Genova, N. P. (2002). Migrant "illegality" and deportability in everyday life. *Annual Review of Anthropology*, *31*(1), 419–447. https://doi.org/10.1146/annurev.anthro.31.040402.085432.
Delgado Wise, R., Márquez Covarrubias, H., & Rodríguez Ramírez, H. (2009). Seis tesis para desmitificar el nexo entre migración y desarrollo. *Migración y Desarrollo*, *12*, 27–32.
Durand, J. (1994). *Más allá de la línea. Patrones migratorios entre México y Estados Unidos*. México DF: Consejo Nacional para la Cultura y las Artes.
Ehrenreich, B., & Hochschild, A. R. (2003). *Global woman: Nannies, maids and sex workers in the new economy*. New York: Metropolitan Books.
Espenshade, T. (1994). Does the threat of border apprehension deter undocumented US immigration? *Population and Development Review*, *20*(4), 871–892.
Federici, S. (2006). Prostitution and globalization: Notes on a feminist debate. In M. Davies & M. Ryner (Eds), *Poverty and the production of world politics: Unprotected workers in the global political economy* (pp. 113–136). London: Palgrave Macmillan.
Federici, S. (2018). *El patriarcado del salario. Críticas feministas al marxismo*. Madrid: Traficantes de Sueños.
Fraser, N. (2007). Feminist politics in the age of recognition: A two-dimensional approach to gender justice. *Studies in Social Justice*, *1*(1), 23–35.
Fraser, N. (2014). Behind Marx's hidden abode: For an expanded conception of capitalism. *New Left Review*, *86*, 55–72.
Fraser, N. (2016). Contradictions of capital and care. *New Left Review*, *100*, 99–117.
Furuseth, O. J., & Smith, H. A. (2016). From Winn-Dixie to Tiendas: The remaking of the New South. In O. J. Furuseth & H. A. Smith (Eds), *Latinos in the New South: Transformations of place* (pp. 1–17). London: Routledge.
Gandini, L., Lozano-Ascencio, F., & Gaspar, S. (2015). *El retorno en el nuevo escenario de la migración entre México y Estados Unidos*. México, DF: Consejo Nacional de Población (CONAPO).
Gaspar Olvera, S. (2012). Migración México-Estados Unidos en cifras (1990–2012). *Migración y Desarrollo*, *10*(18), 101–138.
Glenn, E. N. (2004). *Unequal freedom: How race and gender shaped American citizenship and labor*. Cambridge, MA: Harvard University Press.
Glick Schiller, N., Basch, L., & Blanc-Szanton, C. (1992). Transnationalism: A new analytic framework for understanding migration. *Annals of the New York Academy of Sciences*, *1*(1), 1–24.
Gonzalez-Barrera, A. (2015). *More Mexicans leaving than coming to the US*. Retrieved from www.pewhispanic.org/files/2015/11/2015-11-19_mexican-immigration__FINAL.pdf.
Harvey, D. (1989). *The condition of postmodernity: An enquiry into the origins of cultural change*. Oxford: Blackwell.

Heyman, J. (1995). Putting power in the anthropology of bureaucracy: The immigration and naturalization service at the Mexico–United States border. *Current Anthropology*, *36*(2), 261–287.

Hirsch, J. S. (2003). *A courtship after marriage: Sexuality and love in Mexican transnational families*. Berkeley: University of California Press.

Hondagneu-Sotelo, P. (2001). *Doméstica: Immigrant workers cleaning and caring in the shadows of affluence*. Berkeley: University of California Press.

Hondagneu-Sotelo, P. (2011). Gender and migration scholarship: An overview from a 21st century perspective. *Migraciones Internacionales*, *6*(1), 219–233.

Hondagneu-Sotelo, P., & Cranford, C. (2006). Gender and migration. In J. S. Chafetz (Ed.), *Handbook of sociology of gender* (pp. 105–126). New York: Springer Science and Business Media LLC.

Kalb, D. (2015). Introduction: Class and the new anthropological holism. In *Anthropologies of Class: Power, Practice and Inequality* (pp. 1–27). Cambridge: Cambridge University Press.

Kofman, E. (2014). Gendered migrations, social reproduction and the household in Europe. *Dialectical Anthropology*, *38*, 79–94.

Kofman, E., & Raghuram, P. (2015). *Gendered migrations and global social reproduction*. https://doi.org/10.1057/9781137510143.

Leach, B. (1996). "Working at home is easy for her": Industrial homework in contemporary Ontario. In S. Cole & L. Phillips (Eds), *Ethnographic feminisms: Essays in anthropology* (pp. 139–154). Ottawa: Carleton University Press.

Lee-Treweek, G. (2012). Managing "dirty" migrant identities: Migrant labour and the neutralisation of dirty work through "moral" group identity. In R. Simpson, N. Slutskaya, P. Lewis, & H. Höpfl (Eds), *Dirty work. Concepts and identities* (pp. 203–222). New York: Palgrave Macmillan.

Lee, A. (2018). US-Mexico border militarization and violence: Dispossession of undocumented laboring classes from Puebla. *Migraciones Internacionales*, *9*(35), 211–238.

Levine, E. (2015). Why did Mexico United-States migration begin to decrease in 2008? *Problemas del Desarrollo*, *46*(182), 1–15.

Li, T. M. (2009). To make live or let die? Rural dispossession and the protection of surplus populations. *Antipode*, *41*(S1), 66–93. https://doi.org/10.1111/j.1467-8330.2009.00717.x.

López Castro, G., & Pardo Galván, S. (1988). *Migración en el Occidente de México*. Zamora: El Colegio de Michoacán.

Macías, S., & Herrera, F. (1997). *Migración laboral internacional*. Puebla: Benemérita Universidad Autónoma de Puebla.

Marchand, M. H., & Runyan, A. S. (2011). *Gender and global restructuring: Sightings, sites and resistances* (2nd ed.). Abingdon: Routledge.

Marcus, G. E. (1995). Ethnography in/of the world system: The emergence of multi-sited ethnography. *Annual Review of Anthropology*, *24*, 95–117.

Massey, D. S., Durand, J., & Malone, N. (2002). *Beyond smoke and mirrors: Mexican immigration in an era of economic integration*. New York: Russell Sage Foundation.

Massey, D., Goldring, L., & Durand, J. (1994). Continuities in transnational migration: An analysis of nineteen Mexican communities. *American Journal of Sociology*, *99*, 1492–1533.

Mestries, F. (2013). Los migrantes de retorno ante un futuro incierto. *Sociológica*, *28*(78), 171–212. Retrieved from http://scielo.org.mx/pdf/soc/v28n78/v28n78a6.pdf

Mezzadra, S., & Neilson, B. (2013). *Border as method, or the multiplication of labor*. Durham: Duke University Press.

Mohl, R. A. (2003). Globalization, Latinization and the Nuevo New South. *Journal of American Ethnic History*, *22*(4), 31–66.
Narotzky, S., & Smith, G. (2006). *Immediate struggles: People, power and place in rural Spain*. Berkeley: University of California Press.
Nawyn, S. J., Reosti, A., & Gjokaj, L. (2009). Gender in motion: How gender precipitates international migration. *Advances in Gender Research*, *13*(3), 175–202. https://doi.org/10.1108/S1529-2126(2009)0000013011.
Oso, L., & Ribas-Mateos, N. (2013). An introduction to a global and development perspective: A focus on gender, migration and transnationalism. In L. Oso & N. Ribas-Mateos (Eds), *The International handbook on gender, migration and transnationalism: Global and development perspectives* (pp. 1–35). https://doi.org/10.4337/9781781951477.
Pascual de Sans, Á. (1983). Connotaciones ideológicas en el concepto de retorno de migrantes. *Papers: Revista de Sociología*, *77*, 61–71.
Passel, J., Cohn, D., & Gonzalez-Barrera, A. (2012). *Net migration from Mexico falls to zero—and perhaps less*. Retrieved from www.pewhispanic.org/2012/04/23/net-migration-from-mexico-falls-to-zero-and-perhaps-less/.
Pessar, P. (2005). *Women, gender, and international migration across and beyond the Americas: Inequalities and limited empowerment*. Retrieved from www.un.org/en/development/desa/population/events/pdf/expert/10/P08_PPessar.pdf.
Pew Hispanic Center. (2011). *The Mexican-American boom: Births overtake immigration*. Retrieved 12 September 2019, from www.pewresearch.org/hispanic/2011/07/14/the-mexican-american-boom-brbirths-overtake-immigration/.
Pini, B., & Leach, B. (Eds.). (2011). *Reshaping gender and class in rural spaces*. Farnham: Ashgate.
Rivera Sánchez, L. (2004). Expressions of identity and belonging: Mexican immigrants in New York. In J. Fox & G. Rivera-Salgado (Eds), *Indigenous Mexican migrants in the United States* (pp. 417–446). La Jolla: Center for US-Mexican Studies, Center for Comparative Immigration Studies, University of California, San Diego.
Rivera Sánchez, L. (2007). La formación y dinámica del circuito migratorio Mixteca-Nueva York-Mixteca: los trayectos internos e internacionales. *Norteamérica. Revista Académica del CISAN-UNAM*, *2*(1), 171–203. Retrieved from www.redalyc.org/html/1937/193715169007/.
Rothstein, F. A. (2016). *Mexicans on the move: Migration and return in rural Mexico*. https://doi.org/10.1057/9781137559944.0001.
Sandoval, R., & Zúñiga, V. (2016). ¿Quiénes están retornando de Estados Unidos a México? Una revisión crítica de la literatura reciente (2008–2015). *Mexican Studies/Estudios Mexicanos*, *32*(2), 328–356. https://doi.org/10.1525/msem.2016.32.2.328.328.
Sassen, S. (2002). Women's burden: Counter-geographies of globalization and the feminization of survival. *Nordic Journal of International Law*, *71*(2), 255–274. https://doi.org/10.1163/157181002761931378.
Sassen, S. (2003). Global cities and survival circuits. In B. Ehrenreich & A. R. Hochschild (Eds), *Global woman: Nannies, maids, and sex workers in the New Economy* (pp. 254–274). New York: Metropolitan Books.
Schensul, J. J., & LeCompte, M. D. (2013). *Essential ethnographic methods: A mixed methods approach*. Lanham, Maryland: AltaMira Press.
Sennett, R. (2000). *La corrosión del carácter. Las consecuencias personales del trabajo en el nuevo capitalismo*. Barcelona: Editorial Anagrama, S. A.
Silvey, R. (2004). Power, difference and mobility: Feminist advances in migration studies. *Progress in Human Geography*, *28*(4), 1–17.

Smith, G. (2011). Selective hegemony and beyond-populations with "no productive function": A framework for enquiry. *Identities: Global Studies in Culture and Power*, *18*, 2–38.
Smith, G. A. (1999). *Confronting the present: Towards a politically engaged anthropology*. Oxford: Berg.
Smith, G. A. (2002). Out of site: The horizons of collective identity. In W. Lem & B. Leach (Eds), *Culture, economy, power: Anthropology as critique, Anthropology as Praxis* (pp. 250–266). Albany: SUNY Press.
Smith, G. A. (2018). Elusive relations: Distant, intimate, and hostile. *Current Anthropology*, *59*(3), 247–267.
Smith, R. C. (2006). *Mexican New York: Transnational lives of new immigrants*. Berkeley and Los Angeles: University of California Press.
Smith, B. E., & Winders, J. (2007). We're here to stay: Economic restructuring, Latino migration and place-making in the South. *Transactions of the Institute of British Geographers*, *33*, 60–72.
Thompson, E. P. (1963). *The making of the English working class*. New York: Vintage Books.
van der Linden, M. (2014). Who is the working class? Wage earners and other labourers. In M. Atzeni (Ed.), *Workers and labour in a globalised capitalism: Contemporary themes and theoretical issues* (pp. 70–84). London: Palgrave Macmillan.
van Houte, M., & Davids, T. (2008). Development and return migration: From policy panacea to migrant perspective sustainability. *Third World Quarterly*, *29*(7), 1411–1429. https://doi.org/10.1080/01436590802386658.
Verschuur, C. (2013). Theoretical debates on social reproduction and care: The articulation between the domestic and the global economy. In L. Oso & N. Ribas-Mateos (Eds), *The international handbook on gender, migration and transnationalism: Global and development perspectives* (pp. 145–161). https://doi.org/10.4337/9781781951477.
Vertovec, S. (2004). Migrant transnationalism and modes of transformation. *International Migration Review*, *38*(3), 970–1001.
Villarreal, A. (2014). Explaining the decline in Mexico-US migration: The effect of the Great Recession. *Demography*, *51*(6), 2203–2228. https://doi.org/10.1007/s13524-014-0351-4.
Wolf, E. R. (1982). *Europe and the people without history*. Berkeley: University of California Press.
Wright, M. W. (2006). *Disposable women and other myths of global capitalism*. New York, NY: Routledge.
Zúñiga, V., & Hamann, E. T. (2015). Going to a home you have never been to: The return migration of Mexican and American-Mexican children. *Children's Geographies*, *13*(6), 643–655. https://doi.org/10.1080/14733285.2014.936364.
Zúñiga, V., & Hernández-León, R. (2005). *New destinations: Mexican immigration in the United States*. New York: Russell Sage Foundation.

2 Rural Central Mexico and the East Coast of the United States

Articulating surplus labor and restructured economies

Introduction

In this chapter, we discuss the conditions from which migratory flows to the United States emerged and accelerated in Puebla during the last two decades of the twentieth century. We consider both the impact in rural life of economic restructuring undertaken by the Mexican state beginning in the 1980s and the deindustrialization of the US economy. The analysis captures the articulation, through the supply of cheap and precarious labor, between the state of Puebla, in Central Mexico, and New York City and the Raleigh-Durham corridor in North Carolina. Statistical information from our survey data allows us to compare Zapotitlán Salinas and Pahuatlán de Valle in terms of the emergence and acceleration of migration and staying in the US or returning to Mexico.

We situate migration flows from Puebla to the United States with the disarticulation of rural Mexico, resulting from the progressive liberalization and reorientation of the Mexican economy toward the exterior.

> Mexico, for example, abandoned its already weakening protections of peasant and indigenous populations in the 1980s, in part under pressure from its neighbour to the north to adopt privatization and neoliberal practices in return for financial assistance and the opening of the US market for trade through the NAFTA agreement.
>
> (Harvey, 2003, p. 154)

This transformation subjected the country to structural adjustments under the direction of international institutions, affecting small and medium-sized agricultural producers. The austerity measures dictated by the IMF (International Monetary Fund) included economic stabilization programs to alleviate the debt crisis. Over a period of six years, 743 strategic state companies were privatized, state expenditures were reduced from 30 percent of GNP (gross national product) to 17 percent, and real wages fell 60 percent (Fitting, 2011; Hernández-Navarro, 1992).

In this scenario of the neoliberalization of social life, we identify an increase in Mexican migration to the United States, a privileged path by which transnational

DOI: 10.4324/9780429454196-2

capital incorporated "latent reserves" and residual surplus populations from remote regions of traditional agriculture (Fitting, 2011; Harvey, 2003). This process underpinned accumulation in traditional and new zones of economic expansion in that country (Griffith, 2005; Levine & LeBaron, 2011). In the 1990s, migration increased ten times compared with the preceding decades (Arroyo, Berumen, Sandoval, & Rodríguez-Álvarez, 2010; BBVA Bancomer & CONAPO, 2014). In this chapter, we will show how accelerated migration in Pahuatlán and in Zapotitlán Salinas declined after two decades, creating a short cycle of migration-return within the context of restrictive and criminalizing immigration policies and the pernicious effects of the financial and economic crisis of 2007–2009. These transformations destabilized the lives of these workers and their households on both sides of the border.

The destruction of rural Mexico

Mexico's entry into the General Agreement on Tariffs and Trade (GATT) in 1986, the country's counter agrarian reform of 1992 and the signing of the North American Free Trade Agreement (NAFTA) in 1994 produced profound changes in the accumulation regime and, consequently, the liberalization of the rural labor force in Central Mexico (Appendini, 2001; Fitting, 2011; Otero, 2011; Rubio, 2008). Embracing the neoliberal vision to reduce social spending, technocrats restructured the rural credit system to reduce government funding of agriculture. To accomplish this, farmers were classified with respect to their potential profitability and given differential access to credits according to these criteria. The government classified the 1.1 million subsistence producers as non-creditworthy, assigning them minuscule subsidies from the National Program of Solidarity (Pronasol) (Myhre, 1998). The restructuring of Banrural went along with the disappearance of the Mexican Coffee Institute (INMECAFE), Mexican Tobacco (TABAMEX), Sugar Co. (Azúcar S.A.), and other parastatals formerly charged with channeling subsidies to peasants and the promotion and commercialization of their respective commercial crops (Calderón Aragón & Ramírez Velázquez, 2002).

This led to an unprecedented dependence on imports and the loss of food sovereignty. On the one hand, Mexico became dependent on the importation of basic subsistence grains which were previously produced by small-scale farmers. "The substitution of national production for imports is revealed in the fact that, while in 1990 only 19.8% of national basic grain consumption came from imports; in 2006, 31.5% was imported." (Rubio, 2008, p. 38). The importation of maize, a key symbol of "Mexicanness" (Fitting, 2011, p. 3), doubled between 1993 and 1998 and increased by 50 percent in 1999 (Calderón Aragón & Ramírez Velázquez, 2002, p. 293). "National export and import businesses justified the numerous importations by claiming that national production was insufficient to satisfy the needs of the population." (Calderón Aragón & Ramírez Velázquez, 2002, p. 297).

On the other hand, beginning in the late 1980s, the substantial increase of fruit and vegetable exports from Mexico to the United States and Canada did not generate the jobs necessary to absorb bankrupt peasants (Otero, 2011, p. 385). While the workforce employed in Mexico increased 9.8 percent between 1998 and 2007, in agriculture it decreased 23.97 percent, from 7.5 million to 5.7 million. Other sectors of the Mexican economy did not produce the expected number of jobs to absorb the surplus labor force (Otero, 2011, p. 391).

NAFTA represented the culminating point of the "transnationalization" of national agriculture (Binford, 2004), a process that had been germinating since the 1970s. The liberalization of the importation of machinery and consumer goods favored large agribusinesses dedicated to exporting profitable crops—fruit, flowers and vegetables—to the United States and Canada (Appendini & Torres-Mazuera, 2008). The commercial opening ruined small and medium rural firms producing for the internal market and deepened food dependency on the United States (Rubio, 2001). Fitting (2011, p. 4) warned that Mexico imported its most consumed and culturally valued food, maize, while it exported labor.

Peasant families responded to the destruction of the conditions of social reproduction by producing food for their household's consumption, diversifying economic activities and sending some household members to work in agricultural enclaves in other areas of Mexico (Carton De Grammont, 1982; Lara Flores, 2010). Millions migrated to the United States and Canada (Binford, 2013; Otero, 2011, 2017; Preibisch, 2007). In those countries, workers were employed in low-wage work in construction, services, loading and unloading cargo, informal businesses, in agriculture and in domestic work. In sum, the loss of food sovereignty was accompanied by the loss of labor sovereignty (Otero, 2011, p. 385).

As a result of this process, as Fitting (2011) affirms, new rural subjects emerged. Some reoriented toward agribusiness. Those who could not remake themselves according to neoliberal logics abandoned subsistence agriculture to join migration flows to the United States. In addition to these two subjects, we add a third rural subject, one living in extreme poverty, dependent on subsidies and integrated into a heterogeneous mass of social groups administered by the state in terms of gender, age, ethnicity and disability. This subject is emblematic of the current phase of "selective hegemony," whereby subjects are interpellated by the neoliberal state based on criteria of difference, rather than the welfare state's "expansive hegemony" which created uniform subjects fit for mass production and citizenship (Smith, 2011).[1]

For the case that we analyze, we locate undocumented migrants in this transition. The restructuring of rural Mexico generated additional changes. One notable transformation was the conversion of agricultural land near urban centers or highways into industrial and tourist corridors, residential zones for high and low-income populations and commercial centers (Carton De Grammont, 2004; Velasco Santos, 2017). This process was accompanied by the rapid transition to a service economy, the privatization of water, the reactivation of mining in the hands of transnational companies and the proliferation of illegal businesses, such as prostitution, drug trafficking and gasoline theft. The latter brought with it the increase in organized crime and violence (Fuentes, 2012).

28 *Surplus labor and restructured economies*

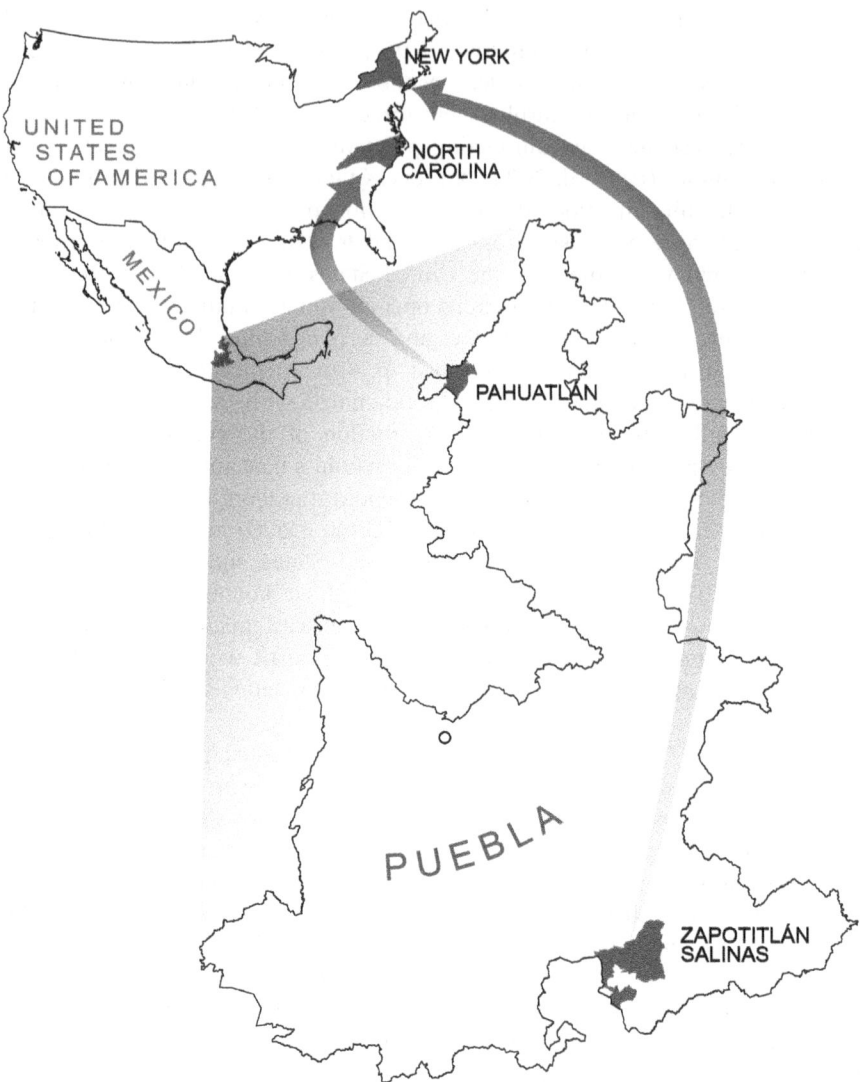

Figure 2.1 Map of Puebla.

Traditionally oriented to the production of raw materials and subsistence goods, after decades of deregulation, privatization and free trade agreements, hundreds of rural towns became producers of cheap, disorganized, and disciplined labor to somewhat mitigate the debacle of neoliberalized rural Mexico. In the increased exportation of labor, the effects of policies that generate an expanded swathe of dispossessed populations and violent regulatory devices combine to create scenes of death and cruelty that shape these "cheap" laborers (De León, 2015; Sider, 2006; Slack, Martinez, Lee, & Whiteford, 2016).

Pahuatlán

The municipality of Pahuatlán (Nahua place name meaning "place of the *pahuas*," a species of avocado) is located 134 km from Mexico City, in the northwestern region of the Northern Sierra of Puebla, in Central Mexico, at an average altitude of 1,600 meters above sea level. In the mountainous landscape of deep canyons and narrow valleys, lush vegetation proliferates, a typical feature of the subtropical humid forest. Most of its inhabitants live in four localities: the county seat, Pahuatlán de Valle, is home to 3,523 people, mostly mestizos. Xolotla and Atla, Nahua localities, have 2,700 and 2,172 inhabitants each, and in San Pablito Pahuatlán live 3,178 Otomíes. The remaining 6,566 inhabitants are spread over 31 localities (Secretaría de Desarrollo Social, 2019), small towns lying among the hills. Despite its rugged landscape, this microregion has been linked to the Mexican Central Plateau since pre-Hispanic times (Galinier, 1987; García Martínez, 1987; Stresser-Peán & Guilhem, 2008).

Since the middle of the nineteenth century, the county seat started configuring itself as a stocking center of agricultural goods from the region, transported by mules to the mining centers of the Hidalguense plateau. The agro-commercial vocation of Pahuatlán was underpinned by the rise of non-indigenous populations who settled in the region, Mestizos, Spanish, French and Italians. However, such vocation was strengthened by the liberalizing policies of the last quarter of the nineteenth century and was later consolidated by the building of a railroad from the city of Tulancingo, Hidalgo, and the opening of a station in 1908 in the neighboring locality of Chila Honey, 15 km from Pahuatlán. The railroad strengthened the economic and social connection of the municipality with the Hidalguenses cities of Tulancingo and Pachuca, as well as with the capital of the country. Thus, Pahuatlán became fully incorporated to the regional, national and international capitalist economy circuits. In this wealth production system, peasants, indigenous peoples and mestizos, progressively driven to the condition of specialized producers of cash crops (Wolf, 1982, p. 385), participated marginally in its distribution.

Two crops that became "planetary goods" (Trouillot, 2013, p. 34), highly profitable given their stimulating effects (Mintz, 1996; Wolf, 1982), dominated the Pahuatecan political economy: sugar cane and, later, coffee. Piloncillo—a sugar cane byproduct, manufactured in rustic wood mills and among the most important indigenous goods since its introduction in the region in the sixteenth century (Ruvalcaba Mercado, 1996) until the mid-twentieth century—was unable to compete with sugar produced in mills with more advanced technological components under state management. The cultivation of the sugar cane and the manufacture of piloncillo harnessed labor from families and peons hired to work in cleaning, cutting, grinding and final preparation. During downtime, large groups of men and families were mobilized to agro-industrial areas in the region or to urban centers.

On the other hand, as Wolf documented for other regions (1982), the progressive specialization in coffee growing, as was the case with piloncillo, was the strength of the smallholders and, at the same time, their weakness. Even though they attempted to meet the increase in demand, they were vulnerable to price oscillation, disasters and environmental contingencies. Earnings depended on the appropriate and timely benefit obtained from the coffee to maintain the quality and aroma of the product, a significant challenge for these isolated and still poorly communicated communities. Since the nineteenth century, when coffee trees were introduced in the area, to the present day, the quality of infrastructure—roads, drinking water, power supply, sewer system, schools, clinics and supply markets—has been extremely uneven. This weak production base forces producers to sell their crops to hoarders or intermediaries from the same localities or the county seat who own the means of transportation and negotiate the price of the coffee beans right after being dried in the sun. Like piloncillo manufacturing, coffee growing demands the intensive use of labor in certain seasons. Women, children and the elderly actively participate in land cultivation and cleaning; peons—men, women and children—join the family unit for product cutting and hauling, hired under the modality of piece-rate payment. The division of labor in which this small commercial production lies gives rise to a selective migration according to age and gender: single women and young men are most prone to migrate seasonally, temporarily or definitively in these areas (see Nolasco, 1985). The transition of an economy based in cane sugar monoculture and piloncillo manufacture to another centered in coffee monoculture constituted a new phase in the integration and subordination of the municipality and the region to the dynamics of national and international capital.

Between 1959 and 1989, the Mexican Coffee Institute (INMECAFE, its acronym in Spanish), a parastatal enterprise, technically and financially directed the so-called social producers all over the country in the Economic Units of Production and Commercialization through a clientelist system of political-party production and control. One of its most important functions was the incorporation of medium and small coffee growers to an export platform regulated by the World Coffee Organization (Hernández-Navarro, 1992; Macip Ríos, 2005; Rus, 1995). Between the 1970s and 1980s coffee growing experienced a boom in the municipality of Pahuatlán propped up by the intervention of INMECAFE. A heterogeneous group of politicians, bureaucrats, merchants, haulers, profiteers and small and medium owners, was able to insert itself at different scales in the chains of intermediaries in the Northern Sierra of Puebla (Arizpe, 1990). Numerous factors intervened in the loss of sustainability of local coffee growing: the end of the International Coffee Organization Agreement, the cancellation of the quota system in 1989, a frost that hit the region in December of that same year, and the beginning of INMECAFE's dismantling at the juncture of the impulse of neoliberal policies.

The dissolution of the parastatal exposed even more the small and medium producers to the abrupt fluctuations of the international market, leaving them more decapitalized and helpless to respond to ups and downs and climatic contingencies, as well as drifting against the actions of brokers and transnational corporations (Velásquez, 2005, p. 190). In Pahuatlán, the heirs of the small agro-commercial bourgeoisie ventured into other commercial businesses: pharmacies, hardware stores, bakeries, grocery stores, transportation, tortilla factories, and construction materials. In addition to a corporation that buys up coffee on a larger scale and exports it to Villa Juárez, small coffee mills linked to the agro-business in the area continue to operate.

Over the past five decades, there has been a transition towards a service-based economy and a relative loss of importance of agricultural activity, mainly that oriented towards producing basic grains for self-consumption or small commerce: corn, bean, chili, peanut, chickpea, citrus and fruit trees, vegetables and herbs for medical use. While in the 1960s and 1970s, 70 percent of the working population was employed in the primary sector, at the end of the first decade of the present century this percentage dropped to 42 percent. On the contrary, in that last decade, the population employed in the secondary sector grew more than 100 percent (INEGI, 1972, 1982, 1990, 2000, 2010). This increase is due to the growth of craft production—a highly feminized activity—and of employment in neighboring cities. The most visible transformation occurred in the first ten years of the new millennium in the tertiary sector with a clear increase in informal trade and services: bureaucrats, teachers, health personnel and, mainly, counter clerks and domestic work. These activities have proliferated under the *Pueblos Mágicos* program (see Chapter 5).

We identify in Pahuatlán a historically modeled social class configuration: on the one hand, a class of owners that monopolized the piloncillo and coffee trade, as well as the small production of huaraches, shoes, farming tools and equipment. At the other end of this class configuration lies a larger and more heterogeneous sector in terms of its social and ethnic origins. Contingents of Otomí and Nahua populations together with non-proprietary mestizos integrate the subaltern sectors: families of peons, smallholder peasants, sharecroppers, domestics, and manual workers. Paraphrasing Roseberry (1991, p. 173), we state that within a sector vaguely defined as "peasantry" on the basis of its origin and/or activity, a "proletarian community" seems to be hiding. They are the heirs of several generations that have worked as peons and day laborers both in local agriculture and in intensive agriculture areas, as well as salaried workers in the

Table 2.1 Pahuatlán: Economically active population by sector (1990–2010)

Year	Sector			
	Primary	*Secondary*	*Tertiary*	*Unemployed/Unspecified*
1990	59.2	20.5	16.9	4.2
2000	50.2	31.0	17.5	1.0
2010	41.6	32.6	24.2	1.2

Sources: Mexican census data, multiple years (1992, 2001, 2011).

automotive, textile, construction and manufacturing industry or in the service sector in neighboring cities. Some authors (Dow, 2005; Galinier, 1987) reported in the 1980s the existence of Otomí migratory flows from San Pablito Pahuatlán to the Southern United States and the continuity of migration within Mexican borders. The youngest—men and women—integrate a "new proletariat," characterized by its flexibility and precariousness, forged in the 1980s and 1990s in Texas poultry farms, California's agricultural fields and in North Carolina's construction and service industry that joined the accelerated migration to the United States in the 1990s.

Zapotitlán

Nestled in a narrow desert valley in the rugged Mixtec region of Puebla, Zapotitlán Salinas (population 2,700) is a rural community 30 km from Tehuacán, an industrial manufacturing and commercial center. The way villagers' labor subsidized regional and national economies reflected the town's subordinate political, economic and social position. Zapotitlán had been an important salt producing center since pre-Hispanic times when salt was used as currency (Castellón, 2006, pp. 70–74). The name of the community refers to the salt-water wells and crystallization ponds (*salinas*) where salt forms through an evaporation process. Throughout the colonial period, Zapotitecos/as supplied New Spain's silver mining industry with salt. The Crown maintained salt production under Indian control and made it illegal for intermediaries to buy or sell it. In salt-producing areas, Indian labor could not be appropriated for other industries, ensuring the mineral's constant supply to the mines (Ewald, 1985, 20, n 15, 24).

In addition to its role in precious metal production, salt from Zapotitlán was an essential element in the diet of livestock—mainly goats—introduced into the Mixteca region by the Spaniards in the sixteenth century. Moreover, caprine products from the region were used in many everyday items throughout New Spain. For example, goat fat was used in the manufacture of candles and lubricants for mining and domestic use. Fat, wool and hides—used in clothing manufacture—were exported to Spain (Mouat, 1980).

Zapotitlán was an important stop on mule train routes. Originating on the Pacific coast, the mule trains traversed the Sierra Madre Occidental connecting agricultural and industrial producers through the provision of local markets and regional commercial centers. A number of perennial fresh-water springs in Zapotitlán supplied the *arrieros* (mule drivers) and their animals, making the village the last resting point before reaching the large market in Tehuacán. When the highway linking Zapotitlán to Tehuacán was built in the 1960s, the *arrieros* were replaced by buses and trucks to move people, animals and goods through the mountainous terrain.

After independence and well into the twentieth century, Zapotitlán produced goats, *ixtle* (maguey fibers) and charcoal for the regional economy.[2] These products tended to overshadow local agriculture as the principal economic activities. During the twentieth century, Zapotitlán, unlike Pahuatlán, was never a target for agricultural development programs and local producers received no subsidies for basic grain production. Erosion, poor soils and scarce rainfall limited farming to yields that provided subsistence a few months out of the year. While men and boys toiled in the *salinas*, in the desert pastures herding goats and in rain-fed cornfields, some adolescent girls found work as domestics in large cities such as Puebla and Mexico City to supplement rural household income.

Over millions of years, petrified salt-water formed travertine and marble deposits underneath or adjacent to the *salinas*.[3] Local men quarried the rock, colloquially known as "onyx," as early as the late-nineteenth century. However, its extraction intensified beginning in the 1960s with the completion of the highway and connection to regional markets. In the early 1960s, quarry owners sold the rock to workshops in Tehuacán, Tecali de Herrera and Puebla, nearby cities and towns situated within a well-established stone-working production network.[4]

The arrival of electricity in 1966 to Zapotitlán made it possible for the first onyx workshops to open. The burgeoning local industry manufactured a variety of handicrafts and some construction materials. Federal electricity subsidies supported the growth of workshops and represented the most significant state intervention into the development of the regional and local industry. The majority of workers previously employed in ranching and salt production shifted into onyx extraction and manufacture from the 1960s to 1980s. Men and boys hauled and cut rock, while women and girls worked as unpaid household labor to polish cut pieces, assemble products and pack the finished product.

The decline of this extraction and manufacture industry—detailed in Chapter 4—was partly due to neoliberal policies. Moreover, the devaluation of the peso in 1994 represented a dramatic blow to workshops already struggling to stay afloat, causing dozens of them to close. International migration to New York City accelerated, shoring up a process that had begun in the previous decade. Remittances became a crucial pillar of subsistence for hundreds of households in Zapotitlán, replacing the income earned from the quarries and the workshops (Lee, 2008).

As was the case in many areas of Mexico, the town underwent a gradual transition from an extraction and manufacture-based economy to a service economy from the 1980s to the 2000s. The remittance economy ushered in new services, both because there was money to pay for them and because the experience of living in the United States contributed to the development of new forms of consumption. Restaurants offering local foods opened alongside pizzerias as return migrants put their cooking skills—acquired in the United States—to use. Although a reliable bus service shuttled people between Zapotitlán and Tehuacán where many studied and shopped, a preference for more individualized transportation services was met with a growing fleet of taxis. Within the town, motorcycle taxis partially displaced walking and bicycles as a quotidian mode of transportation. When dozens of households became equipped with landline telephones in the mid-2000s, replacing the inadequate services offered by the handful of *casetas* (telephone booths) operated in town, the convenience of calling to place food orders and having them delivered by boys on bicycles or motorbikes was widely appreciated. Not surprisingly, these services flourished with the growth of cell phones in the 2010s. An explosion of internet cafes in the 2000s gave way to individual contracts for service in homes. It was often difficult for small businesses offering goods or services to maintain even small levels of profitability and, therefore, remain open. However, there were always families opening businesses, replacing the ones that were forced to close their doors thereby contributing to the shift toward the tertiary sector.

The growth in the tertiary sector was also related to the development of nature and cultural tourism projects. For decades, researchers and visitors had been drawn to the dramatic desert landscape surrounding the town. Its flora and fauna were extensively studied, earning the region international recognition as an important center of biodiversity (centers of plant diversity). Politicians and government bureaucrats supported the institutionalization of the area as part of the Tehuacán-Cuicatlán Biosphere Reserve in the late 1990s. Throughout the 2000s, World Bank funding, channeled through the Mexican federal government, supported the development of local tourism projects to boost local development and ecological conservation (Lee, 2014). Restaurants sprang up along the highway, and a handful of hotels opened to accommodate domestic and international visitors for short stays. The incorporation of the desert into a natural protected area and the transformation of Zapotitlán into a tourism destination is part of the development of the "nature industry" that links the region to other parallel developments in Mexico and elsewhere (Martínez-Reyes, 2016; see also Macip & Zamora, 2012).

The local economic transformations can be traced through changes in the economically active population. The percentage of adults employed in primary activities, such as agriculture and onyx extraction, fell from 28 percent in 1970 to just 16 percent in 2010. The secondary sector, including manufacturing such as the onyx workshops, fell from 67 percent in 1970 to just 49 percent in 2010. Finally, the service sector grew from four percent in 1970 to 34 percent in 2010. (INEGI, 2010, 1972).

The dismantling of state supports for rural agriculture was accompanied by the growth of small programs targeting rural subjects and encouraging them to adopt practices to reduce their impact on the natural protected area. These programs aimed to stimulate local economic development through productive

Table 2.2 Zapotitlán: Economically active population by sector (1990–2010)

Year	Sector			
	Primary	*Secondary*	*Tertiary*	*Unemployed/Unspecified*
1990	25.1	56.9	15.5	1.5
2000	29.9	50.2	18.1	1.3
2010	15.9	49.1	34.5	0.6

Sources: Mexican census data, multiple years (1992, 2001, 2011).

activities: agave cultivation for mezcal production, sheep raising (they were not as destructive of the local vegetation as goats) and cacti fruit harvesting, to name a few programs that came and went in the 2000s and 2010s. These programs operated through "selective hegemony" (Smith, 2011); they targeted the rural poor and women, were frequently tied to election cycles and distributed through family networks or party loyalists. Far from remedying the destruction of rural economies, the scale of the programs never reached a significant proportion of household income. They represented, at best, a modest complementary income. Nevertheless, on the village-level, they represented a significant amount of money, and stories of misappropriation of funds were common, creating tensions and conflicts among families.

While moneylenders among the villagers had always existed, new forms of debt became available. A plethora of micro-lending enterprises recruited groups of women to participate as agents in their own empowerment by financing their small-scale productive activities. While a few used the funds in this way, many used them for subsistence or to buy basic household appliances, covering the weekly payments through remittances or further borrowing from family and friends. National department stores offered credit to purchase clothing, shoes, appliances and electronics, permitting villagers to participate in a "global imaginary of consumption" (Suárez-Orozco, 2003). Villagers also organized themselves in rotating credit associations (Lara, 2010; Vélez-Ibañez, 2010), an arrangement that provided better savings and loan rates than anything available from national banks. However, and perhaps not surprisingly, the proliferation of debt forms brought no relief from debt. Rather, informants explained that they often used one loan to pay off other debts. "I ask for a loan to pay off another one, but I end up covering one hole and creating a bigger one," explained Ignacio. Especially after the economic crisis and the escalation of border and interior enforcement, Zapotitecos/as more frequently patched together income from government programs, deplorable salaries from local jobs and loans from various sources to meet subsistence needs.

Economic restructuring of the East Coast of the United States

Geographic and demographic changes in migratory flows

Between 1990 and 2000, the "new geography of Mexican migration" (Durand, Massey, & Capoferro, 2005) marked a new phase of the 100-year-old history of circulation between the two countries. On the East Coast, the percentage of migrants from Mexico and Central America doubled in a decade. The number of migrants settling in traditional gateways such as California and Texas declined. Instead, the Midwest, Northeast and the South became important new destinations (Griffith, 2005; Hirschman, 2008).

The restructuring of the US economy, from Fordist to flexible production beginning in the 1970s and accelerating in the 1980s, stimulated the transformation in the geography of Mexican migration to the United States (Harvey, 1989). A period of decreasing profitability and productivity of US corporations after the mid-1960s and the oil crisis in 1973 stimulated a major overhaul of production processes and labor control. Deindustrialization of manufacturing centers precipitated an increase in offshore production with flexible production chains coordinated over geographically dispersed areas. Flexible accumulation ushered in the expansion of the service sector, where unionized, industrial workers lost ground to the growth of a casual workforce of part-time, temporary and informal laborers.

The service sector was dominated by producer services, what is known as the FIRE economy (Finance, Insurance, Real Estate). These services required highly skilled workers and numerous low-skilled workers to "service the lifestyles and consumption requirements of the growing high-income professional and managerial class." (Sassen, 1998b, p. 48) Women, formerly as reserve labor, and immigrants, culled from the surplus populations of the Global South, filled low-wage service jobs. The transition to flexible accumulation displaced important segments of the working class across borders, incorporating them into the new configurations of class adapted to the tendencies of deregulation (Friedman, 2015). On the US East Coast, Mexican migrants filled the ranks of this new global proletariat.

Pahuatecos/as in Raleigh-Durham Corridor, North Carolina

Two great forces intervened in the economic reconversion that put the so-called *Nuevo* New South or Latino New South in the 1990s at the forefront of neoliberal globalization and flexible work: on the one hand, the relocation of national and foreign capitals through a combination of tax incentives, low business costs and commercial opening. On the other, the deindustrialization that dismantled forms of production and organization of work in agriculture, steel industries, furniture, carpets and rugs, textiles and clothing, paper, tobacco and chemical plants among others. The loss of jobs was uneven in different sectors and areas of the country. The effects on workers were also dissimilar: according to the level of union organization, some received generous severance packages, while others were dismissed with little compensation. (Minchin, 2012; Mohl, 2003; Popke, 2011).

According to information from the population censuses of the United States, in 1990 the *Nuevo* New South received only 3.6 percent of the Hispanic migrant population. Ten years later, the percentage reached 7.5. Four flows converged in this increase: internal migration from the southwestern United States; others came from Central Mexico and Central America; at the same time, legal migration was promoted through work visas and labor recruitment in traditional areas of Mexican migration. Finally, itinerant agricultural workers who followed the annual crop calendar migrated into the US South (Griesbach, 2011; Levine & LeBaron, 2011). The myth of the disappearance of the neoliberal state was challenged by the decisive state practices that facilitated the encounter between capital searching for profit-making opportunities unobstructed by regulation and abundant "cheapened" laborers from the Global South. Increasingly restrictive US immigration policies and guestworker programs boosted the supply and lowered the cost of Mexican labor (Canterbury, 2012; Kofman & Raghuram, 2015; Mezzadra & Neilson, 2013).

As we have indicated in other works (D'Aubeterre, 2019), North Carolina, one of the 11 states that make up the *Nuevo* New South, formerly the Old South, was considered a "backyard" of abundant cheap, biracialized work, with weak unionization to challenge powerful paternalism; in short, vulnerable communities suitable for investments of any cost (Smith & Winders, 2007; Popke, 2011, p. 247). An improved formula was put into operation for this relaunch by exploiting undocumented migrant workers who misaligned with their presence an age-old biracial, class and gender formation. In sum, the deindustrialization referred to is the historical expression of a specific moment of the unmaking (destruction) of the preceding working class. The other side of the process is the formation of the new working class (Silver, 2014).

Established in 1853, the early development of the city of Durham was associated with the tobacco industry and, in the late nineteenth century, textile and garment factories proliferated. These factories began retreating in the 1970s under the deindustrialization drift. This process encouraged the displacement of important contingents of cheap immigrant laborers of diverse national and ethnic origins (Cravey, 2003; Levine & LeBaron, 2011; Mohl, 2003; Popke, 2011). Immigrant laborers were absorbed by the rural agro-industry—food processing, sawmills and wood production, among the most important—and, more prominently, by the construction sector, the assembly of electronics, subsidiaries of companies with high technological components, laboratories, pharmaceuticals, hospitals, universities and the restaurant industry. The arrival of high-skilled labor, attracted by this expansion and by the city's climate, demanded, in parallel, the provision of housing and care services (Flippen & Parrado, 2012; Kasarda & Johnson, 2006).

Hispanic population in the Durham–Raleigh–Charlotte corridor, North Carolina, grew from 76,726 people, representing 1.2 percent of the total state population in 1990, to 506,203, 6.1 percent of the total population in 2004 (Furuseth & Smith, 2016). It is precisely in that corridor where the bulk of Mexican migration concentrated. In 1990 the Census registered 2,054 Hispanics in Durham county; after a decade, this number grew to 17,039: 75 percent were born abroad and more than 85 percent migrated to the United States after 1990. In 2009, Hispanics already amounted to 12 percent of the total county population, 32,904 people; 90 percent of them undocumented (Flippen & Parrado, 2012, p. 10). The city of Durham was the fourth most populated city of the state with a sustained growth of 16.9 percent during the 2000 decade. In the period between 2000–2008 the population grew from 224,618 to 262,715: 47.06 percent white, 36.53 percent Afro-American, and the rest of diverse origin.

The massive migration of the 1990s from Pahuatlán toward North Carolina was preceded by a pioneer migratory flow to the South of the United States in the 1970s, consisting of young Otomíes from San Pablito Pahuatlán in their seasonal displacements between the Sierra and the poultry and dairy ranches from the south of Texas. This destination served as an important migratory station (Izcara Palacios, 2010) from which waves of workers were redirected toward agrobusiness areas from the New Latino South (Furuseth & Smith, 2016). These circuits connected with the Sierra Norte of Puebla, where workers stayed for short periods of time, integrating into certain phases of the local agricultural calendar only to start again, after a few months, a new cycle of displacements.

In the 1980s Otomíes settled in great numbers in neighborhoods shared with Afro-Americans and Latinos in Old North Durham. This area was degraded and socially stigmatized due to the ethnic condition of their poor occupants. A brief note from 12 December 2008, published in *El Informador*[5] alluded to an area of old apartments inhabited by "Latinos," among them dozens of Otomí families from San Pablito Pahuatlán:

> The Maldita Vecindad [Damned Neighborhood] is how this apartment complex in the city of Durham is known—stated the tabloid—a place mostly inhabited by Hispanic immigrants, given the low cost of its rents. It is a no man's land, everyone does things their own way, the volume of music equipment comes out from everywhere, and beer bottles are the decoration of the place on the weekends. The routine changed on a Saturday when several brave Christians, aiming to reach those hearts without Christ, set up a ramp in the parking lot, and the music band started playing and singing, but its lyrics said something different. The message of Jesus Christ came to the Vecindad to mend the broken souls, to give hope to everyone without it, and faith to those who have lost themselves […].

Over time, Otomíes and Pahuatecos expanded towards the northeast of the city, and to Orange County. In the early years, single men shared apartments, a common and well-documented strategy among immigrants to lower costs (Cravey, 2003; Flippen & Parrado, 2012). Our interviewees in 2013 and 2014 rented single-family homes or married couples sublet rooms to both relatives and non-relatives; children and adolescents were part of these domestic formations of changing contours. Due to the limited availability of public transport, the streets and garages of these neighborhoods are filled with second and third-hand vehicles, essential for the transportation of these workers who are forced to drive without a license given their undocumented status.[6]

Zapotitecos/as in New York

First founded in the seventeenth century, New York became the largest and most important American port by the mid-nineteenth century. It served as the center of a vast transportation network that linked Caribbean and Atlantic ports, cities and towns in the US hinterland via Lake Erie and seaports in England. The growth in the city's manufacturing capacity paralleled its rise as a seaport, particularly with respect to three industries. Sugar, shipped in from the West Indies, was refined in New York, becoming the largest industry in the city during the first half of the nineteenth century and the second largest after mid-century. Cloth from the textile mills of England and, later, New England, was made into ready-to-wear clothes in the scores of garment factories throughout the city. This labor-intensive industry grew significantly throughout the early twentieth century, absorbing thousands of the millions of immigrants that arrived in New York after the Civil War (1861–1865). This same immigrant flow contributed to the demand for ready-to-wear clothing, further contributing to the expansion of the industry. Finally, the printing and publishing industry in the city provided not only pirated copies of the latest English novels, but also newspapers. Information about the latest economic and political developments was highly valued in a city at the center of international trade networks and commodity flows (Glaeser, 2005).

While many immigrants arrived in New York and continued on to settle in the interior of the country, many remained in the city, finding work in manufacturing and a place to live in vibrant ethnic communities. In 1924, the Johnson-Reed Immigration Act "was the nation's first *comprehensive* restriction law. It established for the first time *numerical limits* on immigration and a *global* racial and national hierarchy that favored some immigrants over others." (Ngai, 2004, p. 3, emphasis in the original). The national origin quota system sharply limited the immigration of "undesirable races" from southern and eastern Europe while favoring migrants from northern Europe. In New York, the number of foreign-born declined in proportion to total population.

Owing to US-led economic transformations of Puerto Rico's economy after the country took possession of the island in 1898, migration to New York climbed steadily in the early twentieth century and soared after World War II (Bourgois, 1995, pp. 49–53). The Puerto Rican population grew from 61,000 in 1940 to 817,712 in 1970, representing 10 percent of the city's population (Sánchez Korrol, 2010, p. 1059). Many were employed in manufacturing at the same time that these industries were in decline.

The Immigration and Naturalization Act of 1965 abolished the national origin quota system, establishing instead hemispheric quotas and privileging family reunification. This increased the number of so-called "new immigrants" from Asia, the Caribbean and Latin America, contributing to a growing diversity of ethnic groups in New York. Approximately three million people, one-third of New York City residents, were immigrants in 2010 (Foner, 2013).

The growth of the immigrant population after 1965 occurred during a time of deindustrialization in New York. While the garment industry adapted to flexible production regimes to supply the city's fashion industry and required large numbers of women culled from the ranks of the "new immigrants," the overall number of workers employed was lower when compared with the end of the nineteenth and early twentieth century (Chin, 2005). The decline in manufacturing industries was offset by the city's rise as a global center of finance and business services (Sassen, 2001). The FIRE economy in New York created low-wage service jobs filled by immigrants from Mexico and other countries.

> The concentration of these high-income workers in major cities has facilitated rapid residential and commercial gentrification, which in turn has created a need for legions of low-wage service workers—residential building attendants, restaurant workers, preparers of specialty and gourmet foods, dog walkers, errand runners, apartment cleaners, childcare providers, and so on.
>
> (Sassen, 1998a, p. 48)

The first migrants from Zapotitlán arrived in New York beginning in 1984 and settled in the Soundview, Parkchester and Castle Hill sections of the Bronx. Originally built and settled by Irish, Italian and Eastern European immigrants in the late nineteenth and early twentieth centuries, the majority of these populations migrated to the suburbs in the post-World War II period, opening opportunities for Puerto Ricans, Dominicans and African Americans to settle. The white flight, abandonment and disinvestment which destroyed sections of the South Bronx in the 1970s occurred less frequently in Soundview, Parkchester and Castle Hill (Gonzalez, 2004). In the 1980s, Mexicans, including Zapotitecos, arrived in the area. It was common for men from Zapotitlán to crowd ten or more into one-bedroom apartments, often in pre-war tenement buildings. As they became more familiar with the city, different groups splintered off and recruited newly arrived relatives to settle with them in Washington Heights on the Upper West Side of Manhattan and in Sunset Park in Brooklyn. While Mexicans' geographic dispersal in the city was quite high, their settlement patterns often placed Mexican immigrants as newcomers in neighborhoods with relatively high proportions of Puerto Ricans (Smith, 2006). To adhere to conventions of "respectability" (Skeggs, 1997), single women from Zapotitlán could not live in crowded conditions with unrelated men. Instead, they settled with other immigrant women or, more commonly, with brothers already established in the city.

In the 1980s, when Mexicans, West Africans and other immigrant groups joined the growing Latino population in the Bronx, commentators celebrated the revitalization of the borough (Gonzalez, 2004). Although the increased commercial activity and building renovation were viewed as positive elements, Zapotitecos/as complained bitterly about shouted insults and, occasionally, assaults, by "morenos/as" on the street. Beatriz, who we will meet in Chapter 4, describes how, at her retail job in a clothing store owned by Koreans, she had repeated troubles with Puerto Rican women. "They would insult me and tell me off when I wouldn't sell the clothes to them at a lower price." She described how she had to defend herself when they threatened to wait for her outside the store after her shift or cut in line in front of her at the pharmacy. Security guards herded fistfights into the street so as not to scare off other customers.

The tensions and conflicts among Puerto Ricans and new Mexican immigrant arrivals in New York that Beatriz and other migrants described in their interviews reflected the "human underside to the latest phase in the restructuring of New York's economy" (Bourgois, 1995, p. 169). During the 1980s, the real value of the minimum wage declined by one-third, and the income gap between the minimum wage and the federal poverty threshold grew ten times (New York

State Assembly, 2004). Puerto Ricans and Mexicans competed for jobs while their economic value was plummeting.

> The poverty of [Mexicans'] natal villages makes them a highly disciplined, inexpensive workforce capable of fulfilling the enormous needs that well-paid FIRE sector executives have for personal services: housekeepers, office cleaners, delivery personnel, boutique attendants, restaurant workers. Furthermore, their impoverished rural backgrounds where running water and electricity are considered a luxury make them tolerant of the crushing public sector breakdown endemic to U.S. inner cities. Native-born New Yorkers of any ethnicity are simply not exploitable enough to compete with rural new immigrants for low-wage menial jobs.
> (Bourgois, 1995, p. 169)

The structural violence of the dismantling of life conditions in rural Puebla propelled men and women into New York's workforce displacing native workers by way of their cheapened, "illegalized" labor. These groups often faced off on the streets,[7] their rivalry stemming from Mexicans' self-declared greater capacity for work, a neoliberal subjectivity analyzed further in Chapter 4. An alternative explanation focuses on the simultaneous shift in New York's accumulation regime and the arrival of Mexicans into the city's working classes that prompted a revaluing of waged work and segmentation of the working class along ethnic/racial hierarchies (Federici, 2006). The violence of this process turned factions of the working classes against each other. Meanwhile, the economy hummed along, sustained by cheap, racialized, "illegalized" labor.

The end of accelerated migration: financial crisis and the criminalization of immigration

After the mid-2000s, migration to the United States decreased and return migration increased sharply. Arroyo et al. (2010, p. 13) demonstrate that between 2005 and 2008 there was almost a 50 percent decrease in first migrations from Mexico: from 1.1 million to 560,000. Using Mexican census data, Passel, Cohn, and Gonzalez-Barrera (2012) concluded that migration from Mexico to the US fell from 2.94 million in the 1995–2000 period to 1.37 million in the 2005–2010 period.

Mexican and US government data show sharp rises in return migration and deportations during the first years of the twenty-first century. While from 1996 to 2000 there were 267,150 individuals who returned to Mexico, from 2005 to 2010 this number increased to 825,609, representing a growth of 209 percent in return migration. From 2010 to 2015, 442,503 individuals returned to Mexico, a 46.4 percent decrease over the previous five years, but still significantly higher than the returns registered in the late 1990s (BBVA & Consejo Nacional de Población, 2017, p. 94). With fewer migrations to the US and more returns to Mexico, migration flows between the two countries reached a "net zero" equilibrium from 2005 to 2010 (Passel et al., 2012) and a "below net zero" flow from

2009 to 2014 (Gandini, Lozano-Ascencio, & Gaspar, 2015; Gonzalez-Barrera, 2015; Levine, 2015; Martínez Canales, 2012). The financial crisis of 2007–2009 and US immigration policy were the most important factors behind these significant changes.

Economic and financial crisis

The Great Recession in the United States officially started in December 2007 and ended in June 2009. However, households in the country showed signs of distress before and for many years after this period (Harvey, 2010; Kalleberg & Von Wachter, 2017). In 2006, the rate of home foreclosures increased sharply. Low-income minority areas succumbed first, and, later, middle-class neighborhoods were affected, leaving large tracts of housing abandoned throughout the country. Millions of homeowners defaulted on toxic loans made through predatory lending practices. In total, there were 7.4 million foreclosures between 2007 and 2015, the first year the unemployment rate returned to pre-recession levels (CoreLogic, 2017). By late 2008, the subprime mortgage crisis "had led to the demise of all the major Wall Street investment banks, through change of status, forced mergers or bankruptcy" (Harvey, 2010, p. 2). The excessive deregulation of the financial sector from the 1980s to the 2000s in the United States paved the way for the rise of the so-called "shadow banking system" whose toxic financial instruments, combined with bankers' greed and recklessness, created untold wealth for a few and devastated millions (Harvey, 2010; Tett, 2009). The creation of vast linkages among global financial markets, a process largely consolidated in the 1980s, ensured the spread of the crisis to other parts of the world.

Unemployment increased more rapidly during the recession compared with other recessions in recent decades (US Bureau of Labor Statistics, 2012). Unemployment jumped from 5.0 percent in December 2007 to 10.0 percent in October 2010, slowly returning to 2007 levels by 2015 (US Department of Labor, 2019). Other effects of the crisis continued to linger. Home ownership fell from 68.9 percent in the fourth quarter of 2006, before the recession, to 63.7 percent in the fourth quarter of 2016. It has not recovered to pre-recession levels, achieving only modest increases to 64.8 percent in the fourth quarter of 2018 (US Census Bureau, 2019). The labor force participation rate (LFPR) has also not recovered to its pre-recession level. In November 2007, one month before the recession, 66.0 percent of the population was employed. As of September 2015, the LFPR fell to a low of 62.4 percent and has hovered around 63 percent up until this writing (July 2019) (Federal Reserve Bank of St. Louis, 2019).

The Great Recession had an enormous impact on economic inequality. While upper-income families had median wealth that was greater in 2017 than before the start of the Great Recession, lower-income white and middle-income black and Hispanic household median wealth was reduced almost by half during and after the recession. In 2017, the gap between lower- and middle-income households and upper-income families were the highest ever recorded (Kochhar & Cilluffo, 2017).

The financial crisis had important effects on the labor markets that employed large numbers of Mexican male immigrants. The loss of employment, particularly in construction, accounted for major changes in the demand of unskilled labor from Mexico (Levine, 2015; Villarreal, 2014).

> During the most severe years of crisis (2008–09), Latinos lost a proportionate part—14%, equivalent to 863,800 jobs—of the 6.2 million jobs destroyed in the United States in those years. The most striking case was the construction industry, where Latinos lost 720,000 jobs.
>
> (Levine, 2015)

Aysa-Lastra and Cachón (2012) show that the employment of Latino immigrants was more sensitive to economic cycles when compared to total employed population. That is, the number of Latinos employed grew faster during the expansionary 2000–2008 period and declined more rapidly from 2008 to 2011. While total employment in the United States fell 1.4 percent annually from 2008 to 2011, Latino employment fell 2.6 percent annually during the same time period. Levine argues that the effect of the Great Recession on labor markets is the main factor that has slowed the arrival of migrant workers, especially the undocumented (Levine, 2015). Passel and Cohn (2019) argue that the number of unauthorized Mexican immigrants has declined sharply in the last ten years because more have left than arrived. This population constitutes a minority of the unauthorized population—47 percent—for the first time since the early 1960s. Some recent studies suggest that Mexicans in the United States were hit hard by the recent recession. Unfortunately, discussions on gender, crisis and return have, until recently, been few, eclipsed by the focus on Mexican male circular migration (Rothstein, 2016, pp. 9–10). In Chapters 5 and 6 we will discuss in greater detail how the economic crisis affected Pahuatecos and Zapotitecos in the United States.

Immigration policies and migrant flows: regulating and containing mobile surplus labor

Through the redesign of policies over more than a century, the US immigration regime has, in some moments, contained the flow of immigrants into the country, and, in other moments, selectively regulated legal and "illegal" entry of migrants (De Genova, 2005; Hahamovitch, 2014; Ngai, 2004). Actors with opposing interests intervened in this process, often creating policies with paradoxical, unintended effects in the administration of migrant populations (Calavita, 1992). One of these policies, the Immigration Reform and Control Act (IRCA) of 1986, gave amnesty to undocumented immigrants who had worked and resided continuously in the country since 1982. Under the program, 2.3 million Mexicans obtained legal residence and a path to citizenship.

An unintended consequence of the program was that it did not stem the flow of undocumented immigrants, whose labor continued to be in permanent demand in certain industries (Cornelius, 1998). Pahuatecos/as and Zapotitecos/as, along with millions of other Mexican migrants, arrived in the United States after IRCA. Up until the mid-2000s, migrants apprehended by the Border Patrol were deported back to the border area in Mexico and re-attempted clandestine crossings until they successfully crossed and reached their destination in the US interior (Espenshade, 1994). In this process, which Heyman (1995) termed "the voluntary-departure complex," the US appeared to be making an impressive number of arrests, protecting the country from illegal "aliens" while continuing to import Mexican labor on a large scale. The porosity also allowed for circular migration at intervals of several years among undocumented adults and children.

In the 1990s, during the rapid increase in the number of undocumented migrants present in the United States, the symbolic figure of the "illegal alien" dominated political debates. Politicians used the figure to galvanize their campaigns, promising voters to be "tough" on immigrants (Andreas, 2000). Some policies aimed to deter would-be migrants in high-traffic urban areas by installing more Border Patrol personnel, border walls, night-vision and electronic surveillance equipment. These efforts were part of a prevention-through-deterrence strategy that involved the militarization of the border (Dunn, 1996) to combat undocumented migration and drug trafficking (see also Nevins, 2010). The immediate consequence for migrants was to push them to cross in the deserts and mountains far from urban areas where they would be more easily identified, detained and deported (Cornelius, 2001).

During the 2000s, after the 9/11 attacks and in the context of the War on Terror, significant reorganization of the federal government and increased federal spending bolstered the securitization of immigration and ended the "voluntary departure complex" (Golash-Boza, 2012; Heyman, 1995). The border enforcement apparatus inflicted "specific patterns of trauma" on clandestine crossers (Jusionyte, 2018), making migrants increasingly vulnerable as they crossed the US-Mexican border (De León, 2015; Martínez, Slack, & Martínez-Schuldt, 2018; Slack, Martinez, Whiteford, & Peiffer, 2013, 2015). To avoid detection by the Border Patrol, migrants made longer treks—sometimes up to a week—in the desert, increasing the risk of dying of exposure and dehydration (Lee, 2018; Slack et al., 2016). Under these conditions, criminals and bandits easily preyed on migrants in the borderlands. With the physical, emotional, financial and legal risks for clandestine crossings higher than ever, apprehensions of Mexican migrants at the border fell to lows recorded in the 1960s (Gonzalez-Barrera, 2016). Compounding the trauma, clandestine entries were subject to criminal penalties. When detained at the border, migrants were subject to formal removal proceedings without due process (Lydgate, 2010).

After the mid-2000s, the Illegal Immigration Reform and Immigrant Responsibility Act (IIRIRA) of 1996 was applied vigorously in the interior of the country. This law increased the range of offenses that led to removal, including non-violent administrative infractions. Millions of non-citizens, both undocumented and legal immigrants, were suddenly subject to removal, many without due process (Caldwell, 2019; Golash-Boza, 2012). As a result, the number of removals grew from 165,000 in 2002 to 434,000 in 2013, the year with the greatest number (Chishti, Pierce, & Bolter, 2017). From 2005 to 2015, there were 2.6 million removals of Mexican nationals (BBVA & Consejo Nacional de Población, 2017, p. 83).[8,9]

Immigration policies to contain flows at the border or to remove individuals from the interior are not intended to completely block the United States' access to cheapened labor. With the more porous border from the 1980s to the mid-2000s, scholars speculated that border enforcement separated workers from their dependents in Mexico, thereby ensuring the costs of reproduction of workers' families were borne by the workers, family members in Mexico and the Mexican state (Wilson, 2000). However, in the recent rise of mass deportation in the United States (Martínez et al., 2018), separation of family members with long-standing ties to the country through deportation is not serving the same function with respect to the reproduction of cheap labor. With the growth in the number of US children born to Mexican immigrants in the United States, and Mexicans brought to the US as children and socialized in the country, removals, and the threat of them, terrorize and fracture immigrant workers' families (Boehm, 2016; Caldwell, 2019; Dreby, 2015). Depriving US children of parents to economically provide and care for them or banishing young people to Mexico with the skills and social capital to contribute productively to the United States are practices that do not appear to strengthen US capitalism.

As Heyman points out (2012) border policies are never directly functional for capitalism. Rather, anti-immigrant policies strengthen the material and ideological power of the "illegal," a criminalized category of persons stripped of rights (Gonzales & Chavez, 2012; Heyman, 2014). Border controls combined with interior enforcement "balance the competing political priorities of deporting the undocumented while maintaining a disciplined undocumented workforce in the US" (Goldstein & Alonso-Bejarano, 2017, p. 1). Further, the border shapes "differential mobility with two simultaneous agendas: broad class inequality reaching across borders and nation-to-nation inequality contained within borders." (Heyman, 2012, p. 266). Over time, the post-IRCA flows—of which Pahuatecos/as and Zapotitecos/as incorporated into—were profoundly conditioned by "illegality." They were differentiated from the migrant subjects who were able to benefit from the legalization process of IRCA and start businesses, take part in Mexican and hometown politics, promote and finance luxurious ritual celebrations and vacation in the homeland.

The increasing restrictions and the financial crisis decreased circularity between the two countries as migrants tended to prolong their stays and settle in the United States. The previous temporary residence of Mexican migrants in the US evolved into relatively more permanent residence (Arroyo et al., 2010) that took on the characteristics of "settlement migration" (Griffith, 2005). In Mexico, many return and would-be migrants stayed put. These changes marked the end of accelerated migration from Puebla.

Comparing accelerated migration and return in Pahuatlán and Zapotitlán

As explained in Chapter 1, we administered a modified version of the Mexican Migration Project Ethnosurvey to a 20 percent sample of households in Pahuatlán and a 25 percent sample of households in Zapotitlán. Zapotitlán had a greater percentage of households with migratory experience, 65.3 percent versus 56.3 percent for Pahuatlán. However, Pahuatlán had a greater number of individuals with migration experience per household (2.2) than Zapotitlán (2.0). With fewer overall households participating in international migration, more migrants came from migrant households in Pahuatlán. The vast majority of migrants from Zapotitlán lived in New York City and the surrounding suburbs while the majority of Pahuatecos/as lived in Durham, North Carolina. Men from Zapotitlán were employed primarily in restaurants and other services with a few working in the construction industry. Women from Zapotitlán worked in services as domestics and caretakers, manicurists, restaurant workers and in clothing shops. Pahuatecan men worked primarily in the construction industry while women worked in restaurants, industrial laundry services, manufacturing and cleaning services (homes, offices, hospitals, hotels). In sum, while women from Pahuatlán and Zapotitlán had similar work experiences, men from the two towns had different experiences. Finally, while the rate of staying for Pahuatecan migrants was 74 percent, it was 66 percent for Zapotitlán's migrants.

First international migration

In Figure 2.2, we show the rise and fall of first international migration in the two towns. Accelerated migration begins in the late 1980s in Zapotitlán, in the context of the decline of the local onyx industry, and flows continue to grow steadily throughout the 1990s. In comparison, accelerated migration begins in Pahuatlán in the mid-1990s, triggered by the devaluation of the peso in 1994. In both towns, first migrations reach their highest point in 2001; however, while in Zapotitlán migration remains unchanged until 2004, in Pahuatlán first migration declined abruptly almost 45 percent by 2007. This decline is likely due to the fall in the employment of "Hispanics" in the construction sector (Kochhar, 2008). After the onset of the crisis in 2007, both towns register a significant fall in first migrations with a more rapid descent observed in Pahuatlán.

Gender and first migration

Women make up almost one-quarter of migrants from Pahuatlán (23.4 percent) and Zapotitlán (23.9 percent). In Zapotitlán, women's migration lagged behind men's by about a decade (see Figure 2.3). Only a handful of women migrated in the 1980s. However, in the following decade and up until the mid-2000s, dozens

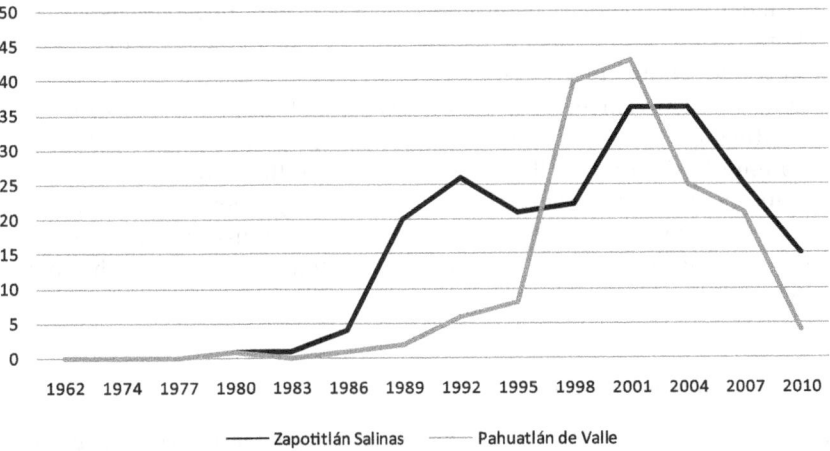

Figure 2.2 First international migration: Pahuatlán and Zapotitlán.
Source: Household surveys conducted in Pahuatlán and Zapotitlán.

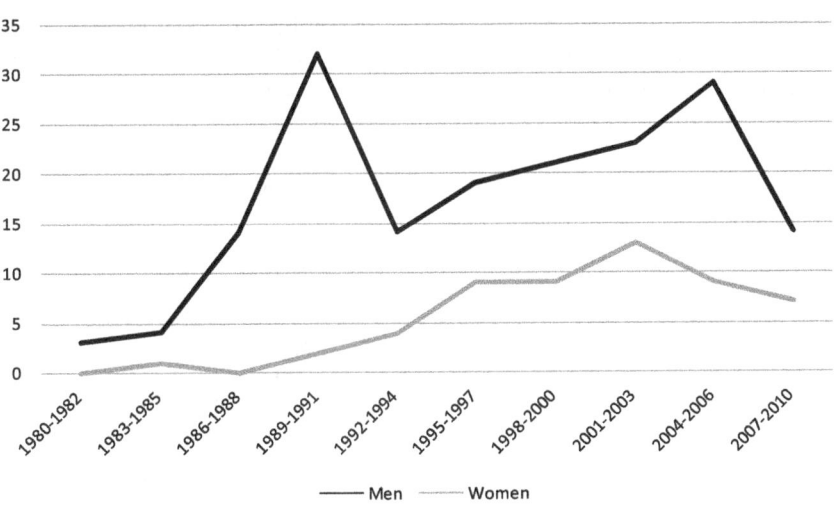

Figure 2.3 Zapotitlán: first international migration by gender.
Source: Household surveys conducted in Zapotitlán.

of women migrated. Their rapid incorporation into migration flows followed the accelerated pattern of the male counterparts, although on a smaller scale. Women's first migrations fell off considerably after the mid-2000s, again, mirroring the pattern of their male counterparts.

These tendencies are replicated with slight nuances in Pahuatlán. It is a late flow compared to that of the men, and their displacements take place in

48 *Surplus labor and restructured economies*

the decade of 1995–2005 (see Figure 2.4). The results in both localities do not contradict what has been reported in other research; however, as we have stated before, only a more detailed analysis allows us to question the conventional idea that women migrate for reunification purposes and only when the men leading the movement have paved a route and a safe insertion for them in the destination place (cfr. Chapters 1, 3 & 5). When speaking about the feminization of migration in this book we allude to the transformations associated with the global reorganization of labor along gender lines, the increase in the participation of women in wage labor in deindustrialized economies and the redefinition of their tasks both within and outside the home (Verschuur, 2013).

Gender and return migration

Of the total returnees to Pahuatlán, a greater percentage of women returned than men during the crisis. From 2008 to 2010, the rate of staying for Pahuatecos/as was 77 percent (23 percent returned). For women, 59 percent stayed in the US (41 percent returned). For men, 78 percent stayed (22 percent returned) (see Table 2.3 and Figure 2.5). The difference in return among men and women is explained by the relatively large number of young mothers with preschool age children, who had resided in the United States for comparatively short periods of time. They returned with their partners and children, that is, these represent family returns. This selectivity in the process of return, as will be analyzed in Chapter 5, responds to the greater difficulties of these women to combine waged work with the care of young children. By contrast,

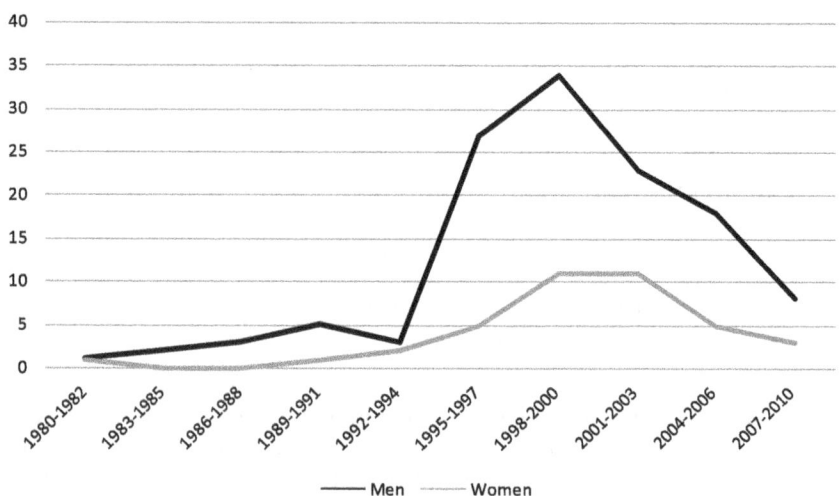

Figure 2.4 Pahuatlán: first international migration by gender.
Source: Household surveys conducted in Pahuatlán.

Table 2.3 Migration profile: Zapotitlán Salinas and Pahuatlán de Valle

	Households surveyed	Migrants recorded in survey	Households with migratory experience	Average migrants per household	US destinations	Employment	Rate of staying in US: active migrants/ total migrants *100
Zapotitlán Salinas	170	209	111 (65.3%)	2.0	New York City (86.6%) California (4.7%)	**Men**: Services: restaurants and markets (78%); construction industry (9%) **Women**: Services: domestic, personal care, restaurants (65%)	66
Pahuatlán de Valle	135	170	76 (56.3%)	2.2	North Carolina (60.9%) California and Virginia (12.6%)	**Men**: Construction industry (61.2%) **Women**: Services: restaurants, domestics, cleaning services (hotels, hospitals) (47.6%); Manufacturing and industrial cleaning services (14%)	77

Source: Household surveys conducted in Pahuatlán and Zapotitlán.

50 Surplus labor and restructured economies

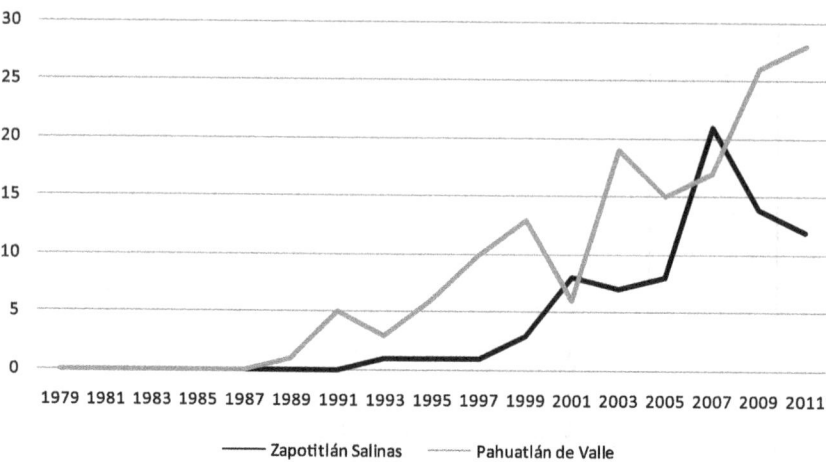

Figure 2.5 Return migration: Pahuatlán and Zapotitlán.
Source: Household surveys conducted in Pahuatlán and Zapotitlán.

the majority of men who returned to Pahuatlán did so alone (see Chapter 5 for details).

During the crisis, the rate of staying in the US for Zapotitecos/as from 2008 to 2010 was 64 percent (36 percent returned) for men, 75 percent (25 percent returned) for women and 66 percent (34 percent returned) overall. Zapotitecas were more likely to stay in New York, a finding that we relate to women's interest in maintaining the relatively high level of social reproduction in the United States when compared with rural Central Mexico. While there were more returns during the crisis years when compared to any other three-year period in the past, there was no massive return to Zapotitlán. The service sector into which men and women from Zapotitlán were inserted in New York experienced some contraction but did not expel massive numbers of workers (see Chapter 6 for details).

With these results, we confront a paradox. Pahuatecos, who worked principally in the construction sector, were more likely to stay in the United States than Zapotitecos, despite the fact that the construction sector experienced the greatest loss of employment during the economic crisis (Levine, 2015). We believe this paradox can be explained by the lower cost of living in North Carolina when compared to New York. According to the Cost of Living Index compiled by the Council for Community and Economic Research, in 2010 it was approximately 60 percent more expensive to live in New York than in Durham (2011). In Chapter 6, we will see how this high cost of reproduction was experienced by some Zapotitecos/as during the economic crisis and how it precipitated return migration in some cases.

Notes

1 Selective hegemony refers to the selective regulatory regimes of the neoliberal context that act upon the contingent of the rural population expelled from the industrial reserve army and transformed into the rural residual population. These regimes reign through dispossession. The state's objective is to articulate production with a democratic body that makes possible over-accumulation, principally through the flow of finance capital. In Mexico, this process originated in the 1990s in the simple reproduction of certain sectors of the indigenous population, not as groups of economic production, but as independent subjects.
2 The production of *ixtle* (derived from the Nahuatl, *ichtli*) involved extracting the fibers from the leaves of the maguey plant and twining them into rope of various sizes (see Cook & Binford, 1990, pp. 83–87, 262, n 9 for further details). In the nineteenth and first half of the twentieth centuries, the sale of *ixtle*, charcoal and goat products, both in Tehuacán and to the southwest, in the Mixtec region, supplemented the income earned from other local industries and subsistence agriculture.
3 The discussion in this chapter and Chapter 4 concerning onyx extraction, the development of the local onyx processing industry and the relationship of these processes to accelerated migration in Zapotitlán was originally discussed in Lee (2008).
4 These regional centers attracted raw materials and finished products marketed nationally and internationally (Secretaría de Economía, 2011). Within this industry, Zapotitlán represented a peripheral production zone of raw material and small artisanal products and some construction materials, such as pieces for mosaic flooring.
5 *El Informador* was the name of a free monthly Christian bulletin published in Spanish, and available in local businesses frequented by Hispanics in Durham (El Informador 2007).
6 Since 2006, North Carolina has increased enforcement of undocumented migration, leading to an active deportation policy. The sheriff's department of Mecklenburg county was the first in the country to start Program 287(g), whereby state and local police are deputized as federal immigration officers. This program mandates that police officers question the migratory status of anyone arrested for committing any crime. If the person does not have the proper documentation, they are turned over to immigration officials and often are deported (Gill, 2010).
7 See (Smith, 2006) for further details of these rivalries and the formation of Mexican youth gangs in New York.
8 Coleman (2007, p. 71, n 5) explains that the immigration laws passed in the 1990s eliminated the term "deportation":

> The concept of "removal" was introduced in its place to do away with the procedural distinctions between "exclusion" (i.e. denial of entrance at the border) and "deportation" (i.e. removal from the interior). The goal was to purge court protections offered under the latter.

9 It is possible that the same individual is removed more than once.

References

Andreas, P. (2000). *Border games: Policing the US-Mexico divide.* Ithaca: Cornell University Press.

Appendini, K. (2001). *De la milpa a los tortibonos: la restructuración de la política alimentaria en México*. México: El Colegio de México, Centro de Estudios Económicos, Instituto de Investigaciones de las Naciones Unidas para el Desarrollo Social.
Appendini, K., & Torres-Mazuera, G. (Eds). (2008). *¿Ruralidad sin agricultura? Perspectivas multidisciplinarias de una realidad fragmentada*. México D.F: El Colegio de México.
Arizpe, L. (1990). *Parentesco y economía en una sociedad nahua*. México: CONACULTA.
Arroyo, A., Berumen, J., Sandoval, S., & Rodríguez-Álvarez, D. (2010). Nuevas tendencias de largo plazo de la emigración de mexicanos a Estados Unidos y sus remesas. *Papeles de Población, 16*(63), 9–48.
Aysa-Lastra, M., & Cachón, L. (2012). Latino immigrant employment during the Great Recession: A comparison of the United States and Spain. *Norteamérica, 7*(2), 7–42.
BBVA Bancomer & CONAPO. (2014). *Yearbook of migration and remittances*. Mexico City: BBVA Bancomer and Consejo Nacional de Población.
BBVA & Consejo Nacional de Población. (2017). *Anuario de migración y remesas: México 2017*. Ciudad de México BBVA Bancomer and Consejo Nacional de Población.
Binford, L. (Ed.). (2004). *La economía política de la migración internacional en Puebla y Veracruz: Siete Estudios de Caso*. Puebla, México: Benemérita Universidad Autónoma de Puebla, Instituto de Ciencias Sociales y Humanidades.
Binford, L. (2013). *Tomorrow we're all going to the harvest: Temporary foreign worker programs and neoliberal political economy*. Austin: University of Texas Press.
Boehm, D. A. (2016). *Returned: Going and coming in an age of deportation*. Oakland: University of California Press.
Bourgois, P. (1995). *In search of respect: Selling crack in el barrio*. Cambridge, UK: Cambridge University Press.
Calavita, K. (1992). *Inside the state: The Bracero Program, immigration and the I.N.S.* London: Routledge.
Calderón Aragón, G., & Ramírez Velázquez, B. R. (2002). De campesino yuntero a jornalero: Neoliberalismo y desarrollo en el campo. In J. A. Segrelles (Ed.), *Agricultura y espacio rural en Latinoamérica y España: Posibilidades y riesgos ante la mundialización de la economía* (pp. 265–322). Madrid: Ministerio de Agricultura, Pesca y Alimentación.
Caldwell, B. C. (2019). *Deported Americans: Life after deportation to Mexico*. Durham: Duke University Press.
Canterbury, D. C. (2012). *Capital accumulation and migration*. Leiden: Koninklijke Brill NV.
Carton De Grammont, H. (1982). La venta de la fuerza de trabajo de los campesinos pobres y acumulación del capital. *Yucatán: Historia y economía, Universidad Autónoma de Yucatán, 34*(6), 30–44.
Carton De Grammont, H. (2004). La nueva ruralidad de América Latina. *Revista Mexicana de Sociología, 66*(Número especial), 279–300.
Castellón, B. R. (2006). *Cuthá: el cerro de la máscara. Arqueología y etnicidad en el sur de Puebla*. México D.F: Instituto Nacional de Antropolgía e Historia.
Chin, M. (2005). *Sewing women: Immigrants and the New York City garment industry*. New York: Columbia University Press.
Chishti, M., Pierce, S., & Bolter, J. (2017). *The Obama record on deportations: Deporter in Chief or not?* Retrieved from www.migrationpolicy.org/article/obama-record-deportations-deporter-chief-or-not.
Coleman, M. (2007). Immigration geopolitics beyond the Mexico-US border. *Antipode, 39*(1), 54–76. https://doi.org/10.1111/j.1467-8330.2007.00506.x.

Cook, S., & Binford, L. (1990). *Obliging need: Rural petty industry in Mexican capitalism*. Austin: University of Texas Press.

CoreLogic. (2017). United States residential foreclosure crisis: Ten years later. Retrieved 29 July 2019 from www.corelogic.com/research/foreclosure-report/national-foreclosure-report-10-year.pdf.

Cornelius, W. A. (1998). The structural embeddedness of demand for Mexican immigrant labor: New evidence from California. In M. M. Súarez-Orozco (Ed.), *Crossings: Mexican immigration in interdisciplinary perspectives* (pp. 113–144). Cambridge, MA: Harvard University Press.

Cornelius, W. A. (2001). Death at the border: Efficacy and unintended consequences of US immigration control policy. *Population and Development Review, 27*(4), 661–685.

Council for Community and Economic Research. (2011). *Cost of living index 2010*. Retrieved from https://census.gov/library/publications/2011/compendia/statab/131ed/prices.html

Cravey, A. J. (2003). Toque una Ranchera, por favor. *Antipode, 35*(3), 603–621. https://doi.org/10.1111/1467-8330.00341.

D'Aubeterre, M. E. (2019). Género, clase y migración: Trabajadoras pahautecas en el Nuevo New South. *Espacio Abierto. Cuaderno Venezolano de Sociología, 28*(1), 87–103.

De Genova, N. (2005). *Working the boundaries: Race, space, and "illegality" in Mexican Chicago*. Durham, NC: Duke University Press.

De León, J. (2015). *The land of open graves: Living and dying on the migrant trail*. Berkeley: University of California Press.

Dow, J. (2005). The Sierra Ñhäñu (Otomí). In A. Sandstrom & E. Garcia (Eds), *Native peoples of the Gulf Coast of Mexico* (pp. 231–254). Tucson: University of Arizona Press.

Dreby, J. (2015). *Everyday illegal: When policies undermine immigrant families*. Oakland: University of California Press.

Dunn, T. J. (1996). *The militarization of the US–Mexico border, 1978–1992: Low intensity doctrine comes home*. Austin: University of Texas Press.

Durand, J., Massey, D. S., & Capoferro, C. (2005). The new geography of Mexican immigration. In V. Zúñiga & R. Hernández-León (Eds), *New destinations: Mexican immigration in the United States* (pp. 1–20). New York: Russell Sage Foundation.

Espenshade, T. (1994). Does the threat of border apprehension deter undocumented US immigration? *Population and Development Review, 20*(4), 871–892.

Ewald, U. (1985). *The Mexican salt industry, 1560–1980: A study in change*. New York: Gustav Fischer Verlag Stuttgart.

Federal Reserve Bank of St. Louis. (2019). Civilian labor force participation rate. Retrieved 29 July 2019 from https://fred.stlouisfed.org/series/CIVPART.

Federici, S. (2006). Precarious labor: A feminist viewpoint. Retrieved 15 April 2019, from https://web.archive.org/web/20090129174238/http://auto_sol.tao.ca/node/3074.

Fitting, E. (2011). *The struggle for maize: Campesinos, workers and transgenic corn in the Mexican countryside*. Durham, NC: Duke University Press.

Flippen, C. A., & Parrado, E. A. (2012). Forging Hispanic communities in New destinations: A case study of Durham, North Carolina. *City and Community, 1*(11), 1–30. https://doi.org/10.1111/j.1540-6040.2011.01369.x.

Foner, N. (2013). Introduction: Immigrants in New York City in the new millennium. In N. Foner (Ed.), *One out of three: Immigrant New York in the twenty-first century* (pp. 1–34). New York: Columbia University Press.

Friedman, J. (2015). Global systemic crisis, class, and its representations. In J. G. Carrier & D. Kalb (Eds), *Anthropologies of class: Power, practice and inequality*. Cambridge: Cambridge University Press.

Fuentes Díaz, A. (Ed.). (2012). *Necropolítica, violencia y escepción en América Latina*. Puebla: Benemérita Universidad Autónoma de Puebla.

Furuseth, O. J., & Smith, H. A. (2016). From Winn-Dixie to Tiendas: The remaking of the New South. In O. J. Furuseth & H. A. Smith (Eds), *Latinos in the New South: Transformations of place* (pp. 1–17). London: Routledge.

Galinier, J. (1987). *Pueblos de la Sierra Norte. Etnografía de la comunidad Otomí*. México D.F.: Instituto Nacional Indigenista.

Gandini, L., Lozano-Ascencio, F., & Gaspar, S. (2015). *El retorno en el nuevo escenario de la migración entre México y Estados Unidos*. México, D.F: Consejo Nacional de Población (CONAPO).

García Martínez, B. (1987). *Los pueblos de la Sierra: El poder y el espacio de los indios del norte de Puebla hasta 1700*. México D.F.: El Colegio de México.

Gill, H. (2010). *The Latino migration experience in North Carolina. New roots in the Old North State*. Chapel Hill: The University of North Carolina Press.

Glaeser, E. L. (2005). Urban colossus: Why is New York America's largest city? *FRBNY Economic Policy Review*, 7–24. Retrieved from www.newyorkfed.org/medialibrary/media/research/epr/05v11n2/0512glae.pdf.

Golash-Boza, T. M. (2012). *Due process denied: Detentions and deportations in the United States*. New York: Routledge.

Goldstein, D., & Alonso-Bejarano, C. (2017). E-terrify: Securitized immigration and biometric surveillance in the workplace. *Human Organization*, 76(1), 1–14.

Gonzales, R. G., & Chavez, L. (2012). "Awakening to a nightmare": Abjectivity and illegality in the lives of undocumented 1.5-generation Latino immigrants in the United States. *Current Anthropology*, 53(3), 255–281.

Gonzalez, E. (2004). *The Bronx*. New York: Columbia University Press.

Gonzalez-Barrera, A. (2015). *More Mexicans leaving than coming to the US*. Retrieved from www.pewhispanic.org/files/2015/11/2015-11-19_mexican-immigration_FINAL.pdf.

Gonzalez-Barrera, A. (2016). *Apprehensions of Mexican migrants at US borders reach near-historic low*. Retrieved from http://pewrsr.ch/1VYPFlk.

Griesbach, K. A. (2011). Local-federal immigration enforcement in North Carolina: Mapping the criminal-immigration overlap. *Norteamérica*, 6, 91–127. https://doi.org/10.22201/cisan.24487228e.2011.3.148.

Griffith, D. (2005). Rural industry and Mexican immigration and settlement in North Carolina. In R. Hernández-León & V. Zúñiga (Eds), *New destinations: Mexican immigration in the United States* (pp. 50–74). New York: Russell Sage Foundation.

Hahamovitch, C. (2014). *No man's land: Jamaican guest workers in America and the global history of deportable labor*. Princeton: Princeton University Press.

Harvey, D. (1989). *The condition of postmodernity: An enquiry into the origins of cultural change*. Oxford: Blackwell.

Harvey, D. (2003). *The new imperialism*. Oxford: Oxford University Press.

Harvey, D. (2010). *The enigma of capital and the crises of capitalism*. New York: Oxford University Press.

Hernández-Navarro, L. (1992). Cafetaleros del adelgazamiento estatal a la guerra de mercado. In J. Mogel, C. Botey, & L. Hernández (Eds), *Autonomía y nuevos sujetos sociales en el desarrollo rural* (pp. 78–96). México D.F.: Siglo XXI Editores y CEHAM.

Heyman, J. M. (1995). Putting power in the anthropology of bureaucracy: The immigration and naturalization service at the Mexico-United States border. *Current Anthropology*, *36*(2), 261–287.
Heyman, J. M. (2012). Capitalism and US policy at the Mexican border. *Dialectical Anthropology*, *36*(3–4), 263–277. https://doi.org/10.1007/s10624-012-9274-x.
Heyman, J. M. (2014). "Illegality" and the US-Mexico border: How it is produced and resisted. In C. Menjívar & D. Kanstroom (Eds), *Constructing immigrant "illegality": Critiques, experiences, and responses* (pp. 111–135). New York: Cambridge University Press.
Hirschman, C., & Massey, D. S. (2008). Places and peoples: The new American mosaic. In D. Massey (Ed.), *New faces in new places: The new American mosaic* (pp. 1–22). New York: Russell Sage Foundation.
El Informador. (2007, December 12). La maldita vecindad. Retrieved 10 March 2008 from www.elinformadornc.com.
Instituto Nacional de Geografía Estadística e Informática (INEGI). (1972). *Tabulados básicos. Estados Unidos Mexicanos. Estados Unidos Mexicanos. IX Censo General de Población y Vivienda, 1970*. México: Instituto Nacional de Estadística Geografía e Informática.
Instituto Nacional de Geografía Estadística e Informática (INEGI). (1982). *Tabulados básicos. Estados Unidos Mexicanos. Estados Unidos Mexicanos. X Censo General de Población y Vivienda, 1980*. México: Instituto Nacional de Estadística Geografía e Informática.
Instituto Nacional de Estadística y Geografía (INEGI). (1990). *XI Censo general de población y vivienda 1990*. Retrieved from https://inegi.org.mx/programas/ccpv/1990/
Instituto Nacional de Estadística y Geografía (INEGI). (2000). *XII Censo general de población y vivienda 2000*. Retrieved from https://inegi.org.mx/programas/ccpv/2000/
Instituto Nacional de Estadística y Geografía (INEGI). (2010). *Censo de población y vivienda 2010*. Retrieved from https://inegi.org.mx/programas/ccpv/2010/
Izcara Palacios, S. P. (2010). La adicción a la mano de obra ilegal: Jornaleros tamaulipecos en Estados Unidos. *Latin American Research Review*, *45*(1), 55–75. https://doi.org/10.1353/lar.0.0099.
Jusionyte, I. (2018). Called to "Ankle Alley": Tactical infrastructure, migrant injuries, and emergency medical services on the US–Mexico border. *American Anthropologist*, *120*(1), 89–101. https://doi.org/10.1111/aman.12967.
Kalleberg, A. L., & Von Wachter, T. M. (2017). The US labor market during and after the Great Recession: Continuities and transformations. *RSF: The Russell Sage Foundation Journal of the Social Sciences*, *3*(3), 1–19. https://doi.org/10.7758/RSF.2017.3.3.01.
Kasarda, J. D., & Johnson, J. H. (2006). *The economic impact of the Hispanic population on the state of North Carolina*. Chapel Hill: The University of North Carolina.
Kochhar, R. (2008). *Latino Labor Report, 2008: Construction reverses job growth for Latinos*. Retrieved from www.pewhispanic.org/files/reports/88.pdf.
Kochhar, R., & Cilluffo, A. (2017). *How wealth inequality has changed in the US since the Great Recession, by race, ethnicity and income*. Retrieved from www.pewresearch.org/fact-tank/2017/11/01/how-wealth-inequality-has-changed-in-the-u-s-since-the-great-recession-by-race-ethnicity-and-income/.
Kofman, E., & Raghuram, P. (2015). *Gendered migrations and global social reproduction*. https://doi.org/10.1057/9781137510143.
Lara, G. (2010). De cajas populares a cooperativas de ahorro y préstamo. Algunas evidencias. *Estudios Agrarios*, *45*, 119–127.
Lara Flores, S. (2010). *Migraciones de trabajo y movilidad territorial*. México D.F.: Porrúa Miguel Ángel Editor.

Lee, A. E. (2008). "Para salir adelante": The emergence and acceleration of international migration in new sending areas of Puebla, Mexico. *Journal of Latin American and Caribbean Anthropology, 13*(1), 48–78.

Lee, A. E. (2014). Territorialisation, conservation, and neoliberalism in the Tehuacán–Cuicatlán Biosphere Reserve, Mexico. *Conservation and Society, 12*(2), 147–161. https://doi.org/10.4103/0972-4923.138413.

Lee, A. E. (2018). US-Mexico border militarization and violence: Dispossession of undocumented laboring classes from Puebla, Mexico. *Migraciones Internacionales, 9*(35), 213–238.

Levine, E. (2015). Why did Mexico United-States migration begin to decrease in 2008? *Problemas del Desarrollo, 46*(182), 1–15.

Levine, E., & LeBaron, A. (2011). Immigration policy in the Southeastern United States: Potential for internal conflict. *Norteamérica, 6*, 5–32.

Lydgate, J. (2010). *Assembly-line justice: A review of operation streamline.* Retrieved from www.law.berkeley.edu/files/Operation_Streamline_Policy_Brief.pdf.

Macip, R. F., & Zamora, C. (2012). "If we work in conservation money will flow our way": Hegemony and duplicity on the coast of Oaxaca, Mexico. *Dialectical Anthropology, 36*, 71–87.

Macip, R. F. (2005). *Semos un país de peones: Café, crisis y estado neoliberal en el centro de Veracruz.* Puebla: ICSyH-BUAP.

Martínez Canales, L. A. (2012). Los migrantes nahuas de Zongolica rumbo a Estados Unidos. *Estado y Sociedad, 19*, 31–35.

Martínez-Reyes, J. E. (2016). *Moral ecology of a forest: The nature industry and Maya post-conservation.* Tucson: The University of Arizona Press.

Martínez, D. E., Slack, J., & Martínez-Schuldt, R. (2018). The rise of mass deportation in the United States. In R. Martinez, Jr., M. E. Hollis, & J. I. Stowell (Eds), *The handbook of race, ethnicity, crime, and justice* (1st ed., pp. 173–201). https://doi.org/10.1002/9781119113799.ch8.

Mezzadra, S., & Neilson, B. (2013). *Border as method, or the multiplication of labor.* Durham: Duke University Press.

Minchin, T. J. (2012). Life and labor in the New South. In R. H. Zieger (Ed.), *Shutdowns in the Sun Belt: The decline of the textile and apparel industry and deindustrialization in the South* (pp. 258–288). Gainesville: University Press of Florida.

Mintz, S. (1996). *Dulzura y poder. El lugar del azúcar en la historia moderna.* México D.F.: Siglo XXI Editores.

Mohl, R. A. (2003). Globalization, Latinization and the Nuevo New South. *Journal of American Ethnic History, 22*(4), 31–66.

Mouat, A. C. (1980). *Los Chiveros de la Mixteca Baja.* México D.F: Universidad Nacional Autónoma de México.

Myhre, D. (1998). The Achilles' Heel of the reforms: The rural finance system. In *The transformation of rural Mexico: Reforming the Ejido sector* (pp. 39–65). La Jolla, CA: Center for US–Mexican Studies.

Nevins, J. (2010). *Operation gatekeeper and beyond: The war on "illegals" and the remaking of the US–Mexico boundary* (2nd ed.). New York: Routledge.

New York State Assembly. (2004). Rewarding work: A fair minimum wage. Retrieved 19 September 2019 from https://nyassembly.gov/comm/WAM/2004MinWage/#toc5.

Ngai, M. (2004). *Impossible subjects: Illegal aliens and the making of modern America.* Princeton: Princeton University Press.

Nolasco, M. (1985). *Café y sociedad en México.* México D.F.: Centro de Ecodesarrollo.

Otero, G. (2011). Neoliberal globalization, NAFTA, and migration: Mexico's loss of food and labor sovereignty. *Journal of Poverty*, *15*(4), 384–402. https://doi.org/10.1080/10875549.2011.614514.

Otero, G. (2017). In pursuit of real utopias: Kerry Preibisch as an organic public sociologist. *Canadian Review of Sociology*, *54*(3), 353–359.

Passel, J., & Cohn, D. (2019). *Mexicans decline to less than half the US unauthorized immigrant population for the first time*. Retrieved from www.pewresearch.org/fact-tank/2019/06/12/us-unauthorized-immigrant-population-2017/.

Passel, J., Cohn, D., & Gonzalez-Barrera, A. (2012). *Net migration from Mexico falls to zero—and perhaps less*. Retrieved from www.pewhispanic.org/2012/04/23/net-migration-from-mexico-falls-to-zero-and-perhaps-less/.

Popke, J. (2011). Latino migration and neoliberalism in the South: Notes toward a rural cosmopolitanism. *Southeastern Geographer*, *51*(2), 242–259.

Preibisch, K. (2007). Local produce, foreign labour: Labour mobility programs and global trade competitiveness in Canada. *Rural Sociology*, *72*, 418–449.

Roseberry, W. (1991). Los campesinos y el mundo. In S. Plattner (Ed.), *Antropología económica* (pp. 154–176). México DF: Alianza Editorial y CONACULTA.

Rothstein, F. A. (2016). *Mexicans on the move: Migration and return in rural Mexico*. https://doi.org/10.1057/9781137559944.0001.

Rubio, B. (2001). *Explotados y excluidos: los campesinos latinoamericanos en la fase agroexportadora neoliberal*. México D.F.: Plaza y Valdés, Universidad Autónoma Chapingo.

Rubio, B. (2008). De la crisis hegemónica y financiera a la crisis alimentaria. Impacto sobre el campo mexicano. *Argumentos*, *21*(57), 35–52.

Rus, J. (1995). Local adaptation to global change: The reordering of native society in highland Chiapas, 1974–1994. *Revista Europea de Estudios Latinoamericanos y Del Caribe/European Review of Latin American and Caribbean Studies*, *58*, 82–91.

Ruvalcaba Mercado, J. (1996). Vacas, mulas, azúcar y café. Los efectos de su introducción en la Huasteca, México. *Revista Española de Antropología Americana*, *26*, 121–141.

Sánchez Korrol, V. (2010). Puerto Ricans. In K. T. Jackson (Ed.), *The encyclopedia of New York City* (pp. 1058–1060). New Haven: Yale University Press.

Sassen, S. (1998a). America's immigration "problem." In *Globalization and its discontents* (pp. 31–54). New York: The New Press.

Sassen, S. (1998b). *Globalization and its discontents*. New York: The New Press.

Sassen, S. (2001). Cracked casings: Notes towards an analytics for studying transnational processes. In L. Pries (Ed.), *New transnational spaces: International migration and transnational companies in the early twenty-first century* (pp. 187–207). London: Routledge.

Secretaría de Desarrollo Social. (2019). Catálogo de Localidades. Retrieved 15 August 2019 from www.microrregiones.gob.mx/catloc/LocdeMun.aspx?tipo=clave&campo=loc&ent=21&mun=109.

Secretaría de Economía. (2011). *Estudio de la cadena productiva del Ónix*. Retrieved from www.2006-2012.economia.gob.mx/files/comunidad_negocios/informacion_sectorial/mineria/CadenaProductivadelOnix.pdf.

Sider, G. (2006). The production of race, locality, and state: An anthropology. *Antropologica*, *48*(2), 247–263.

Silver, B. (2014). Theorizing the working class in twenty-first-century global capitalism. In M. Atzeni (Ed.), *Workers and labour in a globalised capitalism: Contemporary themes and theoretical issues* (pp. 46–69). London: Palgrave Macmillan.

Skeggs, B. (1997). *Formations of class and gender: Becoming respectable*. London: Sage Publications.

Slack, J., Martinez, D., Lee, A., & Whiteford, S. (2016). The geography of border militarization: Violence, death and health in Mexico and the United States. *Journal of Latin American Geography, 15*(1), 7–32. https://doi.org/10.1353/lag.2016.0009.

Slack, J., Martinez, D., Whiteford, S., & Peiffer, E. (2013). *In the shadow of the wall: Family separation, immigration enforcement and security*. Retrieved from http://las.arizona.edu/sites/las.arizona.edu/files/UA_Immigration_Report2013web.pdf.

Slack, J., Martinez, D., Whiteford, S., & Peiffer, E. (2015). In harm's way: Family separation, immigration enforcement programs and security on the US–Mexico border. *Journal on Migration and Human Security, 3*(2), 109–128.

Smith, G. (2011). Selective hegemony and beyond-populations with "no productive function": A framework for enquiry. *Identities: Global Studies in Culture and Power, 18*, 2–38.

Smith, R. C. (2006). *Mexican New York: Transnational lives of new immigrants*. Berkeley and Los Angeles: University of California Press.

Smith, B. E., & Winders, J. (2007). We're here to stay: Economic restructuring, Latino migration and place-making in the South. *Transactions of the Institute of British Geographers, 33*, 60–72.

Stresser-Peán, & Guilhem, O. (2008). *Viaje a la Huasteca con Guy Stresser-Peán*. México D.F.: Fondo de Cultura Económica.

Suárez-Orozco, M. M. (2003). Right moves? Immigration, globalization, utopia, and dystopia. In N. Foner (Ed.), *American arrivals: Anthropology engages the new immigration* (pp. 45–74). Santa Fe, NM: School for Advanced Research Press.

Tett, G. (2009). *Fool's gold: How the bold dream of a small tribe at J.P. Morgan was corrupted by greed and unleashed a catastrophe*. New York: Free Press.

Trouillot, M.-R. (2013). *Transformaciones globales. La antropología y el mundo moderno*. Cauca-Bogotá: Universidad del Cauca, CESO-Universidad de los Andes.

US Bureau of Labor Statistics. (2012). The recession of 2007–2009: BLS spotlight on statistics. Retrieved 29 July 2019 from www.bls.gov/spotlight/2012/recession/pdf/recession_bls_spotlight.pdf.

US Census Bureau. (2019). Housing vacancies and homeownership. Retrieved 29 July 2019 from www.census.gov/housing/hvs/data/histtabs.html.

US Department of Labor. (2019). Bureau of Labor Statistics: Databases, tables and calculators by subject. Retrieved 29 July 29 2019 from https://data.bls.gov/pdq/SurveyOutputServlet.

Velasco Santos, P. (2017). Mezclilla, consumo y la configuración de los sujetos rurales neoliberales en Tlaxcala, México. *Revista San Gregorio, 18*, 34–45.

Velásquez, L. I. (2005). *Impacto socioeconómico de la Biotecnología en la cafeticultura mexicana*. Puebla: Benemérita Universidad Autónoma de Puebla.

Vélez-Ibañez, C. G. (2010). *An impossible living in a transborder world: Culture, confianza and economy of Mexican-origin populations*. Tucson: The University of Arizona Press.

Verschuur, C. (2013). Reproduction sociale et care comme échange économico-affectif. L'articulation des rapports sociaux dans l'économie domestique et globalisée. In *Genre, migrations et globalization de la reproduction sociale* (pp. 23–36). Paris: L'Hartmattan.

Villarreal, A. (2014). Explaining the decline in Mexico-US migration: The effect of the Great Recession. *Demography, 51*(6), 2203–2228. https://doi.org/10.1007/s13524-014-0351-4.

Wilson, T. D. (2000). Anti-immigrant sentiment and the problem of reproduction/maintenance in Mexican immigration to the United States. *Critique of Anthropology, 20*(2), 191–213.

Wolf, E. R. (1982). *Europe and the people without history*. Berkeley: University of California Press.

3 Disarticulation of agriculture, transition to a service economy in the Sierra Norte of Puebla and accelerated migration to the *Nuevo* New South

Introduction

In this chapter we examine the connection of two distant and unequal territories through the provision of cheap and undocumented workers from Pahuatlán in the Northern Sierra of Puebla, in the center of Mexico, to North Carolina, in the *Nuevo* New South (Levine & LeBaron, 2011; Mohl, 2003) during the last four decades. Underpinning this process, we identify a relative surplus population proliferating in an area in which, compared to other states in the country and even within the state of Puebla, the migration rates to the United States were low and moderated until the 1980s. Our analysis of the historical conditions preceding this accelerated, but short-lived, migratory flow in the 1990s, focuses on the contradictory class experiences configured in various sites of exploitation during periods of mobility and immobility of the relative surplus population.

We argue that these mobilities are shaped by the disarticulation and rearticulation of the conditions of reproduction of rural populations under successive waves of capitalist expansion. The narratives of men and women from three generations collected in the field allow us to recognize oscillations and intermittences in this erratic process shaped by displacements in and out of the region and by the rise in migration to the United States in the mid-1990s. The transition from agriculture to manufacturing, to craft production, or to a range of informal activities between one generation and the next, and even throughout the life of these men and women, attests to these comings and goings.

The way persistent and chronic uncertainty is experienced depends on several imponderables of smallholder subsistence production. It also depends on the loss of viability of two crops with commercial value (sugar cane and coffee) that have dominated the political economy of the area under study and the changing relations of these rural populations in Central Mexico with the state (see Chapter 2). Adding to this is the narrow margin of these populations to respond to climate contingencies, crop losses, or to surmount family crises and diseases, which place them in a perennial state of informal survival (Green, 2009). Such uncertainty is shared with rural populations all over the world who have become redundant as neoliberalism marches in its path of dispossession and pillage (Harvey, 1989; Li, 2014; Mezzadra & Neilson, 2013; Pini & Leach, 2011). Such

DOI: 10.4324/9780429454196-3

paths are characteristic of a globalizing process that, far from "homogenizing," points to a greater differentiation because local social reproduction has become unattainable for a considerable segment of these populations.

In this chapter, we insist on the centrality of class in people's lives. We also emphasize that class is not limited to the experience of collective work in a factory, nor to the distinction between owner and disciplined workers, and neither to a "consciousness in itself" that mobilizes the political potential of a given collective (Kalb, 2015; Mollona, 2014; Smith, 2015) (see Chapter 1). We stress the malleability and historical instability of working classes and, at the same time, we highlight the role gender plays in the process of class formation (Narotzky & Smith, 2006). Moving in this direction leads us to acknowledge with Bettie (2003, p. 32) that in late capitalism, class subjectivity is built in a complex manner in relation to gender and ethnic/racial identities. We show the random, unstable and oscillating absorption of relative surplus populations (Marx, 1990, pp. 786, 789) that combine work both inside and outside their regions of origin.

Our ethnographic research also uncovers a process that runs counter to the representation of the male Fordist worker/producer/breadwinner/head of household vs woman/reproducer/dependent on the male's income, that has dominated the "teleological narrative" or "selective tradition" still prevalent in the social sciences (De Genova, 2016; Smith, 2015). Such a masculinized class subject was never fully realized under the expansive waves of Fordist capitalism, and even less so after the dismantling of the welfare state. Furthermore, in the so-called developing countries, this model certainly had focalized and scattered expressions. These insights inform our task of documenting the transformations of the migratory regime linked to the changes in the accumulation pattern, a process that includes the massive incorporation of women in deregulated labor markets (Harvey, 1989; Kofman & Raghuram, 2015; Mezzadra & Neilson, 2013; Oso & Ribas-Mateos, 2013).

The comparatively recent accelerated flows that originated in Central and Southern Mexico to new destinations in the United States, such as the case we analyze here, allow us to identify transitions in the migration of women linked to the deindustrialization of the US economy and job insecurity (Harvey, 2003; Hondagneu-Sotelo, 2011; Sassen, 2002, 2003). In this accelerated migration we identify the combination of the traditional model of individual and cyclic mobility—of male predominance, a "military model of migration" of sorts, usually linked to the agro-industry (Griffith, 2005)—with an emerging mobility scheme of single women or with dependents, which overlaps with the migration of young couples with or without children. This combination frequently results in settlement migrations (Pedone, Gil Araujo, Echeverrí, & Agrela, 2011), sustained by networks that underpin the reproduction processes of workers and their families leading to the development of communities (Griffith, 2005, p. 52).

The initial organization of domestic conglomerates of unaccompanied men gave way in the 1990s to new formations that included men, related to each other or not, without dependents and to conjugal couples that settled temporarily in those "homes." Demographically, Pahuatecan flows supplied these new classes of emerging workers in North Carolina with first-generation adult migrants, as well as children that made up the "1.5 generation." These groups where daily reproduction was organized, acted as a base or station of men who came and went. Their insertion in the construction industry forced them to constantly move between small towns in the region or to other states. The establishment of these new communities of immigrants was related to internal displacements in the *Nuevo* New South and between borders. A series of threads connected these communities, much like a switch, and several households anchored them in the various places between which workers moved (Griffith, 2005, p. 53).

This new mobility pattern of Pahuatecan women, supported by a sustained demand for cheap, unstable, deportable (De Genova & Peutz, 2010; Mezzadra & Neilson, 2013), and therefore severely disciplined labor (Lee, 2015), entailed increased inequalities in reproduction that were "stratified and re-localized on a global scale" (Colen, 1995). We document the conditions that underlie the production of the mother-worker-undocumented migrant subject, whose experience of mobility between two countries was intertwined with precarious work, over-exploitation and gender inequality. We explain the tensions that traverse a new type of binational domestic arrangement, a formation that grew during the last three decades in the context of the decrease of circular migration between Mexico and the United States.

The background of an accelerated migration flow

During our first field trips to the municipality of Pahuatlán in the summer of 2007, our attention was drawn to the long lines of women waiting to exchange dollar remittances in a microbank, the Mexican Association of Credit Unions from the Social Sector (AMUCSS, its acronym in Spanish), established in 2003. The association promoted the saving and investment of remittances in areas of Mexico located far away from urban centers and lacking financial services. From the 1980s, as coffee growing lost viability and pluriactivity gained ground as a compensatory mechanism, the number of households depending on foreign currency increased, with the subsequent activation of informal avenues of dollar remittances based on family and common-origin networks.

The literature about transnational migration recognizes the importance of telephones and electronic media to maintain and reproduce ties with long-distance suppliers (migrant sons/daughters, husbands, fathers/mothers) whose economic support mitigates the precarious situation of many households and communities in Mexico. The rapid incorporation of migration to global financial capital operations takes advantage of the activities surrounding these flows of poor immigrants (agencies that manage remittances, loan and saving systems, telephone and electronic media consumption) to increase their profits despite the ups and downs in the circulation of people and money (Alarcón, 2015; Canterbury, 2012). The impressive circulation of money, goods and news between countries supplying and receiving workers leads one to think that the connection between these remote regions in the national geography is a recent phenomenon, for which globalization is responsible.

However, our research allows us to assert that the region under study slowly began to take shape in the 1940s as a provider of cheap, precarious and "deportable" (De Genova & Peutz, 2010) labor for the economy of the United States. Under the Bracero Program, signed between both countries and successively renewed between 1942–1964, grandparents and parents of contemporary migrants crossed the border by themselves, without dependents, as temporary workers. At first, they were hired to work laying railway tracks and, later, in the agriculture of the US Southwest.

Under the mobility model of single men without dependents, capital takes advantage of the separation between the costs of maintaining the labor force and its reproduction costs. Hahamovitch (quoted in Binford, 2013, p. 2) points out that the "perfect worker" can be attracted and expelled according to the needs of domestic capitalists. Neither the employers nor the state assumes responsibility regarding migrants' previous training or social reproduction. The migrant worker cannot aspire to citizenship nor to the rights associated with it. By inviting "guest workers," nation states seek to import workers that produce surplus value without caring about the real people, their families, needs and expectations beyond the field, the factory or the construction site.

The migratory pattern of unaccompanied men (Alarcón & Mines, 2002) strengthened the narrative of the breadwinner/head of household male and the anchoring of the woman specialized in the reproduction of the group (Cohen, 2005). In Chapter 1 we mentioned the misunderstandings and dissimulation entailed in a superficial reading of this formula underlying migration selectivity on a gender basis. The Bracero program, with a clear gender bias (Cohen, 2005; Flores Álvarez, 2018; Hahamovitch, 2014), set up a subject managed under a temporary mobility regime that was regulated, "not free," and subject to the terms of the agreement and to the requirements of the agricultural cycle. Such a subject is ambiguous insofar as he is neither a slave nor a free worker. For the duration of the program, nearly four and a half million male workers were mobilized (Durand & Massey, 2003). In parallel, it is estimated that during the 1950s there was an average of four undocumented migrants for each hired worker (Chant, 2007), who constituted a "free," irregular labor force without contract. The oscillation between "free" and "not free" work, between regularity and irregularity, resulted in the fragmentation and devaluing of the labor force administered by the Bracero Program (Flores Álvarez, 2018).

In certain regions of the state of Puebla, such as the Mixteca and the Atlixco Valley, there was continuity between the mobility associated with the program and undocumented migration in later years (Macías & Herrera, 1997; Marroni, 2006; Smith, 1995). In other areas, there was a clear break between both moments (Binford, 2003). This is the case of the municipality of Pahuatlán, where a gap of nearly three decades existed between the Bracero migration of men, of little repercussion in the economic life of the municipality, and the accelerated, massive, undocumented migration of the last 30 years. In the 1950s and 1960s, the Bracero migration coexisted with sugarcane production and brown sugar manufacturing. Furthermore, indigenous and mestizo peasants and day laborers were seasonally employed in those years in nearby cities and coffee plantations, as well as in sugarcane and corn fields in the lowlands of the neighboring state of Veracruz.

State-subsidized coffee growing (Macip, 2005), temporary and intermittent employment and informal activities in urban centers contained, to a certain extent, the migratory flows towards the United States in the northwestern part of the Sierra Norte in the state of Puebla. However, agricultural production gradually lost its centrality in the political economy of the municipality of Pahuatlán due principally to the dismantling of the parastatal INMECAFE, that provided assistance to small coffee growers. Other factors were added to the decline of agriculture: a drop in minimum wage, currency devaluation in 1994 leading to the ruin of hundreds of indebted producers and the devastating effects of climate contingencies, plagues and crop loss, from which smallholder coffee growers and other segments of the population linked to the productive chain of coffee were not able to recover.

Pahuatecos' migration to the United States sprang up again, and it accelerated and massified between 1990 and 2005. In a context characterized by the lack of local opportunities, the economic expansion of the US Southeast (Griesbach, 2011; Levine & LeBaron, 2011; Mohl, 2003; Popke, 2011) constituted a promising lifeline for Pahuatecos/as. The negative effects on the local economy were not only felt by coffee growers: the population in general suffered the consequences of this debacle. Don Samuel, a Pahuateco from the county seat and resident of Durham, North Carolina living with his wife and sons since 1998, remembers this critical juncture and the strategies families deployed in the face of the total abandonment by the state of its already weakened role of supporting rural populations:

> My father, in addition to the bakery, sold groceries. My father's business helped me realize how much coffee influenced the economy of the town, and not only the town of Pahuatlán, but all the communities [of the municipality], because when the coffee harvest and the coffee price was high, everybody could afford clothing, they could buy everything: meat, bread. I remember [that] in that time my father's bakery was very successful, but coffee was behind it all. Then there was a frost and all the coffee in the town froze, that was what ruined the town. The town couldn't do anything but send their sons to the north. "There is no future here," they said.
> (Samuel, construction industry worker, Durham, NC, October 2013)

Sons of mestizo coffee growers from the county seat, or families dedicated to traditional trades and commerce, and even teachers and local bureaucrats progressively joined this migratory flow. In short, Pahuatecan migration multiplied and diversified, incorporating men and women from sectors of different ethnic affiliation, class origin and with higher levels of schooling. The turning point of Pahuatecos/as' late, accelerated and undocumented migration to the US Southeast was the rearticulation of a rural-rural flow, which connected this municipality of the mountains with agro-industrial areas in Texas in the 1980s. Such migration still had the military imprint of the Bracero Program, masculine and circular. Between the mid-1980s and the mid-1990s, this flow of undocumented workers redirected itself to North Carolina, progressively subjecting itself to the urban labor market. This market demanded flexible, cheap and unorganized labor in areas of recent capital relocation, especially in the construction sector and in low-paid services where women were over-represented. At the same time, the displacements gradually lost circularity given the increased risks and costs of border crossing, forcing workers to stay in once place longer. In short, the histories of mobility in the region show the tension between forces that retain populations in the territory by creating compulsive social dependency ties and, either successive or overlapping forces that catapult labor to other places. Coffee growing and subsistence production maintained populations in Pahuatlán while the loss of viability of a strategic monoculture devoid of state coverage expelled labor from the region. The pressure exerted by these processes on peasants/artisans and their families yielded absolute surplus value.

Transitions in migratory patterns

In the context of the privatizing policies that characterized the restructuring of both rural Mexico and the sustained growth of a transnational labor force, the households of migrant workers reconfigured themselves, accentuating the importance of kinship and of gender dispositions that ensured the reproduction of communities and households through translocalized practices and cultural and economic policies. "Transnational maternities," "long-distance conjugality," and "check parents" (D'Aubeterre, 2000; Hondagneu-Sotelo, 2011; Hondagneu-Sotelo & Avila, 2003; Mummert, 1999)—among other terms coined in the 1990s and in the last decade to allude to these arrangements—express that, as social arrangements relocate due to the displacements of workers to the United States, the binomial domestic group-household, as a spatial field of intimate cohabitation and daily reproduction, becomes disjointed as well. It is assumed, however, that these are temporary disjunctions, after which everything will return to normal. In these scenarios, more or less temporary arrangements abound to mitigate the instability and uncertainty. Thus, in a few years, reunification and dispersion episodes can occur on both sides of the border. These groups experience many tensions, and marital separations detonate abrupt turns triggered by the distance in the lives of families.

Despite the efforts of national governments to regulate these flows, for example, by granting temporary worker visas, undocumented labor migration has not been eliminated. Nor has migration for the purpose of family reunification. Thus, paradoxically, the increased border surveillance and the risks and costs of border crossing resulted in longer migratory cycles that fostered early processes of conjugal and intergenerational reunification, as well as the formation of first and second unions between young people that spend long periods of time away from their communities of origin and procreate their firstborns in the neighboring country.

The statistics about the composition of Mexican workers' households in the United States allow us to infer the coexistence of these two mobility patterns in the past three decades, during which greater barriers were established to contain the undocumented flows from all over Mexico. The increase of binational domestic formations stands out. According to data from the Pew Hispanic Center, in 2005 there were 1.8 million undocumented children living in the United States, representing 16 percent of the 1.1 million Mexican migrants without legal residence or US citizenship. Furthermore, it was estimated that 3.1 million children who were United States citizens by birth lived in households in which at least one of the parents did not have legal residence (Passel, 2006). To illustrate these transitions, in 1990, 65 percent of Mexican migrants residing in North Carolina were unaccompanied adult men whose age ranged between 18 and 65 years. After a decade, only 42 percent had the same profile. In contrast, in six states from the South and Southeast, including North Carolina, the percentage of young adults and children of Latino origin grew from 2.5 percent in 1980 to 8 percent of the population in 2005 (Minchin, 2012, p. 4). This allows us to infer the existence of transitions towards settlement migration in this so-called "last frontier of Mexican migration" (Furuseth & Smith, 2016).

It is worth analyzing these transformations in the context of the global division of labor focusing on the configuration of a highly stratified transnational reproduction system. Colen (1995, p. 78) argues that stratified reproduction implies a set of physical and social reproduction tasks carried out differentially according to inequalities based on hierarchies of class, race, ethnicity, gender and migratory status. For the cases we analyze, this implies understanding the specific historical and cultural contexts of these hierarchies in both the societies of origin and destination. The physical, mental and emotional reproductive work of raising, taking care of and socializing one's own children and those of others in exchange for the low pay received from other Mexican immigrants or from families in the United States to support households and people (from childhood to old age) is experienced in very different ways, valued and rewarded according to inequalities in the access to social resources. Stratified reproduction, particularly with the commodification of reproductive and care work, reproduces the stratification itself, intensifying the inequalities on which it is based. Many women migrate, Colen argues (1995), in search of work opportunities to improve their life standards and secure education for their children.

Expelled, just like the males, by dispossession processes that in their countries of origin increases the supernumerary population in rural and urban areas, women migrate to support themselves and their families, both in the destination and in their place of origin and, increasingly, to promote the reunification of relatives and closely related people. The notion of stratified reproduction allows us to include in the analysis the strategies pursued by female immigrants within the context of mobility processes taking place between increasingly guarded and dangerous borders. Such strategies seek to combine precarious jobs—underpaid, unstable, part-time, proliferating in the "free trade zones" of a deindustrialized economy (Cobo, 2005)—with the daily care for children, partners and dependents both in their destinations and in their places of origin, where brothers, aging parents and, on many occasions, their own children are left in the care of other women, dependent on their provisions.

Pahuatecan migration from a feminist perspective

During the fieldwork in October 2013 in Durham, North Carolina, we identified aspects that were not captured either in the 2010–2011 survey, nor in the interviews conducted in Pahuatlán throughout more than five years. What stands out is that the first women to travel to the United States and settle in the Southeast were, specifically, single women. Those who had left a child in Mexico under the care of their grandmothers came back shortly after to cross the border again, this time with their children. They recall that, in the early 1990s, crossing the border cost US$1,300. To raise the money, these pioneer young women asked family or friends already established in the United States for loans and paid the loan back with their first salaries. Once this "bridgehead" had been established, consisting of only four women, other single women with or without children felt encouraged to follow them. It was interesting to note that, in our basic social network of women interviewed on both sides of the border, a significant number came from households led by single women—widows or abandoned—who had to face many hardships to raise their children. In other cases, the migration of these single women to the United States was preceded by labor incursions to Mexico City, which set them up as the breadwinners of their homes. In successive interviews we noted the progressive consolidation of interethnic networks of mestizo and Otomí women in the migratory corridor configured in a border area between the states of Hidalgo and Puebla. At the same time, the importance of networks woven between women that enabled the mobility and labor insertion of female relatives and other women from the same region who progressively joined the migratory flow stands out:

> I think that my sister Lucía and her friends were the first to arrive. When they arrived there were already many people from San Pablito and, I think, from another place, San Nicolás, but few from Pahuatlán. My sister's friends came before her, in 1993. They are still here, they are American citizens now: Verónica married an American and another girl, Sofía—who was the one my sister studied with to be a hairdresser and worked together in a beauty salon in Pahuatlán—helped my sister to come here. I came in 95, my sister in 94 and they came in 93.
>
> (Adriana, 36 years old, Durham, NC, October 2013)

Pioneer women traveled between 1992 and 1994, precisely when young male migrants from the municipality were transitioning from rural employment (tobacco and cucumber harvest and lumber industry) to urban employment upon settling in Durham. In those years, the incipient migration of mestizo Pahuatecos/as was far surpassed by the flows of Otomí workers from San Pablito Pahuatlán. Otomíes had accumulated experience in dairy farms and egg production in Texas during the 1980s. A few Otomí women participated in this circuit, preceding the mestizas, some as day laborers while others sold food to the workers, thus lowering reproduction costs (Cravey, 2003; D'Aubeterre & Rivermar, 2014; Griffith, 2005).

The following testimony of a mestiza woman named Lucía allows us to reconstruct the migratory itinerary and the presence of women in the first migrant cohort from the county seat, where agricultural work in the Southeast stands out. Lucía arrived in Durham in 1994, when she was only 17 years old. A year later, she started a relationship with a migrant from Durango. She returned to Pahuatlán only once for a short time to take her young daughter.

> My friends first arrived in Texas, in Nacogdoches, but there were too many people there already. There, everybody worked in ranches, in farms. Then, here, in North Carolina, there were a lot of people [working] in tobacco. My friends, when they came to Carolina, worked in the tobacco harvest. But when I arrived I got in *Servitex* because they were able to find a place there. It was nice for me, because I arrived to an apartment. They didn't have that when they arrived for the first time because they arrived a year before. I never asked them how it was that they left that job to come here, because they lived in ranches.
> (Lucía, 38 years old, Durham, NC, October 2013)

Adriana, Lucía's younger sister, remembers that the migration of single women traveling with male friends, male acquaintances and brothers sparked gossip and suspicion in the town. Adriana, who was single and had a small child, had a good reason to look for a way to make a living outside of Pahuatlán. Female migration finds its full justification when carried out "for the wellbeing of the children": securing their material support when there is no father to take care of their needs legitimates the mobility of single women, their sacrifice and their departure from the town, even risking their life in a dangerous journey to cross the border. When migrating for the sake of others, the decision dignifies she who migrates:

> My sister surprised us, because she was one of our grandparent's favorites. She studied, and she already had a beauty salon there in Pahuatlán. So, when she came here she did surprise us very much and maybe, because of my situation, it was easier for me to make up my mind, because I was a single mother.
> (Adriana, 36 years old, Durham, NC, October 2013)

The justification is more doubtful when single women without children migrate for "selfish" reasons, that is, chasing individual projects, perhaps "vain" personal aspirations. Even the mere wish to "see the other side"—as young males frequently state—turns them into "suspicious migrants" (Juliano, 2002). The story of Lucía reveals the dilemmas surrounding her decision to migrate and the arrangements in her life as a single woman to make it through so much evil-speaking, gossip and suspicions:

> There in the town they said: "They are only going to act all flirty there. What are they going to do there? If they don't even know how to work." People, I think, that's what they thought, but my friends, thank God, they did well. Verónica my friend, had gone back to Pahuatlán to get her daughter, because she left a three-year-old there and she told me: "Let's go." I told her: "No, the thing is I'm going to study." But she told me: "Let's go, it is cool there." And a cousin that was here [in Durham], he only lasted a year here and went back to the town, and he told me "No, don't go to the north. There you are only going to go get married, because men are like vultures there." He says: "They are only waiting to see who comes." Because there were no women, there were only men, I told him: "No, I'm not going to go get married," and that's it. I got the itch to come here; without thinking I just went and told her: "Let's go!"
>
> (Lucía, Durham, NC, November 2013)

Good reputation and respectability are symbolic goods associated with the femininity model of a class (Skeggs, 1997) that must be carefully cultivated when poor women venture into masculinized fields. Not being represented by a male—when migrating as single women—makes them fall into the quicksand of suspicion. In this case, single male households, typically linked to the "military model" of migration and to the barracks of agricultural fields, were displaced as accommodation venues by apartments in urban areas where the first arrivals lived in overcrowded conditions in Durham (Cravey, 2003; Flippen & Parrado, 2012). These venues were considered inappropriate for young single females who could fall prey to sexual harassment by their housemates.

Castañeda and Zavella (2007) document the strategies of female day laborers in Californian agro-industry who are subject to a meticulous social scrutiny including even the careful presentation of their bodies in public, a "remapping task" modeled by instructions of how to be an honest working-class Mexican woman in the United States. The aim of such instructions is to avoid any body language that may be interpreted as a sign of sexual availability by their male counterparts. In Lucía's testimony, one can identify her concern with gaining respectability and acknowledgement for her effort to distance herself from the ways of life attributed to promiscuous women.

> My friends got married shortly after and I was the one who was still single. I was living with many boys from there, from Pahuatlán, who arrived [in

Durham] and lived together. So, when they decided to get married, I said: "What am I going to do? I can't stay here with so many men, because then they are going to say, no, this woman lives here now ... with everyone." That worried me. And then I met two other girls at my job at *Servitex*, they lived alone with their brother and their parents were about to join them, so they told me: "Well, you can come to our place." And, yes, I decided to go to their place and we started to live well there.

(Lucía, Durham, NC, November 2013)

Soon, they all started their married life and, in some cases, brought their young children from Pahuatlán to Durham. Some of the women we interviewed in Durham use the phrase "marrying out of necessity," a strategy for protection or shielding against the advances of men in the house where they resided and, at the same time, for circumventing the economic hardships surrounding these low-income female workers. Deeb-Sossa and Bickham Mendez (2008, p. 16) also identify these practices and discourses among Salvadoran women immigrants in Virginia and North Carolina. Shortly after starting a conjugal relationship, Lucía encouraged her sister Adriana to migrate with her young son. Soon, other relatives followed:

When I finally started living with a man I decided that my sister should come. I told her: "Come over." Not only did she and her son come, my brother and his son came too. They came, and little by little, all the family arrived: my mother and my other little siblings. I was pretty much one of the first in my family to come here.

(Lucía, 38 years old, Durham, NC, October 2013)

This condensed migratory history, reconstructed from the testimonies of Adriana and Lucía, shows the quick consolidation of family, interethnic and common-origin networks as one of the distinguishing features of the accelerated and recent migratory flows from the center of Mexico. These flows take advantage of and quickly add to what previous flows have accumulated. In the previous testimonies we can also identify the interlacing of two female mobility patterns. The first pattern is similar to the "single male military migration" in that it is a migration without dependents, but of limited circularity. This mobility shortly gave way to a second ancillary mobility pattern involving women who had recently started their married life and who, in some cases, traveled with young children born in Mexico. In other words, the family reunification process, unlike what has been observed in other parts of the country, occurs in the early phases of the household's demographic cycle. These young couples continued their reproductive life, giving way to domestic formations, conjugal or not, integrated by binational families, that is, with children born on both sides of the border. The incorporation to the labor market, the first conjugal union, and the paternity/maternity at an early age often overlap in the lives of these immigrants.

Binational families are plagued with difficulties and conflicts that emerge over the years due to greater border controls (cfr. Chapter 2 in this volume) and with the limited circulation imposed on these populations. The tensions these households experience are a defining factor in the explanation of the selectivity of the returns, one of the aspects that will be elucidated in Chapters 4 and 5 of this book. Families are defined by their condition of "semi hostages"—to use the knowledgeable expression of Lynn Stephen (2007)—, a condition that especially affects mothers of preschool children. Given the effects of their illegalization, household heads of these binational family configurations strive to stay in the United States at all costs and to consolidate strategies to live on the edge of citizenship while searching for the recognition of their rights.

Through a variety of strategies, women try to take their children away from the purgatory where disposable workers are piled up. It is worth noting that in the relationship they establish with the state, these female immigrants assume and build their new identities as mother-poor-undocumented, always suspected of deceiving the state. The prejudices towards these racialized populations magnify such suspicion. The relationship these women enter into with the state is an oblique relationship, mediated by the product of their wombs. Perceived as uterus/containers of citizens in the making, undocumented women lack rights of their own and, as is the case with all poor individuals—native or foreign— aspiring to qualify to obtain healthcare or education assistance, they must certify their eligibility by adjusting to the patriarchal equation woman=mother and, what's more, good and sacrificing mothers (D'Aubeterre, 2004).

Female wage labor and stratified reproduction in Durham

Aleida, pride and perseverance

In the context of the decentralization of the productive processes that fathered the organization of labor under the flexible accumulation model, the women from Pahuatlán found precarious part-time and low-paid jobs in industrial laundries, providing janitorial and catering services to large firms and governmental institutions; in restaurant and hotel chains; domestic work and caring for the children of others. Other women, pioneers from San Pablito Pahuatlán, evoke their first and fleeting work experiences in large meat packing companies that provided restaurants and homes with various semi-processed and frozen supplies. This is, as we will see in what follows, the case of Aleida, an Otomí woman from San Pablito Pahuatlán, one of the 32 localities in the municipality, who arrived in 1999, only 20 years old at the time, in Raleigh, North Carolina.

Aleida found work at the Tyson poultry packing plant, where she received a check for US$380 a week in exchange for working 12 hours daily. She started work at four in the afternoon and finished at four in the morning. During the months prior to the Christmas celebrations, after finishing this strenuous working day, she hastily ate a can of corn before she went to work part-time in the manufacture of Christmas wreaths, another one of the county's rural enterprises. Thanks to this second job she was able to send money to her mother in San Pablito who, in those days, took care of her terminally ill father. Even though Aleida did not have a temporary work visa, her profile was similar to that of "single," hyper-mobile (Smith & Winders, 2007) men and women who move without partners or children, under the military migration model, disconnected from reproduction tasks and caring for dependents. Regulated migration, including even political refugees and undocumented migration, run parallel in these sites of cheap labor.

Aleida left the poultry packing plant when migratory documents were required of workers. Another event that influenced her decision was her reconciliation with her husband Martín, from San Pablito, who had been living in North Carolina for a couple of years. When they got back together, they procreated two children in their new home. From the time they settled in Orange County in 2000, in the strip that borders the east of the city of Durham, the couple lived in a ramshackle *traila* (trailer conditioned as housing), a common recourse of poor African American and white families and immigrants (Flippen & Parrado, 2012). Between them both, with plenty of effort, they saved US$13,000 to buy the *traila* and thus save the US$850 rent they paid for a house. In order to lower the maintenance costs, they had to live with relatives, even tolerating the unbearable presence of her mother-in-law, with whom Aleida has never been able to get along.

This couple embodies the most common daily life and reproduction arrangement that we were able to identify in October 2013 in North Carolina among the immigrant families interviewed. It entails, usually, the coexistence of a male linked to the construction industry and a wife-mother-worker in the restaurant industry, services or janitorial work who have had children in the United States. Women with a longer migratory trajectory have a similar family constellation with the addition of an adolescent son or daughter born in Mexico. During the last 12 years, Aleida was a faithful worker in the Bojangles chain, well-known for its chicken and biscuits, a cheap fast food menu that makes life easier for thousands of workers overwhelmed by extreme schedules, taxing part-time job combinations and extra hours. Aleida's workday started at 4:30 in the morning. She prepared the biscuit dough in the kitchen and, when finished, continued with the preparation of hundreds of refrigerated chicken parts. Mexican, Central American and African American women predominated in the food preparation and cleaning, as well as in customer service. Aleida showed us with pride the badge she was awarded for her exceptional ability to make dough, the distinctive mark of this fast food chain with "Southern flavor." At 6:00 am she made a cell phone call to her husband: Martín changed diapers, prepared bottles and took Alexander to the babysitter's home, a Guatemalan woman from the neighborhood of about a hundred *trailas*, hidden in a woody corner of a secondary road. Martín quickly left for work in a fence installation company to start a workday that kept him away from home until late at night. In the meantime, Gaby, the couple's 11-year-old daughter, got herself ready and then waited for the school bus that picked her up at 7:40 am. Aleida left Bojangles at 3:13 pm; if needed, on her way home, she picked up some groceries in the small Latino shops located along the way. Before 4:00 pm she picked up little Alexander and, once home, started making dinner or, simultaneously, cleaning the house and doing laundry while following the plot of Mexican soap operas on a huge television screen that captivated Gaby, distracting her from her schoolwork.

Elena: migration to the North as maternal sacrifice

Unlike Aleida, the Pahuatecan mestizas interviewed did not mention having work experience in the rural food packing industry. Instead, for most of them, restaurant chains are nowadays a "refuge labor market niche," that is, a choice for those who cannot choose (Juliano, 2002). The extreme flexible conditions in this industry allow the youngest women—single, separated or abandoned with children—to "put together hours here and there," a part-time in one chain and a part-time in another. This strategy allows them to reach the prized 40 hours or slightly more a week, with which they try to meet their daily consumption—living with austerity, buying clothes in second-hand shops, buying in Latino stores—to, eventually send money to the town or, as in the case of Aleida, build a house as a final refuge at the end of her work trajectory in the United States.

Overwhelmed by debts, Elena—31 years old, divorced and with two children born in Durham—in 2011 sold a small business that she and her ex-husband set up years before in Pahuatlán with the savings from their first time in North Carolina in the late 1990s and early years of the last decade. The business was already untenable in 2010: its few profits went into paying for the premises and restocking the merchandise. After selling the business, Elena set off to North Carolina for the second time. Once settled in Durham, some Pahuatecos/as gave her shelter: "The apartment was small, with only one bedroom, the living room and the kitchen. I stayed in the living room, my friends in the room, but I paid very little" (Elena, 31 years old, Durham NC, November 2014). Thanks to this support, Elena reactivated as a single and free worker, confident that she had left her children in good hands with their grandmother in Pahuatlán. "I didn't find work quickly, I was unemployed for about two months, because I arrived in August, when it's a bit slow. And, also, because I didn't have a car, I couldn't move. There was work all right, but far away" (Elena, 31 years old, Durham NC, November 2014). Finally, she found work in a sock packing plant, with low pay on a piece-rate basis: "There were days when we earned 50 dollars and others when we earned 90 and there were days when we earned 16 dollars a day, that's how the check came" (Elena, Durham, NC, November 2014).

Day by day she increased her discipline to work intensely, secure modest consumption and support social reproduction processes in her distant town. The flexible worker's body is redesigned to maximize its productive capacities and contain its potentialities and reproductive needs. To this end, the work and social reproduction costs are transferred to other places and people and, therefore, are not contemplated in the salary calculation of these cheap workers (Binford, 2013; Cravey, 2003).

> I worked in the morning in the packing plant and in the afternoon in the burgers until eleven. As soon as I could, I bought a second-hand car for two thousand dollars. Then, I started to send money to my children, even if it wasn't much I'd send it to them, that's why I needed to have two jobs. That's what I got used to, because that's the only way, because with one job it's just for getting by, I would've stayed in Pahuatlán for that, just to get by eating and living.
>
> (Elena, Durham NC, 2014)

In 2012, reunited with her two adolescent children, Elena abandoned her condition as a single worker, hypermobile and without dependents—that is, as a "perfect worker"—to configure herself as a "single, low-income mother" before the state, looking for recognition and aiming to create conditions for raising her children.

> When my children came we rented here, we bought the beds, I couldn't furnish it quickly either, as I would've wanted, I didn't have the money. Because when you're going to rent a house you have to pay the electricity deposit, since it's the first time, you have to pay the rent deposit.
>
> (Elena, Durham NC, November 2014)

In addition to securing a house, clothing and utensils, Elena managed their entrance to schools, healthcare and access to basic governmental support:

> First, I applied for food stamps, so that they would give my children food. Now I have a card that they give to everyone who's low-income and have children, small children. My daughter is 16, I think this will be the last year that they will give her [food stamps]. It's 200 dollars per child a month, they only give me 250 for both. We applied for the school lunch program, because I'm a single mother they approved it. We are low-income, they give [lunch] to low-income children.
>
> (Elena, Durham NC, November 2014)

In 2013, Elena worked four days a week in a Tobacco Road chain restaurant, in Chapel Hill, where her shift ran from 9:00 in the morning to 3:00 in the afternoon. After taking a short break and having a snack in her van, she worked in the kitchen of The Cheesecake Factory six days a week from 4:00 pm to 11:00 pm. On Fridays and Saturdays, the workday in the factory extended well into early morning, overtime for which she was never paid extra, as stipulated by law; instead, she was paid 80 percent at best. How can we identify in these life stories the fields in which these super-exploited female workers display micro practices, albeit confusing and complex, circumscribing potential class confrontations? As Gavin Smith (2015, p. 81) states "[A] class does not sit alone; it is made by the force of its opposed class." However, in the identification of class we need to go further: "The unfolding of our potential, the development of what we might be against the reality of what we currently are, is a struggle against the conditions that exist in the present, in order to make them into new possibilities" (Smith, 2015, p. 81). With evident anger, Elena alluded to one of her frequent confrontations with the managers over work accidents caused by the lack of proper maintenance of work tools.

> The day the manager came I told him "here in the contract it says that you have to give us the tools we need for working." The fryer was broken for three months, and until Melvin came, I think he spoke to the owner, they kind of fixed it. But it only worked for a month and it's broken again. I tell him "why don't you replace them? why don't you sell them?" He tells me "because there's no money." The thing is they don't want things to go to waste. Plus, the less expenses the store has, the more bonuses the manager gets.
>
> (Elena, Durham NC, November 2014)

With two adolescent children and without a stable partner with whom to share the monthly rent of US$560 and other expenses, Elena would not be able to move forward if it were not for her two jobs. Because of the debts to go back to the United States, the purchase of the second-hand car, and the pressure to send money to her aging mother in Pahuatlán, she had to put her project to finish building a house in her hometown on hold, anticipating that, given her migratory status, she might have to leave the country at any time. In October 2013 she spent her days buried in doubts and bitterness that she tried to hide, so her relationship with her children would not turn sour. She blamed herself for leaving them alone for long periods, she was barely able to steal hours from her sleep to make the food her children reheated upon coming home from school. "They watch too much television," Elena laments, but she is unable to support the development of other formative activities because she, after all, "is here for my children, but can't do it all." Keeping her children in the education system is a challenge, even if this means that their desired upward mobility will be spurious (Jiménez & Assusa, 2017) and will not always result in better salaries. However, receiving an education will at least entail the abandonment of the humiliating manual occupations of their mothers.

Lucía, a model worker

Lucía arrived in Durham in 1994; one year later she started a relationship with a man from Durango, a state in Northern Mexico. Soon, the conjugal relationship turned extremely violent, to the extent that she had to ask the police to intervene. The police imposed a restriction on her former partner, and, in the end, he was deported. During the time she lived alone with her young daughter, Lucía requested state aid as a single mother. In addition to food stamps, she received a subsidy for the rent of her home and daycare. She also received money from her sister in exchange for taking care of her nephews and cleaning her sister's house.

In 2013, when we interviewed Lucía for the first time, she was 38 years old, had fewer economic hardships and a new partner. She worked at a laundry shop eight hours daily from four in the morning to three in the afternoon, five days a week. Once her workday was over, she drove her old van to the neighborhood she shared with Mexicans, African Americans and Central Americans. She picked up her two-year-old daughter, whom she left in the care of a fellow Pahuatecan for US$75 a week. She did some domestic work before picking up her 12-year-old daughter Mariana, born in Pahuatlán, from her clarinet class. Despite the costs of the daily commute between her home, her workplace and the community center, she boasted of sponsoring the girl's vocation.

From 2010, Lucía worked in the laundry services room of a cleaning company, which offers a wide range of services in North Carolina, for several well-known pharmaceutical companies—Bayer, Novartis, Bios, Hospira, who order services and medical equipment supplies. When Lucía entered the laundry services, she started earning US$9 per hour; the maximum amount she could earn was US$12 as a manager or section leader, who earned an additional 70 cents per hour. When Lucía left her former job in a uniform and linen rental company, she earned US$12 per hour. At the new company she earned US$10.50, a little less than at the other, but she managed to put more hours in. Working 40 hours a week was quite a feat, she asserted. The majority of the laundry room staff was made up of women, about 30, mostly Mexican and Central American. From 2010, the company demanded workers fold the sheets standing up; every two hours, workers took a ten-minute break, plus they had half an hour to eat.

Despite these working conditions, Lucía hoped to retire in that company. She shared expenses with her new partner, a construction worker from the State of Mexico, who is also divorced, with children in Mexico. In 2013 they paid the rent of a small house by subletting a room to two single migrants. In 2014, when we interviewed the couple again, they had settled with their three children in a *traila* Lucía had bought years before. The *traila* was renovated thanks to the greater liquidity enjoyed by "dual income" families (Fraser, 1997). She knows that her new conjugal relationship has brought greater stability to her life, but also two small children that limit her mobility and anchor her in a full-time, underpaid job. However, an ace up the sleeve for women like Lucía, is the recourse of the rights of children born in the United States, which can be wielded before the state. It is a risky bet, considering the cuts to social spending, the increased restrictions of the immigration policy of the United States and the exacerbated racism of the last decade.

Amanda's loneliness

Amanda, an Otomí woman, was only 13 years old when she arrived in Mexico City to employ herself as a domestic worker. Five years later, in 1999, a few months pregnant, she crossed the border with her boyfriend Carlos. Carlos, also from San Pablito Pahuatlán, already had a trajectory as a construction industry worker in North Carolina, where the Sanpablitos concentrated in house and apartment painting services (Rivermar & Flores, 2015). In 2013 when we interviewed Amanda, she was 33 years old and had been living in Durham for 15 years, where her two children were born. Unlike other Pahuatecos/as, Amanda and Carlos did not invest what they had saved all those years in building a house in their hometown:

> We haven't built a house in the town because here, in Durham, we bought a house, because we have been here most of our life, and the children were born here. We have finished paying for it, so as Carlos says: "every sacrifice has its reward," because we worked a lot. Well, I worked a lot before. When I came here I worked at a cleaning company, from 7:00 in the morning until 9:00, 8:00 at night. Sometimes my children were already asleep when I came home.
> (Amanda, Durham, NC, October 2013)

The first years in Durham were very difficult. As is usual among these poor migrants when they start their life in their new destination, the young couple shared a room with single men related to Carlos. Given the flexible, conjunctural and versatile nature of kinship ties, the fusion processes, the building and strengthening of intimate ties that underpin family conglomerates throughout a cycle are replaced over time by opposite processes. These latter processes are fission processes that loosen or erode intimate ties, segregating the parental or community aggregate in domestic groups with "nuclear" tendencies. As D'Argemir Comas & Pujadas Muñoz (1991) state, this occurs frequently in situations of ascending social mobility and search for social differentiation, once the critical stages of emigration and settlement are overcome.

The conjugal trajectory of Amanda and Carlos was an example of this erratic process with multiple exits and uncertainties: the beginning of organized life as a conjugal aggregate was a significant challenge. In households led by construction industry workers, the conjugal interaction was usually interrupted by frequent separations imposed by work contracts both in and out of state. The fluctuations in work demands in the construction industry, especially during the economic upheaval of 2007–2009, meant that males must take part in temporary displacements. Amanda describes the work conditions and absences of her husband:

> Just now Carlos came back from Pennsylvania, he was gone for six weeks. He says he was very tired, he worked Saturdays and Sundays, starting at 7:00 or 6:30 in the morning and finishing until 9:00 at night, so he didn't have any time off. The contractor has properties nearby, in Virginia and there in Pennsylvania as well. I suppose he trusts my husband or likes how they work, that's why he asks them to go do the job there. And he didn't come back at all for six weeks.
> (Amanda, 33 years old, Durham, NC, October 2013)

Given the frequent absences of the men, the women cared for the children and carried out the daily maintenance of the home by themselves. Living in loneliness, sometimes being unable to travel from one place to another due to the lack of a vehicle or a driver's license, with difficulties accessing services given their lack of competence in English, there were bitter memories for the first Pahuatecas and Otomíes who settled in Durham in the 1990s. Amanda had to deal with loneliness and isolation during her first years there, before finding work cleaning houses and having her own vehicle.

> I'm usually alone, because in the company where he used to work before, he went to Virginia, to Charlotte. When Carlos' father died, he left me here alone, when my children were very young. He went to Mexico [for two months] and I couldn't find a job, it seems like all the doors I go to are locked for me, I mean the only thing left for me to do was cry or I don't know what to do. It's difficult to live here and not know anyone and even worse when one doesn't speak the language. This place isn't for me, I spent almost my entire life in Mexico City and coming here and seeing all this, it's totally different. There, you see people, but here nothing, when one comes here, one doesn't have a car. One struggles to get a ride. Now there are many people who speak Spanish, but before, if you don't speak English, you had to wait one, two, even three hours for an interpreter. When I got pregnant with my oldest son I felt so useless when I had to go to a clinic or a store. Now it is very different from when getting here for the first time, there are many Hispanics.
> (Amanda, 33 years old, Durham, NC, October 2013)

The individual and group movements of these migrants, as reported by Griffith (2005, p. 53) associated with the rhythms of the construction and agro-industry, combined with the growth of the resident population, enabled the consolidation of internal markets in these *sui generis* communities of recent settlement in the New South. These community arrangements offer rides for those without vehicles or driver's licenses, cheap home cooked meals, health and childcare, and other daily consumption services; in short, they provide ways of establishing community ties.

Conclusions

We assert in this chapter that the migrations of recent decades and the growing participation of women—single, married, with or without children—at the beginning of their reproductive life, were inscribed in the neoliberal reorganization of labor and the configuration of a new proletariat in reconverted areas under the neoliberal transformation, such as the case of the New Latino South documented here. In the context of new accumulation schemes, a close relationship was discovered between capital delocalization and redesigned immigration regimes that selectively managed the mobility of the cheap workforce. Such processes are underpinned by active state policies that have strengthened speculative capital and dismantled conditions of reproduction and every form of social security.

The accelerated character of this flow was expressed in the rapid transition from a circular and temporary settlement migration that gave way to the formation of family arrangements integrated by couples at the beginning of their reproductive cycle. The mother-worker-undocumented subject, configured in this context, was signified by an unresolved contradiction: as with the men, they were coveted by capital as a cheap labor force and, at the same time, are an object of persecution and deportation due to their migratory status. However, by considering how production and social reproduction articulate in the shaping of these subjects, other tensions in their lives come to light.

In their attempt to make effective the citizenship rights for their children, these female workers underpin their identities as mothers in their claims and daily struggles in different arenas—schools, clinics, hospitals, churches and civil associations. However, given the ruthless neoliberal attack on social reproduction, they are despised, as the rest of the state-dependent population, for being undocumented foreigners who make undeserved use of taxpayers' resources, and are criminalized for it as well. In practice, these selective interventions shift the tension between capital and labor toward a frequent division and hostility between salaried and non-salaried sectors of the working class and among racialized groups (Fraser, 1997; Mollona, 2014; Sider, 2006). While as mothers they consider these claims legitimate, they are forced to hide due to their condition of "unwanted foreigners," just as the men are hardly able to articulate a class identity and recognize themselves in the struggles of workers against capital.

This contradiction takes place in the context of the tension between the increased spatial-temporal flexibility demanded from low-wage workers and the need to settle in one place demanded by social reproduction (Smith & Winders, 2007). In short, this is a subject that abandons its condition of "perfect worker," hyper-mobile, without dependents, circulating between one place and the other, under the referred model of military mobility, to become a subject that makes itself hyper-visible outside the production sites, before the state, involved in multiple routines as working mothers and, at the same time, breadwinners for dependents on both sides of the border.

References

Alarcón, R. (2015). Digitalización, clase social y formación social electrónica en El Salvador rural. In A. Fuentes (Ed.), *Conflictos y sujetos emergentes. Episodios en la transformación rural neoliberal* (pp. 19–56). Puebla: Benemérita Universidad Autónoma de Puebla.

Alarcón, R., & Mines, R. (2002). El retorno de los "solos": Migrantes mexicanos en la agricultura de Estados Unidos. In M. E. Anguiano & M. Hernández (Eds), *Migración internacional e identidades cambiantes* (pp. 43–70). México, DF: El Colegio de Michoacán y el Colegio de la Frontera Norte.

Bettie, J. (2003). *Women without class. Girls, race, and identity*. Berkeley, Los Angeles, London: University of California Press.

Binford, L. (2003). Migración acelerada entre Puebla y Estados Unidos. In E. Masferrer & J. Mondragón (compilers), *Etnografía del estado de Puebla, Puebla centro* (pp. 58–67). México D.F.: Gobierno del estado de Puebla, Secretaría de Cultura del estado de Puebla.

Binford, L. (2013). *Tomorrow we're all going to the harvest. Temporary foreign worker programs and neoliberal political economy*. Austin: University of Texas Press.

Canterbury, D. C. (2012). *Capital accumulation and migration*. Leiden: Koninklijke Brill NV.

Castañeda, X., & Zavella, P. (2007). Changing constructions of sexuality and risk: Migrant Mexican women farmworkers in California. In D. A. Segura & P. Zavella (Eds), *Women and migration in the US–Mexico borderlands: A reader* (pp. 249–268). Durham, NC: Duke University Press.

Chant, S. (2007). Género y migración. In S. Chant & N. Craske (Eds), *Género en Latinoamérica* (pp. 389–428). México D.F.: CIESAS.

Cobo, R. (2005). Globalización y las nuevas servidumbres de las mujeres. In C. Amorós & A. de Miguel (Eds), *Teoría feminista: de la Ilustración a la Globalización* (pp. 265–300). Madrid: Minerva Ediciones.

Cohen, D. (2005). Masculinity and social visibility: Migration, state spectacle, and the making of the Mexican nation. *EIAL: Estudios Interdisciplinarios de America Latina y El Caribe, 16*(1), 119–132.

Colen, S. (1995). Like a mother to them: Stratified reproduction and West Indian childcare workers and employers in New York. In F. Ginsberg & R. Rapp (Eds), *Conceiving the New World Order: The global politics of reproduction* (pp. 78–102). Berkeley: University of California Press.

Cravey, A. J. (2003). Toque una ranchera, por favor. *Antipode, 35*(3), 603–621. https://doi.org/10.1111/1467-8330.00341

D'Argemir Comas, D., & Pujadas Muñoz, J. J. (1991). Familias migrantes: Reproducción de la identidad y del sentimiento de pertenencia. *Papers Revista de Sociología, 36*, 33–56.

D'Aubeterre, M. E. (2000). *El pago de la novia: Matrimonio, vida conyugal y prácticas transnacionales en San Miguel Acuexcomac*. México D.F.: El Colegio de Michoacán, BUAP.

D'Aubeterre, M. E. (2004). Procreando ciudadanos: Trabajadoras indocumentadas mexicanas residentes en California. *Canadian Journal of Latin American and Caribbean Studies, 29*(57–58), 147–172.

D'Aubeterre, M. E., & Rivermar, M. L. (2014). From Amate paper making to global work: Otomí migration from Puebla to North Carolina. *Latin American Perspectives, 41*(3), 118–136. https://doi.org/10.1177/0094582X13519426

De Genova, N. (2016). The "natives point of view" in the anthropology of migration. *Anthropological Theory, 16*(2–3), 227–240. https://doi.org/10.1177/1463499616652513

De Genova, N., & Peutz, N. (Eds). (2010). *The deportation regime: Sovereignty, space, and the freedom of movement*. Durham, NC: Duke University Press.

Deeb-Sossa, N., & Bickman Mendez, J. (2008). Enforcing borders in the Nuevo South: Gender and migration in Williamsburg, Virginia, and the Research Triangle, North Carolina. *Gender and Society, 20*(5), 613–638.

Durand, J., & Massey, D. S. (2003). *Clandestinos. Migración México-Estados Unidos en los albores del siglo XXI*. México D.F.: Universidad Autónoma de Zacatecas/Miguel Ángel Porrúa.

Flippen, C. A., & Parrado, E. A. (2012). Forging Hispanic communities in new destinations: A case study of Durham, North Carolina. *City and Community, 1*, 1–30.

Flores Álvarez, J. (2018). *"Nos fuimos a la braceareada con la esperanza de ganar un centavo más". Masculinidades, movilidad laboral y experiencia de clase en un pueblo*

minero zacatecano. (Thesis M.A. in Sociocultural Anthropology). Benemérita Universidad Autónoma de Puebla, Instituto de Ciencias Sociales y Humanidades.
Fraser, N. (1997). *Justice interruptus. Critical reflections on the "postsocialist" condition.* London: Routledge.
Furuseth, O. J., & Smith, H. A. (2016). From Winn-Dixie to Tiendas: The remaking of the New South. In O. J. Furuseth & H. A. Smith (Eds), *Latinos in the South. Transformations of place* (pp. 2–17). London: Routledge.
Green, L. (2009). The fear of no future. Guatemalan migrants dispossession and dislocation. *Anthropological, 2*(51), 327–341.
Griesbach, K. A. (2011). Local-federal immigration enforcement in North Carolina: Mapping the criminal-immigration overlap. *Norteamérica, 6,* 91–127. https://doi.org/10.22201/cisan.24487228e.2011.3.148
Griffith, D. (2005). Rural industry and Mexican immigration and settlement in North Carolina. In V. Zúñiga & R. Hernández-León (Eds), *New destinations: Mexican immigration in the United States* (pp. 50–74). New York: Russell Sage Foundation.
Hahamovitch, C. (2014). *No man's land. Jamaican guest workers in America and the global history of deportable labor.* Princeton: Princeton University Press.
Harvey, D. (1989). *The condition of postmodernity: An enquiry into the origins of cultural change.* Cambridge, MA & Oxford, UK: Blackwell.
Harvey, D. (2003). *The new imperialism: Accumulation by dispossession.* Oxford: Oxford University Press.
Hondagneu-Sotelo, P. (2011). Gender and migration scholarship: An overview from a 21st century perspective. *Migraciones Internacionales, 6*(1), 219–233.
Hondagneu-Sotelo, P., & Avila, E. (2003). "I'm here but I'm there": The meanings of Latina transnational motherhood. In P. Hondagneu-Sotelo (Ed.), *Gender and US immigration: contemporary trends* (pp. 317–340). Berkeley: University of California Press.
Jiménez, C., & Assusa, G. (2017). Desigualdades de corta distancia? Trayectoria y clases sociales en Gran Córdoba, Argentina. *Revista Mexicana de Sociología, 79*(4), 837–874.
Juliano, D. (2002). La inmigración sospechosa y las mujeres globalizadas. In C. Gregorio & B. Agrela (Eds), *Mujeres de un solo mundo: Globalización y multiculturalismo* (pp. 123–134). Granada: Universidad de Granada, Instituto de Estudios de la Mujer.
Kalb, D. (2015). Introduction: Class and the new anthropological holism. In J. G. Carrier & D. Kalb (Eds), *Anthropologies of class: Power, practice, and inequality* (pp. 1–27). Cambridge: Cambridge University Press.
Kofman, E., & Raghuram, P. (2015). *Gendered migrations and global social reproduction.* New York: Palgrave/Macmillan.
Lee, A. (2015). En Estados Unidos no tienes libertad. La gran recesión y migración de retorno en Zapotitlán Salinas, 2007–2011. In M. E. D'Aubeterre & M. L. Rivermar (Eds), *Lo que dejamos atrás ... lo que vinimos a encontrar. Trabajo precario, nuevos patrones de asentamiento en Estados Unidos y retorno a México* (pp. 135–169). Puebla: Benemérita Universidad Autónoma de Puebla, Instituto de Ciencias Sociales y Humanidades.
Levine, E., & LeBaron, A. (2011). Immigration policy in the Southeastern United States: Potential for internal conflict. *Norteamérica. Revista Académica del CISAN-UNAM, 6,* 5–32.
Li, T. M. (2014). *Land's End: Capitalist relations on an indigenous frontier.* London & Durham: Duke University Press.
Macías, S., & Herrera, F. (1997). *Migración laboral internacional: Transnacionalidad del espacio social.* Puebla: Benemérita Universidad Autónoma de Puebla.

Macip, R. F. (2005). *Semos un país de peones: Café, crisis y estado neoliberal en el centro de Veracruz*. Puebla: ICSyH-BUAP.

Marroni, M. da Gloria. (2006). Migrantes mexicanas en los escenarios familiares de las comunidades de origen: Amor, desamor y dolor. *Estudios Sociológicos, XXIV*(72), 667–699.

Marx, K. (1990). *Capital: A critique of political economy (Vol. 1)*. London: Penguin Books.

Mezzadra, S., & Neilson, B. (2013). *Border as method, or the multiplication of labor*. London & Durham: Duke University Press.

Minchin, T. J. (2012). Life and labor in the New South. In R. H. Zieger (Ed.), *Shutdowns in the Sun Belt: The decline of the textile and apparel industry and deindustrialization in the South* (pp. 258–288). Gainesville: University Press of Florida.

Mohl, R. A. (2003). Globalization, Latinization, and the Nuevo New South. *Journal of American Ethnic History, 22*(4), 31–66.

Mollona, M. (2014). Informal labour, factory labour or the end of labour? In M. Atzeni (Ed.), *Workers and labour in a globalised capitalism: Contemporary themes and theoretical issues* (pp. 181–209). Basingstoke: Palgrave Macmillan.

Mummert, G. (1999). "Juntos pero desapartados": Migración transnacional y la fundación del hogar. In G. Mummert (Ed.), *Fronteras fragmentadas* (pp. 451–473). México: El Colegio de Michoacán.

Narotzky, S., & Smith, G. (2006). *Immediate struggles: People, power and place in rural Spain*. Berkeley: University of California Press.

Oso, L., & Ribas-Mateos, N. (2013). *The international handbook on gender, migration and transnationalism: Global and development perspectives*. https://doi.org/10.4337/9781781951477.

Passel, J. (2006). Size and characteristics of the unauthorized migrant population in the U.S. Retrieved from http://pewhispanic.org/reports/report.php?ReportID=61

Pedone, C., Gil Araujo, S., Echeverrí, M. M., & Agrela, B. (2011). *Hijos huérfanos con padres vivos. Políticas y discursos públicos sobre migración, familia, género y generación en contextos de inmigración/emigración: Europa, España, Ecuador y Colombia*. Draft paper presented at the III Congreso Annual de La Red SPANED, Pamplona, Spain. Retrieved from http://unavarra.es/digitalAssets/149/149677_100000Pedone

Pini, B., & Leach, B. (2011). *Reshaping gender and class in rural spaces*. Farnham: Ashgate.

Popke, J. (2011). Latino migration and neoliberalism in the US South. Notes toward a rural cosmopolitanism. *Southeastern Geographer, 51*(2), 242–259.

Rivermar, M. L., & Flores, M. L. (2015). Migración y explotación: Mestizos y Otomíes en la industria de la construcción de la costa este de Estados Unidos. In M. E. D'Aubeterre & M. L. Rivermar, *Lo que dejamos atrás ... Lo que vinimos a encontrar. Trabajo precario, nuevos patrones de asentamiento en Estados Unidos y retorno a México* (pp. 77–108). Puebla: BUAP, ICSyH.

Sassen, S. (2002). Women's burden: Counter-geographies of globalization and the feminization of survival. *Nordic Journal of International Law, 71*(2), 255–274. https://doi.org/10.1163/157181002761931378

Sassen, S. (2003). Strategic instantiations of gendering in the global economy. In P. Hondagneu-Sotelo (Ed.), *Gender and US immigration. Contemporary trends* (pp. 43–61). Berkeley: University of California Press.

Sider, G. (2006). The production of race, locality, and state: An anthropology. *Anthropologica, 48*(2), 247–263.

Skeggs, B. (1997). *Formations of class and gender. Becoming respectable*. London: Sage Publications.

Smith, B. E., & Winders, J. (2007). We're here to stay: Economic restructuring, Latino migration and place-making in the South. *Transactions of the Institute of British Geographers*, NS *33*, 60–72.

Smith, G. (2015). Through a class darkly, but then face to face: Praxis through the lens of class. In J. Carrier & D. Kalb (Eds), *Anthropologies of class: Power, practice, and inequality* (pp. 72–88). Cambridge: Cambridge University Press.

Smith, R. (1995). *"Los ausentes siempre presentes." The imagining, making and politics of transnational migrant community between Ticuani, Puebla, Mexico, and New York City*. (Thesis Ph. D.), Columbia University.

Stephen, L. (2007). *Transborder lives: Indigenous Oaxacans in Mexico, California, and Oregon*. Durham: Duke University Press.

4 "I was motivated to do everything"

Undocumented "entrepreneurs of the self" in New York

Introduction

This chapter turns to the emergence and acceleration of migration in Zapotitlán. Through the accounts of women and men situated along different points of the transnational circuit, this chapter traces villagers' experiences with changing political economic regimes in Zapotitlán and New York City. Some Zapotitecos/as responded to the economic crisis in Mexico of the 1980s by migrating to the United States, while others, especially women, increased their participation in waged work, particularly in recently established garment factories that produced for domestic and international markets. As the crisis deepened in the 1990s with the devaluation of the peso, migration accelerated, and many more men and women migrated north to work in New York's expanding service sector. Providing for families' basic needs appeared to be "progress" against the backdrop of worsening conditions of social reproduction in Mexico. As low-waged service workers, Zapotitecos/as struggled to meet the basic social reproductive requirements for their families. In the final section, the discussion turns to the forms of discipline which traverse gendered, "illegal" subjects laboring as restaurant workers, domestics and garment factory workers.

We lived from the rocks! Onyx and labor in Zapotitlán

Chapter 2 provided some details about the history of Zapotitlán Salinas, an important salt producing center for the colonial mining industry. Salt also played a central role in the diet of goats. The region's caprine industry produced various products for industry and household use up until the revolutionary period in the early twentieth century. *Barbacoa*, goat meat cooked for hours in an underground oven, continues to be a favorite local dish. In addition to goats, villagers produced *ixtle*—fibers from the agave plant used for making ropes—and charcoal. These products were sold for cash or traded for other foods and goods in the regional market in Tehuacán. Salt, goats, ixtle and charcoal were pillars of the local economy in a region where rain-fed agriculture provided food for only part of the year.

DOI: 10.4324/9780429454196-4

After the mid-twentieth century, some local families with access to travertine (known as "onyx") and marble quarries, hired their family members and neighbors to extract rock. Before electricity arrived in the town in the 1960s, the rock was sold in Tehuacán and other regional processing centers. However, in the late 1960s, the first workshops opened in Zapotitlán and produced handicrafts and some construction materials. Owners paid workers piece rate and often withheld a portion of workers' weekly earnings in order to ensure they would return the next week. Subordinating labor through these means counterbalanced the tendency for workers to look for better wages in the competitive local labor market. "We lived from the rocks!" one former workshop owner explained to me. The majority of workers shifted from ranching and salt production to onyx extraction and manufacture from the 1960s to the 1980s.

Overall, Zapotitlán's incorporation into the regional stone industry through the provision of low-cost labor and rock reinforced local social differentiation. While workshop owners sought to retain labor, they also sought to undersell workshops selling similar products. Quarry owners fought incessantly over the borders among quarries to prevent the theft of onyx. Although some individuals suggested local onyx producers form a cooperative to stave off the predatory practices of intermediaries, individual short-term gain appealed more to the town's *caciques*, political bosses. Without authorities to adjudicate the conflicts over property ownership, conflicts turned violent from time to time and political bosses demanded, and received, compliance from villagers with relative ease. Disputes over quarry ownership encouraged extracting rock as quickly as possible. This process, however, resulted in inefficient use of the rock and undervalued sale prices.

The lost decade: economic crisis and the decline of onyx

As discussed in Chapter 2, the Mexican oil crisis of 1982 sent the country into economic and political shock. Beyond the rise in the cost of basic subsistence, Zapotitecos/as experienced the crisis as the beginning of the decline of the onyx industry owing to various factors. First, demand for onyx products fell as household earnings declined. Second, the supply of local rock diminished because of internal disputes over quarry ownership. This forced workshop owners to buy raw material from external sources, thus raising the cost of production. Third, workers began to migrate to the United States, making it difficult for workshop owners to find and train workers. Fourth, in the 1990s, cheaper Chinese imports began to replace onyx products in national markets. Finally, as part of the neoliberal structural adjustment policies, the state eliminated electricity subsidies for workshops. Electricity prices increased 16 percent from 1991 to 1992 and 32 percent from 1995 to 1996 in real terms.[1] Although workshops withheld payments in protest, the government refused to grant reprieves to all but a few of the largest and most prosperous workshops. The majority had to contend with higher operating costs and debts left over from the unsuccessful protest. As a result, many owners closed up shop and left for the United States (Lee, 2008).[2]

Garment factories in Zapotitlán: the "complementarity" of women's labor

In an effort to attract foreign investment in export manufacturing, the Mexican government implemented the Border Industrialization Program in 1965 and the In Bond Plant Program in the 1970s. These programs instituted the tariff laws and fiscal incentives that permitted the development of maquiladoras in the country (Fernández-Kelly, 1983, p. 25). In theory, ex-Braceros expelled from the US at the end of the guest worker program in 1964 were to constitute an important part of the workforce for the new plants, thereby stemming undocumented migration to the US. However, in practice, firms contributed to the formation of a new proletariat by employing a majority of adolescent daughters and single mothers as operators on assembly lines. In general, female maquiladora workers lacked employed male relatives in their households. Managers and supervisors preferred women's docility and dexterity, a discourse that transformed their economic necessity and structural vulnerability into biological and psychological "truths" in an effort to speed production and increase profits (Fernández-Kelly, 1983; Iglesias, 1985).

In an effort to recruit lower-cost labor, Mexico expanded the maquiladora system to other parts of the country in the early 1970s, through "decentralization" (Fernández-Kelly, 1983, p. 38) or "peripheralization" (Escobar Latapi & Martinez Castellanos, 1991; Rothstein, 2007, pp. 68–69). The state reinforced the industry during the 1980s to offset the shocks of the 1982 oil crisis and the IMF-led economic restructuring that followed. Further, maquiladoras contributed to the abandonment of import-substitution industrialization and the opening of the Mexican economy by attracting transnational capital (Flores Morales, 2008, pp. 61–70). While garment production for the national market had existed in Tehuacán since the 1960s and 1970s, the growth of the maquiladora export sector in the 1980s and 1990s boosted the city's apparel industry. Tehuacán, Puebla's second-largest city, had earned the unofficial title of blue-jean capital of the world by the late 1990s (Barrios Hernández & Santiago Hernández, 2003, pp. 29–30).

Beginning in the 1980s, the first garment factories opened in Zapotitlán, employing dozens of adolescent girls, and single and married women. Subcontracted by larger firms in Tehuacán looking to boost production at a minimum of cost, these clandestine shops offered meager salaries and none of the workers' benefits required by law. The entry of garment factories coincided with the fall in the purchasing power of men's wages earned in the quarries and onyx workshops. *La necesidad*—the need for income—relaxed gendered norms about women's "proper place" in the home and reduced domestic conflicts for the women who sought employment. Despite low, "complementary" wages, the local garment factories appealed to many women because they did not have to pay for transportation to work. Some women opted for the slightly better pay and benefits offered in Tehuacán's legally registered maquiladoras once they gained experience in local factories.

Although unmarried daughters turned over all or a portion of their salary to their parents, working in the factory could be experienced as "freedom" from the restrictive norms of the household that dictated their daily chores and movements in the town. Daughters who maintained some control over their wages might gain limited prestige for providing clothing for household members or for being a sponsor for a neighbor's baptism or wedding. Their subordinate position in the household, however, was not reconfigured. Others handed over their salary to their parents who might give them a small allowance while using the majority for household expenses. María, who was 13 at the time she began to work in a maquiladora in Zapotitlán, explained that the work was "nice" (*bonito*) because of the friendships she made and the freedom she was granted by her mother to play basketball with her girlfriends after work. The work was also difficult (*pesado*) and tiring (*cansado*). After a couple of years, she left the garment factory to take care of her sister's children. She explained that this was much easier than standing all day in the factory. Their mother, María's sister, labored as a domestic worker in Chicago (María, 17, Zapotitlán Salinas, April 2003).

Despite greater freedoms to socialize outside the home and factory, work in the maquiladora represented an increase in women's overall workload because waged work was added to their obligatory reproductive work. This second shift (Hochschild, 1989) was especially onerous for home workers. In an attempt to push an even greater amount of the cost of production on the workforce, factories allowed women with children and at least two years' experience to opt for the more "flexible" arrangements of working from home. The clothing factory distributed packages of materials for assembly while workers paid for the sewing machines and electricity used in their homes. Factory managers also required women to pay for the transportation of the materials and finished products to and from the women's homes. The "flexibility" of watching children during the day and working late into the night was attractive, although the exhaustion and fatigue took a devastating toll on all the garment factory workers, especially affecting home workers' wellbeing.

I would clean the house quickly: domestic work and the reproduction of rural households

Many women alternated between work in maquiladoras and domestic work, before and after marriage. Carolina, the daughter of peasants, migrated to Mexico City in 1986, when she was 17, to work in a maquiladora and, later, as a live-in domestic worker. Carolina managed to send half of her salary to her parents, who used the money to pay for the maintenance of her younger siblings back in Zapotitlán. She cleaned house and cared for two young children in a middle-class neighborhood. When the family would retreat to their weekend home in a nearby town early on Saturday morning, Carolina explained her routine.

> I would clean the house quickly. It had three floors and I was all alone. When they were away, I would wash the curtains with *Downy* and re-hang

the curtains while they were still wet. On Saturday afternoon, I would leave for my house [in Zapotitlán, about 4–5 hours by bus]. When they got back from Cuernavaca, the whole house would smell like *Downy* and they would say "Carolina has been working very hard!"

(Carolina, 30 years old, Bronx, NY, November 2004)

She laughed, pleased that her employers recognized and appreciated her hard work, signaled by the smell of fabric softener permeating the house. When the female head of household had breast augmentation surgery, Carolina cared for her. "I was the nurse! They did not hire anyone to take care of the *señora*. I did all the household chores quickly and I had time left over to take care of her." When Carolina told them that she was going to migrate to New York, her employers told her that they did not know what they would do without her.

Structurally, the labor-power of domestic workers, devalued through racialized, gendered and classist discourses proclaiming the inevitability and naturalness of servile labor (Davis, 1981; Durin, 2017), was infinitely replaceable in a country where nearly half of the population lives in moderate or extreme poverty. Carolina, like virtually all domestic workers, subsidized the reproduction of her employers' position in the Mexican urban middle-class, a position marked by the distinctions of employing *"chachas"*[3] and buying vacation homes and plastic surgery (Bourdieu, 1984). She constructs herself as indispensable to the family, through the way she attends to their every need, even when these needs go beyond what her employers normally expect of her. She seeks to be always available, proud of the job she does to please, a servant rather than a worker (Amorós, 2008, p. 311). Her emotional and affective competencies were partly accounted for by her gendered socialization in a peasant household as servile labor to parents and brothers. At the same time, Carolina's disposition to serve was potentiated as a member of the new working classes expelled from subsistence production and petty commodity production in rural towns through the neoliberal policies that dismantled living conditions in places like Zapotitlán.

Whether through the affective and emotional labor of domestic work, assembling and packaging onyx artifacts, or manufacturing clothes in the factory or at home, women from Zapotitlán were socialized into waged work characterized by long hours and low pay. Garment factories exposed women to manufacture characterized by flexible production. They incorporated into the new working classes created through the shocks of the 1980s debt crisis and the destruction of rural economies through economic restructuring. Many of these women left Mexico to incorporate into labor markets in the US remade through neoliberal restructuring that required the flexibility and availability many women were familiar with through their waged work in Mexico.

"Progress" in worsening conditions: the emergence of international migration in Zapotitlán

I sewed clothes at home so that I would not have to leave my children alone. I never wanted to separate from them, until things got too difficult.

Because of the poverty, hunger and living from charity, I wanted to progress. For this reason, I went to New York.

(Gilda, 29 years old, Zapotitlán Salinas, January 2012)

Given the worsening conditions of social reproduction in the 1980s and 1990s, it became more and more difficult for households to pay expenses through the work available in local labor markets. With rising prices for food and other necessities, local wages maintained families at a bare minimum. Onyx workers could afford food and other indispensable household and ceremonial expenditures, but they could not make improvements to housing or afford to educate their children beyond primary or middle school. Maquiladora wages, already substantially reduced by their assignation as "complementary" to men's wages, did not keep pace with the cost of living. Single mothers, like Gilda, were especially vulnerable to sinking deeper into poverty. Despite the fact that Gilda worked from home and accepted clothing and other goods from her neighbors, she was not able to cover all the needs of her family. For workshop owners, the rising costs of production, the shrinking of markets for onyx products and the accelerating migration of the workforce caused many of them to close their doors.

It was in this context of the decline of local wages—a reflection of the generalized crisis in Mexico—that international migration became an attractive option. Although many migrants discussed how migration allowed them and their families to "progress" and "succeed" (*salir adelante*), the vast majority of migrants "dreamed" (American style) about providing for their families' basic needs: food, housing, education and health care. Providing for families' basic needs *appeared* to be progress against the backdrop of worsening conditions for social reproduction. If migrants were successful in inserting into US labor markets, they might succeed temporarily at beating back poverty. Despite the celebration of the development potential of remittances in the 1990s and 2000s, migration produced dependency, not development, in rural Central Mexico (Binford, 2003; Reichert, 1979; Wiest, 1984).

The first migrant from Zapotitlán, Luis, a 20-year-old quarry worker, left in 1984 with his brother's brother-in-law. This man, from Izucar de Matamorros, had been to the US several times to work in restaurants in the Bronx section of New York City.[4] A year later, Luis financed the trips of his two brothers, also quarry workers, and some cousins and friends, who worked in the workshops. Six months passed until another small group of men from Zapotitlán joined their compatriots in New York. This "military-style" migration pattern (Griffith, 2005) characterized international migration from the town from 1984 to 1987; five or six men—principally young and unmarried—would leave every six months. The "success" of these first groups of migrants, combined with worsening local conditions, motivated more to go north. By 1988, larger groups of 10–15, that included a few women, left every few months, and workshop owners began to feel the effects of a dwindling labor pool.

The collapse of onyx and the devaluation of the peso: the acceleration of international migration

Many migrants who departed in the 1980s believed that migration would only be a temporary part of their working lives. However, after the peso devaluation in 1994—where the currency lost approximately half its value overnight—the local onyx industry permanently declined. Zapotitecos/as viewed international migration as the most viable solution to meet a family's basic needs. As a result, the town's migrant pool quickly diversified. College graduates and professionals joined ex-onyx and ex-maquiladora workers in restaurants, markets, domestic work, clothing factories and construction sites in New York. Young couples with or without children, and unaccompanied women with or without children migrated alongside men who arrived without dependents.[5] From 1988 to 2010, of the 51 women who migrated, 60 percent were single without children or single mothers. From 1985 to 1991, only 3.8 percent of migrants were women. However, from 1992 to 1998, 27 percent of the migrant flow was comprised of women, and from 1999 to 2006, women made up 30 percent of the flow.

The peso devaluation coincided with a steady ramp-up of Border Patrol presence on the US–Mexico border, as discussed in Chapter 2. Before the mid-2000s, it was not uncommon for unaccompanied men and women to circulate back and forth every three, four or five years. However, undocumented men and women with US-born children tended not to circulate in order to avoid detention at the border and jeopardizing their chances of reunifying with their children in the US. After the mid-2000s, the further militarization of the border (Lee, 2018; Slack, Martinez, Lee, & Whiteford, 2016) as well as the increase in interior detention and deportation (Cantor, Noferi, & Martinez, 2015), exacerbated the "bottling-up" effect, and reduced circularity and first migrations to the United States. Zapotitecos' arrival after the Immigration Reform and Control Act (IRCA) of 1986 ensured that they were locked out of virtually any path to recognition as legal immigrants.

"Learn how to sew so you can get a job": Zapotitecas and labor market insertion in New York

The first migrants from Zapotitlán arrived in New York beginning in 1984 and settled in the Soundview, Parkchester and Castle Hill sections of the Bronx, as discussed in Chapter 2. Most migrants found work through their relatives and friends from Zapotitlán. Occasionally they used temporary agencies or worked as *equineros*, day laborers gathered on street corners (*esquinos* in Spanish) waiting to be hired. Others resorted to being *esquineros* on a part-time basis to find work on their days off from their regular jobs.

Results from the Ethnosurvey administered to a 25 percent sample of households in Zapotitlán[6] showed that of 156 migrant men on their first migration, 138 (88 percent) worked in New York City and Spring Valley (a suburb of the city).

The remaining individuals were scattered among California (Los Angeles and Monterey), Chicago, Tennessee, Atlanta, Florida and Texas. Of the 138 in New York, 74 (54 percent) worked in restaurants, 33 (24 percent) worked in services (supermarkets, convenience stores and carwashes), and 12 (9 percent) worked in construction. The percentages of workers in each category did not change significantly from first migration to last migration, the only two moments registered in the survey with respect to employment information.

Of 47 female migrants, 42 (89 percent) worked in New York City and Spring Valley and the remaining women lived in Chicago, Los Angeles and Pennsylvania during their first migration. Of the 42 in New York, 11 (26 percent) worked in private homes as caretakers or domestics, seven (17 percent) worked in beauty salons, six (14 percent) in dry cleaning or clothing factories, five (12 percent) in restaurants, and four (10 percent) in supermarkets and other retail establishments. Only four (10 percent) reported that they were homemakers and not looking for paid work. The vast majority of women who migrated to the US from Zapotitlán were wage earners. The sample size of women with a last migration was too small to draw any conclusions about changes in occupation between first and last migration.

Conditioned by the legal construction of their personhood as "illegal aliens," undocumented men and women toiled long hours, in dangerous and taxing conditions for meager wages. Despite the value they created for small and medium-sized firms in the city, they remained officially invisible. Usually paid in cash, no official record existed of migrant workers' individual contributions. They remained permanently excluded from the social protections that citizens and some legal immigrants enjoyed.

Eva: garment factories in New York and *tristeza* (sadness)

By 1988, the first woman from Zapotitlán left for New York. Eva, a single mother, traveled regularly to Tijuana, a northern border city, to sell onyx and embroidered blouses. She had learned to embroider in a course given to women in the village. Once they had gained the necessary skills, garment workshop owners from a nearby town subcontracted women in Zapotitlán as home workers to embroider blouses. Eva, along with other men and women from the region, sold the blouses in tourist destinations throughout the country. In Tijuana, she could see the fence that marked *la linea* (the border) between the two countries and told others that one day she might go to New York. Everyone cautioned her that it would be too dangerous for an unaccompanied woman. However, Eva thought about building a house that would be better than the wood shack she shared with her daughter.

On one of her trips to Tijuana, she crossed over into San Diego with the help of a smuggler and then flew to New York. Four male relatives from Zapotitlán, already established in New York, helped pay her way. Because she knew how to sew, she found work immediately in a garment factory owned by a Korean woman.[7] She worked nine hours per day, Monday through Saturday for US$210 (US$3.88/hour, slightly above the federal minimum wage of US$3.35/hour in the 1980s).

After five months in New York, four other women from Zapotitlán arrived, inspired by Eva's success. Three of them found work in the same garment factory. After several months, she moved to another factory owned by a Dominican man and made US$230 each week for the same number of hours. Whenever women told her they were going to go to New York, she responded: "Fine, go, but learn how to sew first so that you get a job." (Eva, 55 years old, Zapotitlán Salinas, September 2003). Eva's insistence on women acquiring sewing skills before they migrated lends weight to the idea that women from Zapotitlán migrated primarily to work and not as dependents on male relatives.

New York's garment industry had always relied on immigrant workers and their children as an essential labor source. Their lack of social capital restricted their flight into more remunerative labor markets. As a result, new waves of immigrants were required to replenish workers who either aged out of work or found better jobs after a period of acculturation and incorporation (Waldinger & Lapp, 1992). While the industry declined in the decades after World War II, immigrants from Latin America and Asia established themselves by opening small factories that were contracted by larger garment manufacturing firms. Smaller firms, headed mostly by immigrants, were well-suited to recruiting labor from immigrant communities and, therefore, adapted more easily to changing production conditions, characteristics which explain their relative success in a competitive industry (Waldinger, 1984).

Immigrants from Mexico, like Eva, furnished the low-waged labor required by small immigrant-owned firms in New York. She evaluated her meager wages and difficult working conditions (as did other immigrant laborers) by relying on a dual frame of reference, that is, with reference to worse conditions in their home countries (Waldinger, 1984, p. 104; Waldinger & Lichter, 2003, p. 40). Meager wages and difficult working conditions are understood by Mexican immigrants in relation to Mexican wages and working conditions shaped by the neoliberal dismantling of livelihoods in rural areas (Binford, 2009). For Eva, working in a sweatshop in New York presented one of the only paths to "acquire the income necessary for a minimally dignified life" (Binford, 2009, p. 505) given the increasing precarity and informalization of work in rural Mexico in the 1980s and 1990s.

After a few months working in the second garment factory, Eva was overcome with "tristeza" (sadness). The months-long separation from her daughter took an emotional toll, and she had to take frequent bathroom breaks, a symptom of her worsening diabetic condition. Under these circumstances, it was difficult to continue working at the required speed in the garment factory. While Eva told me that she decided to leave voluntarily when she became sick, it is not uncommon for operators to be forced to leave, under more or less direct pressure, when they do not make production quotas because of illness or injury (Fernández-Kelly, 1983, pp. 113–114; Wright, 2006, pp. 33–42).

Melissa Wright's elegant analysis of the myth of the third-world disposable woman explains how the myth naturalizes the deterioration of women's bodies through factory work. Women's bodies become a form of industrial waste that will necessarily and inevitably be disposed of and replaced. "The myth explains this unlucky fate as a factual outcome of natural and cultural processes that are immune to external tampering" (Wright, 2006, p. 2). Although women produce enormous value, they do so through their own destruction. When Eva could no longer make the quota, she left her job and joined a Pentecostal church where she received food baskets in return for her volunteer work. A parishioner hired her as a nanny to care for her two children for US$130 per week. This represented a substantial reduction in pay; however, the "lighter" working conditions made it easier for her to manage her diabetes. Eva, like Maria (mentioned above) and Gilda (discussed below) found "refuge" from the bodily wear and tear of manual jobs in remunerated reproductive work in private homes.

After a year and a half in New York, Eva returned to Mexico. With the money she had saved from working in the US, she built a small house in Tehuacán and almost finished another in Zapotitlán. Eva was satisfied with what she had accomplished by migrating: "I never finished my house, but at least I have a solid house of cement. I wanted to go back a few years later with my daughter, but because my health got worse, I had to resign myself to the house that I had."

Her sister, however, commented that Eva came back worn out (*acabada*) from working long hours and being away from home, attributing the wasting from Eva's diabetes to the experience of migration (see Chapter 6 for more discussion about return migration and illness). She complained that Eva returned without "doing anything" (*no hizo nada*), that is, without permanently improving her living conditions. She implied that Eva's trip had not been worth the heartache of separation and the wear on her body.

Powerful tropes among villagers establish normative behavior that disciplines migrants. "Legitimate" reasons to leave the village include the goal to "salir adelante," to progress and improve living conditions. This process entails hard work and sacrifice, both in terms of suffering in the United States as well as the suffering of family members from separation (Abrego, 2014). Because there is much at stake, the sacrifice must lead to success, measured primarily in terms of the amount of money migrants invest in regular remittances, clothing, housing, vehicles and, for a few, a business—all things that can be seen publicly and evaluated through gossip. If they cannot prove their success, migrants are subject to disqualifications. *No hizo nada* (he/she did not accomplish anything), *anda perdido* (he/she is lost i.e., in drugs, for example), *dan lastima* (he/she evokes pity) are some of the colloquial forms of these disqualifications. The constant evaluations of success and failure that circulate in the transnational migrant circuit act to shore up a normative discourse of the hard-working migrant, one that disciplines the population (Cordero Diaz, 2007).

Gilda: "fast hands" and "doing the work of two people"

To avoid disqualification, it was imperative to demonstrate one's capacity to work. The flexible laborers forged out of the rural surplus population of Central Mexico continually adapted to the demands of flexible labor markets in New York. Upon her arrival in New York, Gilda met a woman from Brazil who took her to clean houses. However, the woman explained to Gilda that she would pay her when she learned to do her job well. Robbed of her wage, Gilda quit working for the Brazilian woman and worked for a Guatemalan woman who told her she could pay her US$6 per hour to clean houses. While she was proud of earning her first US$18 after a three-hour shift, Gilda knew that she could earn more.

> I was not satisfied making 6 dollars an hour. It was very little money. I heard that men earned 10 dollars an hour at the corner [working as day laborers]. So I went to the corner, because I didn't have any contacts. And if you don't speak English, no one will hire you. I went to the corner at 6 in the morning and I stood there with all the men. I saw how they ran and got into the cars. At first, I didn't understand. One day I ran and I got inside the truck, and the driver asked me, "What? Why you?" They asked me if I knew how to paint and I said "yes." The man felt sorry for me. Even though I was a woman, he gave me a job. They gave me a brush and a bucket to prepare the paint. I started to paint ceilings, walls; I painted everything.
> (Gilda, 50 years old, Zapotitlán Salinas, January 2012)

Although the corner was a decidedly masculine space and the jobs offered there tended to be for men,[8] Gilda staked out a place for herself. Working "like a man" for a while, she was able to earn more money per hour. After a few weeks, an elderly woman hired Gilda off the corner to do some alterations. Satisfied with Gilda's work, she hired her full-time to work as a domestic in her home paying her US$10 per hour. Working Monday through Friday, eight hours a day, Gilda cooked, cleaned, ironed and eventually bathed and cared for the woman as her health deteriorated.

Gilda's material and affective labor to ensure this elderly woman's wellbeing (while leaving her own children in the care of her father and sisters in Zapotitlán) can be understood through the optic of global care chains (Hochschild, 2000; Yeates, 2012, p. 137). The concept of global care chains calls attention to how reproductive labor has been globalized alongside economic globalization, allowing for its expansion, particularly in the context of the withdrawal of state services and increasing welfare restrictions (Ehrenreich & Hochschild, 2003; Truong, 1996). Millions of migrants like Gilda labor in the reproductive tasks abandoned by the state and by women entering the workforce in migrant destination countries.

In addition to her caretaking job during the week, Gilda worked at a social hall on the weekends washing dishes from 8:00 pm until 4:00 am earning US$8/hour.

"I always had a job. I was always working. If I would have had more hands, I would have worked more."

Gilda returned briefly to Zapotitlán when her son graduated from secondary school. She begged him to continue to study, explaining to him that she had migrated and worked in New York so that he could study. However, he insisted that he would not study and would not be left "alone"—without his mother—in Zapotitlán. Her son insisted that if Gilda did not take him to New York, he would spend all her remittances on diversions, wasting precious resources. Reluctantly, Gilda returned with him and went back to her job as caretaker for the elderly woman. She stayed in that job for another two years until the woman passed away. Afterward, she found a job in a restaurant kitchen where she worked for eight years performing virtually every task and climbing the hierarchy from dishwasher to kitchen manager.

> I was motivated to do everything! They told me: "Gilda has fast hands." I helped my boss a lot. With me, he saved three persons' salaries and I helped him a lot with the work. An African American man started work and I showed him how to use the machine. Later, I got a woman a job there. I gave other Hispanic people jobs, including many women. One helped me with the silverware, another with the dishes. But no one was as fast as I was. Then I started to help the cook prepare the pizzas and take them out when they were done. Then the woman who served soup got sick and they asked me to take over her job. I served the soup and the salads. It was two jobs in one.
> (Gilda, 50 years old, Zapotitlán Salinas, January 2012)

With respect to her tasks as a kitchen manager, she proudly proclaimed, "I had the satisfaction of hiring and firing people!" Gilda's insertion into the flexible labor markets for service workers in New York required her to constantly adapt to a number of jobs that required varying amounts of mental, emotional and physical labor. She was, perhaps, most proud of her restaurant work. She boasted about her "fast hands" and disposition to help out in any way. She understood that these traits were of great use to her employer. She molded herself into a self-exploiting, flexible worker, always ready to do any task required of her in the kitchen. Gilda embodied the flexible, ready-to-do-anything worker, a so-called "unskilled" worker molded to be satisfied with the temporary, part-time offerings of the low-waged service labor market.

In interviews, Gilda referenced her capacity for arduous, tedious work, a capacity that enabled her to reach the highest levels of restaurant kitchen administration. Through the idea of "doing the work of two people," she affirms her moral worth as a worker. In the context of the criminalization of "illegality," being an industrious worker is a strong claim to belonging to the American nation-state. It is often used as a marker in negative opposition to other Latino groups—particularly Puerto Ricans in the New York context—who have the rights of citizenship yet not the "hunger" to work like poor, Mexican immigrants, according to many Zapotitecos. In this "immigrant analogy" (Smith, 2006), Puerto Ricans' "dependence" on the government—i.e., their use of public assistance—is seen as an essentialized characteristic of being averse to working, and, therefore, a moral failure.[9] In an attempt to overcome this marginalized status, Zapotitecos/as boast about their capacity for work. *They* are the ones that have a legitimate right to be in the United States, despite their official status as "illegal aliens."[10]

Hard work not only allows Zapotitecos/as to be full, moral beings in the absence of legal personhood, but also dispels doubts about being "bad" or "failed" migrants. Spouses, children, extended family members, and friends all weigh in on whether someone has accomplished something through migration, putting pressure on individuals to demonstrate their success. The "bad" migrant discourse—a disciplinary apparatus wielded by *paisanos* to shame each other—metes out punishment for not conforming to the norm of hard work.

However, it is not the only detectable discourse. The willingness to go beyond the requirements of the job and to align one's efforts to please supervisors, managers and owners corresponds to a self-optimization impulse. Having "fast hands" and "doing the work of two people" are proud narratives of workers who feel they have accomplished important things. Helping bosses by ensuring that things run smoothly so the restaurant can open on time are positive narratives, a hallmark of a subject who is always optimizing. We will return to this idea in the final discussion of the chapter.

Carolina: "I have worked like a man!"

Carolina, after working as a domestic worker in Mexico City, migrated to New York City in 1990. Her brother worked in New York and helped pay her smuggling fees. "I went without thinking! I was always the most adventurous one in my house! I was doing very well in Mexico City. I was sending money home to my family and I earned well." She began work a few days after arriving as a live-in domestic servant to a Dominican woman with two young children, a job for which she had already acquired experience in Mexico City. Carolina earned US$200 per week and continued sending money home to her parents to support them and her younger siblings. Although she experienced migration as "adventure," her labor was necessary to pay for a portion of the subsistence of her parents and younger siblings. An "adventure" perhaps, but one with the obligation to work and support other family members.

After two years of working, she became pregnant and moved in with the father of her child, an arrangement that lasted only a few months when he abruptly announced that he was returning to Mexico. Abandoned by her partner, she returned to live with the Dominican woman who promised Carolina that she and the baby could stay with her without paying rent in exchange for her labor as a nanny and housekeeper. Although Carolina complained in the interview that this was a difficult situation because she had no money of her own to buy any "extras" for herself or the baby, she felt that she had no other option for her infant daughter. She stayed with the woman until her baby was about a year old. With the woman's help, Carolina applied for public assistance. Carolina's unpaid domestic labor—subsidized by public assistance—allowed her employer to provide low-cost labor to the New York service economy. Carolina's non-wage relationship to capital illustrates the heterogeneity of a working class which includes both paid and unpaid labor (Carbonella & Kasmir, 2015). Further, the various "hidden" dimensions of her work—as an undocumented, live-in domestic without a salary—should not impede us from a full consideration of her position as a classed and gendered subject (Bettie, 2003), invisibly subsidizing the low wages of another woman through her reproductive labor.

Eventually, close relatives invited Carolina to move in with them. Although she received public assistance, it did not cover all her expenses. She would have to work. The dismantling of welfare programs beginning in the 1970s and the associated belief that meager benefits were no longer entitlements but should instead be exchanged for labor maintained benefits at a bare minimum (Goode & Maskovsky, 2001).[11] She found an immigrant woman to care for her daughter while she worked in a *bodega*, a convenience store, stocking shelves. After several months, she worked cleaning a movie theater from 12:00 am to 9:00 am, six days a week. "There were 12 theaters to clean and each of the bathrooms had 15 stalls. It was hard work, and we had to work fast. Everything had to be clean by morning. The men were faster at this work and they helped me finish on time." (Carolina, 30 years old, Bronx NY, November 2004). Her health suffered from the night shifts because she was not able to sleep during the day. She became sick from the strong chemicals used in her job, combined with lack of sleep and caring for her child.

Carolina eventually met a man from Zapotitlán, Fernando, with whom she had two children. When I met Carolina in 2004, her eldest daughter was starting secondary school and her two youngest children were four and six. In addition to her children, she cared for two small children full-time in her two-bedroom apartment near the Mosholu subway stop in the Bronx. Fernando worked in Manhattan, on Canal Street, delivering food to office workers in Lower Manhattan. He paid his transportation to work, the rent and food for the family. Carolina's salary was destined for clothes, school supplies and personal products. She visited a Pentecostal church once a week for a free meal and food to take home. Ordering housewares and some clothes from catalogs allowed her to pay "little by little," so that she could afford basic goods for her growing family.[12]

Carolina internalized the idea that reproductive work did not "count" as work. She commented that women—even those from Mexico—could be very difficult. They were always *echando piedras*, making hurtful comments. "In this country, I have worked in everything. There are women who say to me, 'I have never seen you work!' But I have worked like a man!" (Carolina, 30 years old, Bronx NY, February 2005). Here, Carolina referred to her work stocking shelves in the convenience store and cleaning the movie theater. The "hard-working immigrant" trope defends one's moral worth as a worker—doing "men's work"—against the idea that women are *only* involved in reproduction.

Beyond the complaint that other immigrant women have not seen Carolina work outside the home, she had to defend herself against the idea that she has not *done anything*—built a house or started a business—back in Mexico.

I have *not done anything*. The only inheritance that I will leave my children is their education. This is the only thing with which they can defend themselves. My cousin built a huge house in Mexico. But my idea is this: I will give them education, even though others criticize me that I have *not done anything*. I give my children what I can. I don't give them everything. I buy books and food for them. I have a little account in the bank for an emergency. This is my idea. They will decide what to do with their future.

(Carolina, 30 years old, Bronx NY, November 2004)

As an immigrant with US-born children, Carolina oriented her life toward the United States, placing her hopes in her children's social mobility through education. This clearly defined life project drew criticism from other Mexican immigrants because she had "not done anything" back in Zapotitlán that would demonstrate her "success." Instead, Carolina wanted to raise her children in the US where she believed they would have better life opportunities. However, social mobility through education was and is difficult to attain for children of Mexican immigrants because of their marginalized status in the city's hierarchy of immigrant groups.[13]

Beatriz: "even if you don't know how to do it, just say you do"

Women with children in Zapotitlán who desired to migrate had to tread carefully between the motivation to improve their families' condition and the possibility of people seeing them as if they had abandoned their children. The shame of being a single mother in this community, where the purity of the Virgin Mary was and is held as the exemplary mode of being for unmarried women, turned migration into a path to redemption. When she was 14, Beatriz left school to work in one of the local maquiladoras, from 8:00 am to 7:00–8:00 pm, contributing her salary of 300 pesos (US$30) to her household where she lived with her parents. After four years, she became pregnant, worked until she had her baby, and returned to work when her baby was four months old, leaving him in the care of her mother. This arrangement continued until the baby was a year and a half old. At that point, Beatriz left for New York to live with her brothers who had established themselves in the city previously. She left the boy in the care of her mother because she felt the risks of the clandestine crossing were too great for him. Along with economic necessity, the shame and disillusionment that her parents felt at her "failure" (*fracaso*) to live up to the standards of a "decent" woman was a key factor in Beatriz's decision to migrate.

> My parents were irritated and offended that I failed [became pregnant before marriage]. They told me that if I had to make a living in New York, so be it. They told me: "You might not make it; you could die. They say that they abuse women. Anything could happen to you!" I told them: "I am not afraid and I want to take the risk."
>
> (Beatriz, 29 years old, Zapotitlán Salinas, June 2011)

The numerous risks associated with clandestine migrations for undocumented migrants crossing the US–Mexico border were viewed, by Beatriz's parents, as forms of punishment for her failures—*her cross to bear*, in local vernacular. Beatriz courageously assumed these risks to achieve a higher purpose: to support her son as a transnational mother (Hondagneu-Sotelo & Avila, 1997). Selfless motherhood, *la mujer abnegada*, even of the transnational type, could perhaps offer moral redemption for her "mistakes."

Beatriz left her young son with her mother and arrived in Yonkers, New York, a town in Westchester County, in 2002, to live with her brother who had arrived several years earlier. Fleeing the moral stigma of *fracaso* and the need to send back money for the expenses her mother incurred while caring for her son as well as her mother's diabetes medications, Beatriz recalls the fear she felt at having to find a job in an unknown city. Another woman encouraged her by telling her: "Don't be afraid, or else you won't learn." Fear could make it difficult for her to learn to be a productive, flexible worker, adapted to the needs of the service economy. After a few weeks of walking around and asking for work in the businesses that lined the suburban streets, she found employment in a Mexican restaurant washing dishes. For six months, she worked 12 hours per day, earning US$4 per hour, until a gang murdered a Mexican immigrant outside the restaurant, after which she no longer felt safe at her job.

A co-worker from the restaurant recommended her to the owner of a restaurant along the Hudson River. Going to work required a one-hour commute on the bus, but the upscale area made Beatriz feel much safer. Beatriz was charged with cleaning the restaurant from 8:00 am to 4:00 pm daily, although she quickly discovered that her limited English made her the target of ridicule of a Korean manager.[14] The constant ridicule motivated Beatriz to take English classes in the afternoon after work. Once she could "defend" herself in English, the manager left her alone. She was the only person hired to clean the restaurant, ostensibly because previous workers were unable to deal with him. Beatriz relied upon her ability to work hard at a fast pace to do what was expected of her. "When I started the job, there was no one else to clean, so I had to come in early in order to quickly finish cleaning the dining rooms so that the restaurant could open at 11."

Within months, she had managed to deal not only with the workload but also with the difficult manager, a feat that allowed her to earn some autonomy with respect to the timing of certain tasks. She told the Korean manager: "Ok, I will clean your office, but on the days that I want to, not when you tell me to." She constantly looked for ways to pick up additional hours on holidays and overtime during the summer high season, a way to earn double the salary that the "generous" Italian owners offered even to an undocumented worker like Beatriz.[15] She was the ultimate flexible worker, adapting to long hours in the summers and reduced hours—and less pay—in the winters. Working only a few hours a day a few days a week in the winter made it difficult for Beatriz to earn enough to pay her expenses in Yonkers and send money home for her mother and son. However, the promise of more pay in summer kept her hanging on to her job. She bore the ensuing hardships of the ebb and flow of the flexible restaurant industry.

When Beatriz became pregnant, her employers told her to look for two women who would take over the cleaning and whom she would oversee. She became their manager and shifted around the restaurant performing "light" work. When she was eight months pregnant, she decided to quit. Her bosses gave her a "bonus" of two weeks' pay and told her to come back whenever she was ready.

After the baby, she decided not to return to the restaurant. "It was going to be too difficult because I did not have anyone to take care of my daughter. So I would have to start from scratch." She found another undocumented Mexican woman to take care of the child and found work in a clothing boutique owned and managed by Koreans not far from her apartment. Although she had never sold clothing before, she explained how sometimes it was necessary to tell people that she could do the work: "Well, if you need the work, even if you don't know how to do it, just say you do, so they give you the work and when you get the job, work hard!" She earned considerably less money than she was earning at the restaurant, US$5/hour, and had to pay childcare, US$25/day. However, her bosses agreed to give her Tuesdays off to allow Beatriz to take her daughter to doctors' appointments if it became necessary. By taking only one day off, Beatriz explained, "... [the business] isn't affected nor am I." Being able to negotiate this gave Beatriz a sense of control over her work within a situation where she had few options. "I work 6 days a week, 9 hours a day. They don't give me Saturday or Sunday off. And if I get sick, well, I still need the money, so I will work in whatever I can." Although attending to customers took up most of her time, she also repaired damaged clothing, made bank deposits and did other administrative tasks without extra pay. Beatriz's English skills allowed her to assume work in different tasks required by retail. Knowing that her personal treatment of each customer was key to good sales, Beatriz explained how she helped people pick out clothes that looked good on them. She knew she was successful because they would come back to seek her help again. "I always tried to be as polite as possible with people."

"Illegality" and entrepreneurialism: constructing subjects at the intersection of techniques of power and of the self

> Personal autonomy is not the antithesis of political power, but a key term in its exercise, the more so because most individuals are not merely the subjects of power but play a part in its operations.
>
> (Rose & Miller, 1992, p. 174)

Beatriz, Gilda, Carolina and Eva manifest a variety of positions with respect to their relationship with capital through their productive and reproductive labor. While the women's labor and migration trajectories demonstrate the ways in which flexibility, precarity and disposability traverse their working lives on both sides of the border, they also show how they have moved through different class positions with respect to the wage relationship. Carolina, whose in-home childcare was devalued by other immigrants who claimed that they had never seen her work, represents a crucial element in the reproduction not only of the future workforce, but also of the current workforce because her labor "liberated" other immigrant women for work in New York's service economy. Carolina's flexibility to care for her own family and other women's children permitted the adaptation of various workers to precarious, low-waged work. Gilda, Eva and Beatriz were liberated from unpaid reproductive labor because family members in Zapotitlán assumed care of their dependent children. However, Gilda and Eva took on remunerated reproductive work in New York to "rest" from toiling in sweatshops and restaurant kitchens.

Extending the hard-working immigrant discourse, migrants extolled the virtues of their abilities to work autonomously. Migrant women were proud of their work, took initiatives to perform at high levels over extended periods and talked about how they staked out some autonomy in what were extremely difficult working conditions. They sought to cultivate their supervisors' satisfaction by working fast, taking on additional tasks and being always available through high and low seasons. They "did men's work" and managed others to ensure that restaurants, movie theaters, and convenience stores were clean, food was prepared and other peoples' children content. The desire for autonomy forms part of the construction of a neoliberal, flexible worker who has internalized the idea that she is not deserving of citizenship or social protections. This subject is deserving of (a meager) salary and nothing more.

Through a Foucauldian lens, the hard-working Mexican immigrant discourse is a truth claim that produces subjects, like Gilda and Beatriz, who conform to expectations of normative behavior (Foucault, 1978). From an analysis of how subjects were produced through regulation and control, Foucault turned his attention to how neoliberal subjects play an active role in their own formation as "entrepreneurs of the self" (Dilts, 2011; Foucault, 2008). In *Psychopolitics: Neoliberalism and New Technologies of Power*, Byung-Chul Han suggests that this subjectivity corresponds to the post-industrial, immaterial and networked forms of production common under finance capital (Han, 2017). According to Han, disciplinary society corresponded to the rise of industrial capitalism. Institutions such as the family, schools, prisons, hospitals, military barracks and factories disciplined workers through experts' discourses constructing the norms of acceptable behavior. Han argues that the restricted movements of workers through these confining institutions and policed discourses imposed limits on productivity.

With the rise of finance capitalism, the post-industrial, immaterial and networked forms of production required the constant breaking down of barriers. The subject was subjugated less through external discipline than a being constantly working on itself, optimizing its performance. Han (2017) argues that the subject under finance capitalism is more like a project, constantly being sculpted into better and better form. The self-exploited being is "free" to improve, attempting to reach an always-receding finish line. This represents a more efficient form of subjectivation and subjugation, because the class struggle turns inward. The subject struggles against her/himself. Collective class struggle is abandoned and replaced by a repressive individualism in which problems are internalized and can only be resolved by the individual working on him or herself.[16]

Although IT workers, traders, and other professionals associated with finance and technology are the paradigmatic workers in the new economy, the evidence from undocumented Mexican migrants who work preparing food, cleaning houses and stocking shelves points to the fact that they, too, have succumbed to an internal self-exploitation regime. They constantly push themselves to do more and to do it better and faster. Gilda's fast hands that did the work of two people, and Beatriz, who, even though she did not know how to do the work, said "yes," and aimed to please, represent how psychopolitics have become a dominant force even among the workers occupying the lowest, most vulnerable, precarious, disposable and deportable spaces of the social hierarchy.

At the same time, we would be remiss to suggest that psychopolitics is the only force shaping the subjectivity of undocumented workers. Immigration policies, both the surveillance of the border and interior enforcement, construct the "illegal" subject limiting immigrants' mobility and wellbeing in the United States (De Genova, 2005). These policies, conceived during the Fordist, industrial capital era to restrict the movement of both legal and illegal labor, weigh like a nightmare on the neoliberal, mobile subjects discussed in this book. The border walls, drones, detention centers, etc.—brought into being during the flexible accumulation phase of capitalism—are instruments of Foucauldian disciplinary power. Migrants discuss the terror of disciplinary control they encounter at the border, forcing them to walk through the desert for days, without food and water, in an attempt to evade detection and detention. At the same time, the militarization of the border created the conditions for risky, expensive human smuggling operations and the diversification of criminal groups who prey on migrants.[17]

The disciplinary control regime at the border has spawned numerous academic and popular critiques. However, what has received less critical attention is the self-exploiting, migrant-entrepreneur who, although undocumented with miserable wages, is available, indeed is disposed, to throw herself into her work, always doing more, always optimizing what she is doing for the good of the enterprise. The neoliberal, undocumented entrepreneur's subjectivity—the hard-working immigrant—shores up her moral right to belong in US society through her hard-earned contributions to productive and reproductive labor. Here the technology of the self—the self-exploiting, entrepreneur service worker—is integrated into the technologies of domination and power—i.e., the construction of the "illegal" subject through punitive immigration policy. For Eva, Gilda, Beatriz and Carolina, these technologies infiltrate the body. The illegal self is redeemed—for an uncertain period of time—by and through the evermore laboring, optimizing neoliberal self.

Notes

1 These figures, adjusted for inflation, were calculated using data for household electricity rate prices provided in the Balance Nacional de Energía 2003, Secretaría de Energía, Mexico DF. I thank Ernesto Aguayo for providing the data and helping with the calculations.
2 The relationship between the local onyx industry and accelerated migration in Zapotitlán draws on Lee (2008).
3 Diminutive of "muchachas" (girls), a derogatory and infantilizing reference to female domestic workers.
4 In the Mixtec region of Puebla, where Izucar de Matamorros is located, poor agricultural conditions and a lack of public investment forced residents to work in regional agricultural labor markets and, later, in the United States in the 1950s during the Bracero Program (Rivera Sánchez, 2007). While the first Mixtec migrants arrived in New York in the 1940s and 1950s (Smith, 2006), larger Mixtec migrant networks emerged in New York in the 1960s (Rivera Sánchez, 2007). The timing of the insertion of these pioneer migrants allowed many of them to apply for permanent residency after IRCA became law in 1986. Luis, the first migrant from Zapotitlán, accompanied an experienced migrant from this region to New York City and was able to take advantage of extensive networks established in previous decades to find housing and a job, a fact that benefited the men and women who migrated after him. However, the majority of Zapotitecos/as could not regularize their migratory status because their arrival to the United States occurred after the Immigration Reform and Control Act (IRCA) of 1986.
5 In 2003, people reported that Zapotitlán's priest was urging newly married couples to migrate together to the United States so that wives would not be left behind.
6 See Chapter 1 for methodological details.
7 Margaret Chin details economic and social relations between Korean owners and Mexican workers in New York City's garment industry (Chin, 2005).
8 See Ordóñez for a detailed portrayal of the lives of male day laborers in California (Ordóñez, 2015).
9 Arlene Dávila describes how the media and public discourse in New York represent Mexican immigrants "as a relatively homogenous community of vulnerable workers, striving to maintain their identity as 'good immigrants' by working hard, keeping their cultural traditions, and maintaining their transnational connections back home" (Dávila, 2004, p. 156). Mexican leaders in the city deflect anti-immigrant sentiment by embracing this representation. However, Dávila points out that this discourse tends to reinforce the idea that Mexicans' value rests only on their production and consumption. Further, by drawing on Bonnie Honig's insights, Dávila points out that "this type of representation helps to reinstate popular and always contradictory ideals of democracy and meritocracy, while antagonizing groups in benefit of the status quo" (p. 162).
10 In her insightful ethnographic study of Asociación Tepeyac, Anthropologist Alyshia Galvez examined how Mexicans in Bronx Catholic parishes articulated citizenship claims through their devotion to Our Lady of Guadalupe. Drawing on Christian humanism's assertion of each person's inherent rights and dignity, activists and migrants struggle for inclusion by appealing to a higher moral law that supersedes immigration policies of the nation-state. At the same time, the undocumented migrant worthy of rights draws on an individual who embodies hard work, along with family values and dignity (Galvez, 2010).
11 Goode and Maskovsky (2001) discuss how economic polarization, political demobilization of the poor and market triumphalism embraced by neoliberal politicians were responsible for the rollback of the social safety net created through the New Deal and the War on Poverty. The notions of cost-effectiveness, competition and efficiency

ushered in during the transition to flexible accumulation undergirded efforts to eliminate so-called Big Government and promote private-sector solutions to poverty (Goode & Maskovsky, 2001).
12 Fernández-Kelly noted the prevalence of Avon sales among women in Ciudad Juárez's working-class neighborhoods (1983, p. 159). She argues that Avon sales and debts represented a redistributive mechanism among the maquiladora workers. Among female factory workers in Guangzhou, Aihwa Ong mentions how corporations like Avon "engender new needs and desires that socialize Chinese workers to the norms of mass consumption" (Ong, 1999, p. 40). In the context of class and gender, it is important to note how a company like Avon benefits by paying on commission through catalog orders and thereby evades the hire of a permanent workforce to sell its products. This represents an additional mechanism by which women subsidize the expansion of capitalist enterprise with poorly remunerated work.
13 Social mobility through education, however, was difficult to attain for Mexicans in New York. In the early 1990s, census data showed that 47 percent of Mexicans aged 16 to 19 were not in high school and had not graduated, more than twice the rate for the next-highest groups: Dominicans and Puerto Ricans (Rivera-Batiz, 1996). Data from the 2010 census showed that this number had fallen to 41 percent. However, no other immigrant group in the city had a dropout rate above 20 percent, and the average was 9 percent for all groups (Semple, 2011). According to sociologist Robert Smith, the insertion of Mexican immigrants—mostly poor and undocumented—into labor markets in New York as unskilled, low-waged service and construction workers limited the education-based mobility of their immigrant and second-generation children. Mexicans' dispersal across industries and jobs in New York had a negative impact on social mobility and development of social capital (Smith, 2006, pp. 26–27).
14 See Kim (1999) and Smith (2006) for additional information about the relationships between Korean employers and Mexican workers. Mexican workers are paid much less than Korean co-ethnic workers in Korean-owned businesses and are seen as suitable workers for unskilled tasks. This hierarchical relationship can cause conflicts in the workplace.
15 Smith (2006, p. 37) explains that Italian Americans may have positive attitudes toward Mexicans as "fellow immigrants and Catholics, struggling as their own grandparents did," especially when there are few Mexicans in their neighborhoods.
16 We thank Leigh Binford for help with the development of this idea.
17 Immigration policy operates at the border and throughout the interior of the country. In a Foucauldian sense, migrants are never safe from the panopticon of Immigration and Customs Enforcement (ICE). Yet, the objective is not to remove immigrant labor entirely, but to instill fear in migrants wherever they are, thereby creating a tractable and docile workforce (Goldstein & Alonso-Bejarano, 2017).

References

Abrego, L. (2014). *Sacrificing families: Navigating laws, labor and love across borders*. Stanford: Stanford University Press.

Amorós, C. (2008). Globalización y orden de género. In C. Amorós & A. de Miguel (Eds), *Teoría feminista: De la Ilustración a la globalización. De los debates sobre el género al multiculturalismo* (pp. 301–330). Madrid: Minerva Ediciones.

Barrios Hernández, M., & Santiago Hernández, R. (2003). *Tehuacan: Del calzon de manta a los blue jeans*. Tehuacán, Puebla: Comision de Derechos Humanos y Laborales del Valle de Tehuacán, A.C.

Bettie, J. (2003). *Women without class: Girls, race, and identity*. Berkeley: University of California Press.

Binford, L. (2003). Migrant remittances and (under)development in Mexico. *Critique of Anthropology, 23*(3), 305–336.
Binford, L. (2009). From fields of power to fields of sweat: The dual process of constructing temporary migrant labour in Mexico and Canada. *Third World Quarterly, 30*(3), 503–517. https://doi.org/10.1080/01436590902742297.
Bourdieu, P. (1984). *Distinction: A social critique of the judgement of taste*. Cambridge, MA: Harvard University Press.
Cantor, G., Noferi, M., & Martinez, D. E. (2015). *Enforcement overdrive: A comprehensive assessment of ICE's criminal alien program*. Retrieved from http://immigrationpolicy.org/special-reports/enforcement-overdrive-comprehensive-assessment-criminal-alien-program.
Carbonella, A., & Kasmir, S. (2015). Dispossession, disorganization and the anthropology of labor. In J. G. Carrier & D. Kalb (Eds), *Anthropologies of class: Power, practice and inequality* (pp. 41–52). Cambridge: Cambridge University Press.
Chin, M. (2005). *Sewing women: Immigrants and the New York City garment industry*. New York: Columbia University Press.
Cordero Diaz, B. L. (2007). *Ser trabajador transnacional: Clase, hegemonía y cultura en un circuito migratorio internacional*. Puebla, México: ICSyH-BUAP.
Dávila, A. (2004). *Barrio dreams: Puerto Ricans, Latinos, and the neoliberal city*. Berkeley: University of California Press.
Davis, A. (1981). *Women, race and class*. New York: Random House.
De Genova, N. (2005). *Working the boundaries: Race, space, and "illegality" in Mexican Chicago*. Durham, NC: Duke University Press.
Dilts, A. (2011). From "entrepreneur of the self" to "care of the self": Neo-liberal governmentality and Foucault's ethics. *Foucault Studies, 3*(12), 130–146.
Durin, S. (2017). *Yo trabajo en casa: Trabajo del hogar de planta, género y etnicidad en Monterrey*. Ciudad de México: Centro de Investigaciones y Estudios Superiores en Antropología Social.
Ehrenreich, B., & Hochschild, A. R. (2003). *Global woman: Nannies, maids and sex workers in the new economy*. New York: Metropolitan Books.
Escobar Latapi, A., & Martinez Castellanos, M. de la O. (1991). Small-scale industry and international migration in Guadalajara, Mexico. In S. Diaz-Briquests & S. Weintraub (Eds), *Migration, remittances and small business development*. Boulder, CO: Westview.
Fernández-Kelly, M. P. (1983). *For we are sold, I and my people: Women and industry in Mexico's frontier*. Albany: State University of New York Press.
Flores Morales, M. de L. (2008). *"No me gusta, pero es trabajo": Mujer, trabajo y desechabilidad en la maquila*. México D.F: Plaza y Valdés.
Foucault, M. (1978). *History of sexuality* (Vol. 1., Trans M. Hurley). New York: Pantheon.
Foucault, M. (2008). *The birth of biopolitics: Lectures at the College of France, 1978–79* (Trans G. Burchell). New York: Palgrave Macmillan.
Galvez, A. (2010). *Guadalupe in New York: Devotion and the struggle for citizenship rights among Mexican immigrants*. New York: New York University Press.
Goldstein, D., & Alonso-Bejarano, C. (2017). E-terrify: Securitized immigration and biometric surveillance in the workplace. *Human Organization, 76*(1), 1–14.
Goode, J., & Maskovsky, J. (2001). Introduction. In J. Goode & J. Maskovsky (Eds), *New poverty studies: The ethnography of power, politics, and impoverished people in the United States* (pp. 1–34). New York: New York University Press.
Griffith, D. (2005). Rural industry and Mexican immigration and settlement in North Carolina. In R. Hernández-León & V. Zúñiga (Eds), *New destinations: Mexican immigration in the United States* (pp. 50–74). New York: Russell Sage Foundation.

Han, B.-C. (2017). *Psychopolitics: Neoliberalism and new technologies of power*. London: Verso.

Hochschild, A. R. (1989). *The second shift: Working parents and the revolution at home*. New York: Penguin Books.

Hochschild, A. R. (2000). Global care chains and emotional surplus value. In W. Hutton & A. Giddens (Eds), *On the edge: Living with global capitalism* (pp. 120–146). London: Jonathan Cape.

Hondagneu-Sotelo, P., & Avila, E. (1997). "I'm here, but I'm there": The meanings of Latina transnational motherhood. *Gender and Society, 11*(5), 548–571.

Iglesias, N. (1985). *La flor más bella de la maquiladora*. México, D.F: Secretaría de Educación Pública y Centro de Estudios Fronterizos del Norte de México.

Kim, D. Y. (1999). Beyond co-ethnic solidarity: Mexican and Ecuadorean employment in Korean-owned businesses in New York City. *Ethnic and Racial Studies, 22*(3), 581–605.

Lee, A. (2008). "Para salir adelante": The emergence and acceleration of international migration in new sending areas of Puebla, Mexico. *Journal of Latin American and Caribbean Anthropology, 13*(1), 48–78.

Lee, A. (2018). US–Mexico border militarization and violence: Dispossession of undocumented laboring classes from Puebla, Mexico. *Migraciones Internacionales, 9*(35), 213–238.

Ong, A. (1999). *Flexible citizenship*. Durham: Duke University Press.

Ordóñez, J. T. (2015). *Jornalero: Being a day laborer in the United States*. Oakland: University of California Press.

Reichert, J. (1979). *The migrant syndrome: An analysis of US migration and its impact on a rural Mexican town*. Department of Anthropology. Princeton, NJ: Princeton University.

Rivera-Batiz, F. (1996). *The education of immigrant children: The case of New York City*. New York. Immigrant New York Series, International Center for the Study of Migration, Ethnicity and Citizenship, New School for Social Research.

Rivera Sánchez, L. (2007). La formación y dinámica del circuito migratorio Mixteca-Nueva York-Mixteca: Los trayectos internos e internacionales. *Norteamérica. Revista Académica Del CISAN-UNAM, 2*(1), 171–203. Retrieved from www.redalyc.org/html/1937/193715169007/.

Rose, N., & Miller, P. (1992). Political power beyond the state: Problematics of government. *The British Journal of Sociology, 43*(2), 173–205.

Rothstein, F. A. (2007). *Globalization in rural Mexico: Three decades of change*. Austin: University of Texas Press.

Semple, K. (2011). In New York, Mexicans lag in education. *New York Times*.

Slack, J., Martinez, D., Lee, A., & Whiteford, S. (2016). The geography of border militarization: Violence, death and health in Mexico and the United States. *Journal of Latin American Geography, 15*(1), 7–32. https://doi.org/10.1353/lag.2016.0009.

Smith, R. C. (2006). *Mexican New York: Transnational lives of new immigrants*. Berkeley & Los Angeles: University of California Press.

Truong, T.-D. (1996). Gender, migration and social reproduction: Implications for theory, policy, research and networking. *Asian and Pacific Migration Journal, 5*(1), 27–52.

Waldinger, R. (1984). Immigrant enterprise in the New York garment industry. *Social Problems, 32*(1), 60–71.

Waldinger, R., & Lapp, M. (1992). Why immigrants stay in fashion: Insights from New York's garment industry. *Policy Studies Review, 11*(2), 97–105.

Waldinger, R., & Lichter, M. (2003). *How the other half works: Immigration and the social organization of labor*. Berkeley: University of California Press.

Wiest, R. E. (1984). External dependency and the perpetuation of temporary migration to the United States. In R. C. Jones (Ed.), *Patterns of undocumented migration: Mexico and the United States* (pp. 110–135). Totoway, NJ: Rowman & Allanheld.

Wright, M. W. (2006). *Disposable women and other myths of global capitalism*. New York: Taylor & Francis Group.

Yeates, N. (2012). Global care chains: A state-of-the-art review and future directions in care transnationalization research. *Global Networks, 12*(2), 135–154.

5 Deceleration of migration and the selectivity of return migration in the Northern Sierra of Puebla

Introduction

Between 2007 and 2009, the most critical years of the so-called great crisis, employment in the masculinized construction sector in the United States, where the majority of Hispanic migrants work, dropped 25 percent. In contrast, foreign-born Hispanic women experienced an employment gain of almost 10 percent in personal, laundry and private household services (Rothstein, 2016, p. 11). The differential drop in employment according to gender was also reflected in the number of migrant returns to Mexico (Arroyo-Alejandre, Berumen-Sandoval, & Rodríguez-Álvarez, 2010; Woo Morales & Flores Álvarez, 2015). The new international division of labor expresses itself in the marked differences in employment and return according to gender and national origin during the years of economic recession. Various processes are interwoven behind these differences: the global increase of women in wage labor in deindustrialized economies, the redefinition of their responsibilities both in and out of their households, socio-demographic changes, population aging, and welfare state restructuring in the destination countries (Verschuur, 2013). The lethal effects of structural adjustment programs in impoverished countries and regions that supply so-called cheap labor also lie behind the differences in migrants' employment and return. Immigrant labor is highly coveted for reducing production costs in certain economic sectors of destination countries or to relaunch or reorient economies of vast regions, as is the case of the so-called *Nuevo* New South.

Going beyond the idea of gender as an individual attribute (cfr. Chapter 1), we conceptualize it as a fundamental structural element of migration, shaping a variety of practices, identities and institutions involved in the configuration of migration flows. New perspectives in the field unearthed the complex relationship between gender, migration and social reproductive crisis. We agree with Fraser (2017, p. 22) that

> *every* form of capitalist society harbors a deep-seated *social reproductive* 'crisis tendency' or 'contradiction.' On the one hand, social reproduction is a condition of possibility for sustained capital accumulation; on the other

hand, capitalism's orientation to unlimited accumulation tends to destabilize the very process of social reproduction on which it relies.

According to Williams (2014, p. 12), for Fraser

> most analyses of the current capitalist crisis are gender blind and asserts the obverse, that feminism lacks a framework to link social changes affecting gender relations to this crisis [... Fraser] suggests that we need an integrated approach to understand how these dimensions relate to each other.

Coinciding with Fraser's claim, several feminist authors (Farris, 2019; Kofman & Raghuram, 2015; Verschuur, 2013; Williams, 2014), among others, consider the relationship between migration and the crisis in social reproduction, along with the crises in ecology and finance, as the main pillars of the contemporary crisis of global capitalism.

In this chapter, we analyze the deceleration of a migratory flow to North Carolina and the selective return to the municipality of Pahuatlán, in Central Mexico, inspired in these debates about the crisis in social reproduction. The empirical foundation of the discussion is provided by information obtained from interviews with 51 returnees in the municipality of Pahuatlán and in the Northern Sierra of Puebla, between 2007–2010 and 2010–2014, as well as in Durham and Orange County, North Carolina, in 2013 and 2014. Interviews are complemented by the results of a survey applied to 135 households in Pahuatlán. We assume that the reinstatement of the returnees in their places of origin—transitory or at times definitive—does not constitute a "triumphant moment [that] puts things back where they were" (Pascual de Sans, 1983, p. 72). As Rivera Sánchez states (2015, p. 246), return does not necessarily imply going back to the family origins and to the [unmodified] birthplace. On the contrary, it includes a series of displacements not only of the spatial-territorial kind, but also positional and, fundamentally, biographical. Return entails a relocation in the social space. From our perspective, Pahuatecan migrants' return before and after the economic and financial recession in the United States expresses the oscillating relationship of surplus populations with capital, trapped in the sway between full employment, underemployment and unemployment on both sides of the border. Such a relationship can be grasped in the ethnographic record both in individual and group work trajectories, in the same generation or intergenerationally. In addition, both at the macro and the micro level, return entails destabilization and reorganization of reproductive processes in binational households integrated by citizens and non-citizens wielding uneven rights, hindering—or at times facilitating—the mobility of the group, or of some of its members, between both countries.

In the following section, we present the theoretical coordinates framing our reflection. Next, we discuss the selectivity of returning to Mexico or staying in the United States and the context in which these men and women went back to Mexico. In the last section, we analyze return considering the two migration modalities identified in the municipality of Pahuatlán: the mobility of workers without dependents who return to Mexico alone and family return migration.

Crisis, return and social reproduction

When we started our field trips in the municipality of Pahuatlán in 2007, researching the impact of migration in educational trajectories, residents believed that migration to the United States was over. Bad news spread regarding job loss in the construction sector in North Carolina, the primary destination of Pahuatecans. Some were returning or had stopped going altogether and, furthermore, a few had been deported. In 2010, we started a new project on return migration in the area. We tried to find out whether remittances had decreased due to job loss, how many people returned, and who returned. We investigated how these populations were remade in an environment where well-founded fears spread about how things could get worse both for Pahuatecan families that depended directly on the dollar salaries of absent providers, and for other segments indirectly benefiting from these remittances (cfr. Chapter 6 of this volume).

At the same time, the fieldwork carried out in Durham in 2013 and 2014 allowed us to realize that the impacts of the recession on Pahuatecan immigrants and their families in both countries lasted beyond July 2009, when the crisis was officially over. As part of our research, we interviewed men who went back to Pahuatlán during those difficult years, by themselves or with their wives and children. They stated that the main reasons for going back to Mexico included pay cuts and job loss in the construction sector in North Carolina and other neighboring states where they sought work (South Carolina, Tennessee, Virginia and Florida). In addition, the impossibility of renewing their driver's licenses, due to greater restrictions imposed on undocumented immigrants (Gill, 2010; Griesbach, 2011) affected the routines of these illegalized, flexible and hypermobile construction workers. Twenty-seven-year-old Roberto managed to attain the coveted position of subcontractor and oversaw the mobilization of a crew of undocumented immigrants, although he was still an *ilegal* (illegal). He alluded, as did almost every returnee we interviewed, to the effects of the crisis. Mexican newcomers were to blame for the cheapening of labor-power in that sector:

> In addition to the drop in employment, as time goes by, many people are coming. They come, they work for two, three years, I hired them. The mistake is that, in order to get the job, if I charged five thousand per house, they charged four thousand, then another one comes and charges three thousand, another comes and charges two thousand. In addition to the drop in employment, one keeps making it cheaper, which is what angers gringo workers the most. Because if they used to earn, let's say, very cheap, ten dollars an hour, now we go and do their work for five dollars, and that angers them.
>
> (Roberto, Pahuatlán de Valle, October 2008)

Unlike male returnees and those interviewed in Durham, allusions to the uncertainty exacerbated by the degradation of the reproductive conditions of households predominated in the stories of the women we interviewed. They spoke of debts and the difficulties they faced in paying rent, covering children's expenses and sending money to their hometown. Those who stayed in North Carolina in 2013 and 2014 with children born in both countries were trapped in the predicament of returning to Mexico or staying in a country where they were defined by a paradoxical condition: even if they were mothers of citizens, they themselves lacked that status.

Among them is Julia, 40 years old, married to a Pahuatecan construction worker, and mother of three adolescent daughters. Her eldest was born in Mexico and she crossed the border with her parents when she was very young. In 2013, the family was still living in Durham even though Rafael, the father, had lost his job in 2008. When we interviewed Julia, she told us with a hint of grief about the difficult situation her family was still going through since the height of the crisis. Her eldest daughter was paid to look after an elderly woman but lacked work benefits. The youngest daughters, although they continued their high school studies, took low-wage jobs during the holidays to earn some pocket money. The house, the furniture and household goods showed signs of decay. Their deteriorating condition would not likely return to the favorable conditions that prevailed during the construction boom. In those years, Julia's family managed to celebrate their daughter's 15th birthday along with many guests. Photos of those times reflected the satisfaction of their aspirations. Julia and her niece Adriana, who we referred to in Chapter 3, a fellow survivor of the crisis still living in Durham in a mixed-status household, spoke of the damages and the attempts to mitigate them.

> Work became very scarce in those years! We had to borrow money at the financial institution. When we arrived, lots of people were eager to buy gold. Back then we bought it for about ten dollars per gram and when I pawned it, in 2008, at the pawn shop, they paid me 18, 20 dollars per gram. That was a good investment! We paid the rent with that, the person renting us the house waited for up three, four months, and we paid this person little by little until we finished paying.
>
> (Julia, Durham, NC, October 2013)

The effects were multiple and uneven. They were visible not only in the rise of inequality regarding proprietary classes but also in the growth of differences between migrant workers, with or without papers, and their citizen counterparts. It was a heavy blow to workers' faith in legal documentation as the key for enjoying, albeit with many sacrifices, the life standards of middle classes in the United States. Neither Adriana nor Julia were able to understand why the crisis had also ruined many immigrants with legal status and many years of living in the US, thwarting their aspirations of social mobility by destroying the control on the livelihoods they had worked so hard to gain. The crisis also instilled new fears about the medium-term future of their families in that country. It did so by wrapping these migrants who hoped to remove their children from poverty in the elusive mysteries of mortgages and other credit instruments of financial capital that, behind their promises of salvation, hid unsuspected risks and new forms of dispossession (Harvey, 2004).

> We have Mexican friends that are American citizens already and that, at that time, when the crisis came, had already been living for about ten, eleven years in their homes and lost them because they couldn't afford them. They filed for bankruptcy. We were all affected by the crisis, not only us [undocumented Mexicans]. But, obviously, citizens, where were they supposed to go if they are Mexican-American citizens? Many people opted for going back to their country, but they come back again, or the husband comes back and the wife stays there.
> (Adriana, Durham, NC, October 2013)

The women's bewilderment at the failure of legal migration status and citizenship to "save" families during the crisis was intertwined with allusions to the collapse of their life conditions during those years. The crisis of 2008–2009 triggered improvised family arrangements and the selective return to Mexico. We tried to untangle these complications by focusing not only on the site of the production of goods and the insertion of these cheap workers in the deindustrialized US economy, but also by broadening our gaze to the space of labor-power (re)production. In such a space, gendered and racialized activities and relationships proliferate, oriented to maintaining life and developing human potentialities mainly, but not only, in the family and kinship arenas.

Focusing on the reorganization of social reproduction activities entails recognizing the inhumanity of the processes that produce differences between working classes (Carbonella & Kasmir, 2015). Such differences are amplified in moments of crisis in their articulation with gender, race and ethnic formations, as shown in Roberto's aforementioned testimony, by blaming Mexican workers for the collapse of the construction industry. Indeed, in the junctures where subaltern classes are remade, competition emerges between natives and non-natives for the available jobs. This situation enables "[…] capitalists to maintain wage discipline and to inhibit working-class solidarity by means of the application of a logic of divide and rule" (Farris, 2019, p. 124). A struggle ensues between different segments, previously produced as different—in both countries under the same capitalist logic—even before they reach the competitive labor market in the United States (Bhattacharya, 2019, p. 117). The deepening of those differences was one of the outcomes of the 2007–2009 crisis. While some were expelled, thrown again to segments of the relative surplus populations, others managed to overcome the storm with varied costs. In the following section, we turn our attention to unraveling the selectivity of return and discussing how gender intervenes in shaping these experiences in which working classes are remade.

The selectivity of staying-return

In Chapter 3 we alluded to the blurry contours of single male domestic formations in the Durham-Raleigh corridor. The incorporation of women seeking to develop social and work ties and become visible in schools and community and health centers remodeled these formations throughout the years. As Cravey (2003, p. 618) argues, "[t]he novel ways in which [transnational migrants] organize labor within these households ... allow them to cut certain costs and to hold other costs below the norm for nonmigrants living in North Carolina." Drawing on Marx, Bhattacharya reminds us that "[...] for this peculiar commodity labor-power [...] there enters a historical and moral element in the determination of its value" and that these life standards have no predetermined upper limit, insofar as the needs to be satisfied are historically modeled by the working classes' struggles (2019, p. 117). In short, under capitalism, the reproduction of working classes is always a necessarily differentiated and differentiating (re)production, in line with the needs of accumulation. "... [w]orkers produced at lower cost elsewhere," Cravey reminds us, "provide a substantial savings to employers' contexts such as the United States" (2003, p. 618).

Migratory flows usually provide labor-power originating from places with lower levels of welfare in which the capital from the destination countries has not invested—or has invested little—in their reproduction. In that regard, the countries and regions that become labor reserves subsidize countries and regions that concentrate wealth. Cravey (2003, p. 618) concludes that "it is clear these migrants provide several subsidies to capital: a generational subsidy, a daily or short-term subsidy, and racialized workplace practices and wages." However, even salary differentials, whereby a Mexican worker in certain sectors of the US economy earns up to ten times more than in Mexico, can be reduced in moments of crisis. Canterbury (2012, p. 47) argues that

> [... it ...] is the level of capital accumulation in a country and not economic growth in the immediate period, which matters most to people in taking their decision to migrate to that country, even as the country experiences an economic crisis. With a high level of capital accumulation a country will be able to sustain its standard of living relative to other countries despite the fact that it is in economic and financial crises.

Let us recall that in the years before and after the economic recession, as the number of Mexican unauthorized immigrants in the United States decreased,[1] unauthorized immigrants from other parts of the world showed slight increases, especially the flows stemming from Central America and Asia (Passel & Cohn, 2018).

How can this apparent paradox be explained? Given the historical levels of accumulation in the United States, net social security in that country is more solid and capable of mitigating unemployment and low salaries of immigrant workers relatively successfully, even in times of economic recession (Canterbury, 2012). It is worth noting that the net social security rate is uneven not only between the countries of origin and destination, but also between the different destination regions, a central factor in the selectivity of staying-return. Likewise, there is a marked differentiation between segments of the working classes corresponding to their access to goods and services that enable their social reproduction. Race, gender and migratory status condition this access. Reified and essentialized categorizations legitimize and naturalize socially produced differences. This explains why the value of native labor-power is higher than that of racialized and illegalized migrant workers. Both the differences between native workers and immigrants, and between regions (e.g., those existing between the tri-state area of New York and the *Nuevo* New South) are related to processes of working-class formation in each country, which, in turn, are shaped by aspirations and struggles with capital to limit the degradation of life conditions. All this molds differentiated life standards and habits among the various segments of class (Bhattacharya, 2019; Farris, 2019).

The shared experience of having lived in unequal environments, more or less remote but interconnected, intervenes in the selectivity of staying-return, thus configuring a dual frame of reference (Hahamovitch, 2003). Many first-generation migrant workers endure precarious working conditions partly because they compare salaries and life conditions in the United States with those from their countries of origin. Given the relatively high rate of exchange of the US dollar in the peripheral countries, migrants have the real or illusory feeling that they earn more than they would in their countries of origin. Canterbury refers to this condition as "the tyranny of the exchange rate in the capitalist system" (2012, p. 50). This is how Samuel, a construction worker, explained it to us. Samuel, despite the blow of the economic recession, was still living in the city where he settled in 1994. He fathered four children with Herminia, a fellow Pahuatecan, who had a cleaning job. His testimony illustrates the common reasoning of immigrants based on the dual frame of reference that justifies risking everything to cross the border.

> If you go now here and buy a hamburger, it's going to cost you five, six dollars. The drink, one dollar. It's very hard to understand when you say: "Well, at least here I earn the six dollars of the hamburger in an hour." Earning the lowest salary, one has made enough money to eat. And in Mexico, when you want to go to McDonald's, the hamburger costs at least 80 Mexican pesos. When is a peasant going to be able to earn 80 pesos in a day?
> (Samuel, Durham, October 2013)

However, it is not only about the obvious income differences and work conditions between both countries. In the explanation of the selectivity of staying-return intervene both structural factors linked to production—salaries and working conditions—and those related to the reproduction of the broader life conditions of workers and their families mediated by marital status, demographic cycle and household composition. Equally fundamental are the state institutions that intervene in these social reproduction circuits and the market as provider of goods, services and care. From this perspective, "we see emerge myriad capillaries of social relations extending between work place, home, schools, hospitals—a wider social whole, sustained and co-produced by human labor in contradictory yet constitutive ways" (Bhattacharya, 2017, p. 74).

The immigrant traveling without spouse or children, similar to the military migration pattern, circulating between both countries with varying degrees of restrictions, may be more prone to return when the dual frame of reference erodes as a result of unemployment or underemployment. The male undocumented migrant traveling alone does not require social assistance nor housing for his dependents (wife and children). He does not get pregnant, nor file for maternity leave or postpartum care and, above all, does not bear citizens. On the contrary, under the model of family migration, women work hard to make themselves visible before the state to provide welfare for their children. In those cases, migrants build social arrangements that underpin settlement and struggle to overcome their condition as illegal aliens, deportable and disposable, which may eventually transform into anti-capitalist struggles (Bhattacharya, 2019).

During our fieldwork in North Carolina, we observed that members of Pahuatecan households with school-age children often settled in that state. They activated various strategies to mitigate their pauperization, tilting the scale toward staying in the United States despite the degradation of work in the years of the recession. Our ethnography confirms the primordial role of women in households linked to the decaying construction sector. In those years, Pahuatecan women, mostly employed in the service sector, continued providing for their homes and, eventually, when their working hours were reduced, worked part-time or became involved in various activities to earn income. These activities included food preparation at home for workers, pawning or selling goods, caring for other women's children in their neighborhoods, saving among friends and relatives, and catalog sales, to name the most common strategies. The Pahuatecans who remained in Durham belonged to households with children born here and there, with longer residence in the US, stronger roots and greater access to social security. They also tried to protect children born in Mexico, sparing them the risks of a new border crossing in case of re-emigrating to the US.

> I think that something that made one endure the storm a little was having family here, in Durham. There were entire families that left. They sent what they earned to Mexico and they kept something to eat and survive here. Those people who left were more a hundred percent there, but when one has children, one is more a hundred percent here. In my case, I have four children who were born here. The four of them go to school and, from people we know or that have left, we hear what the situation is like over there, and we know it's best that we stay here.
>
> (Samuel, Durham, October 2013)

For people with school-age children, staying in the United States seemed, by far, more convenient. The perception of the superiority of the US education system over the Mexican system corresponds to Mexican's experience of the high levels of capital accumulation in the United States. Therefore, as Canterbury (2012) argues, these immigrants, convinced that education is a safe path for social mobility, feel strongly committed to their children doing well in school so they may develop successful academic trajectories and abandon the denigrating manual jobs of their parents and grandparents. Of course, only first-generation migrants may draw this comparison, given their experience of living in both countries.

In February 2010, we interviewed 25-year-old Adela in the Nahua community of Atla. When she finished secondary school, Adela moved to Mexico City to work as a domestic and in 2003 she migrated to North Carolina. There she reunited with her boyfriend Enrique, a fellow Ateco, construction worker, who had established in Wilmington years before. In that port city, they bore a daughter. In 2008, Enrique was deported, and the family group returned to Atla. When Adela went back to Mexico after Enrique's deportation, she was two months pregnant. Her son was born in Pahuatlán's municipal health office. Adela compared the care she received in Durham with that of Mexico:

> Even though we are Mexican, they treat us better there at the hospital or at the clinic. There, when babies are born, it is much better than here, they give us what they call WIC and Medicare for the children and for the mother, they give us everything. And if one has no money, one can go and ask and they pay the bill. Here [in Atla], when having a baby, one must pay.
>
> (Adela, Atla, July 2010)

These immigrants value not only the quantity and quality of the goods consumed despite their low salaries, but also the relative superiority of the education and health system as resources that make their children's upbringing possible, compared to the lower investment of the state in their countries of origin. However, for these illegalized populations, the reduced advantages of a depleted welfare state in the destination countries may vanish suddenly. Benefits disappeared abruptly when public spending decreased during the crisis, or migrants were deported. As reported in European countries (Bastia, 2011), after a recession period, both female and male workers are willing to sell their labor-power well under reproduction costs or the standards reached before the crisis.

This extends to the arena of social reproduction given the adverse effects on wellbeing that come with it. While financial capital transfers the cost of the crisis to the users of its services, the state reduced its spending in areas fundamental for households. Despite the recovery of recent years, Julia, to whom we referred above, admitted that life conditions in North Carolina worsened between 2008 and 2013: "We have government clinics, where we only pay the minimum. But now it's more expensive: US$45 per appointment. Before 2008, the appointment was US$23 and when we arrived [in the mid-1990s] it was US$10" (Julia, Durham, NC, October 2013).

Unlike mixed-status households, with adolescent children and a longer time of residency in Durham, households composed of young couples in the initial stages of the demographic cycle with preschool children born in North Carolina had, after several attempts, to give up the dream of living as a model marital family. In our sample, these households were the most prone to return to Pahuatlán.

What did they find upon their return?

Elena, whom we already talked about in Chapter 3, alluded to the difficulties endured by Pahuatecos/as living in North Carolina during the years of the crisis faced with the dilemma of staying or returning.

> Well, there are a few who are returning, but some are starting to arrive [in Pahuatlán] given their situation over there. Those who have been there for a short time, maybe get scared easier because they don't know, they can't stand it, they've never experienced a crisis. Because this isn't the first crisis, for example, each year life is really shitty. There are going to be raids or there were raids. Someone got caught, someone came. They get scared and they come to Mexico. Those who don't, they make do, they go to another state or wait until the crisis is over. At any rate, three days of work are enough for the whole family to eat or whatever.
> (Elena, Pahuatlán de Valle, March 2009)

The export of Pahuatecan workers in the 1990s provided some relative stability during two decades for the reproductive conditions of a segment of the community that depended, directly or indirectly, on the remittances from North Carolina. Due to the exchange difference, commerce and local housing, construction boomed. The expanding tastes in consumer goods and basic services spread to households with and without migrants. Families who monopolized commerce during the past decades obtained the greatest benefits. The offer of private health and education services in urban centers of the region flourished with the demand originating in these towns receiving remittances, while state coverage or the quality of local services deteriorated. Given this dependency, the US 2007–2009 economic recession rapidly took a toll on the economy of these households in this corner of the Sierra.

In 2011, we interviewed 35-year-old David who had recently returned to Pahuatlán after two years of working in construction in North Carolina. Upon his return, he set up a blacksmith workshop in the county seat. When we interviewed him, he was the municipal government secretary. Like other businesses directly or indirectly supported by remittances, David's workshop did not generate the expected income:

> In the last year my work as blacksmith dropped almost 50% because most of our jobs are for people living in the United States who are building their

houses here. If dollars don't come in, construction work stops and all the other work here, too. There are no dollars coming in! There are some that are coming in, but only for the family to survive.

(David, 35 years old, Pahuatlán de Valle, April 2011)

As a result of the Mexican State's abandonment of its already weak protection of indigenous and peasant populations—producers and consumers of basic goods—a compensatory policy was implemented 40 years ago through successive programs of selective intervention. In practice, these programs have configured new fragmented subjects, making up a dissimilar contingent of "extreme poor."[2] Under intervention schemes appropriate to structural adjustments, these programs transfer a significant portion of their operating costs to the beneficiaries themselves, especially women who will be jointly responsible for their achievements and failures. As is the case elsewhere, in Pahuatlán those populist neoliberal state interventions have produced contradictory results (Molyneux, 2006). In practice, this effort has resulted in the criminalization of "vulnerable" populations due to their "addiction" to this aid and for "wasting" a social wealth they have not contributed to generating. Beneficiaries are despised for the irrationality of their consumption habits. A woman living in the most degraded areas of the municipal seat expressed a recurring opinion among residents:

Youth and children don't do much, most have the support of *Oportunidades*. Parents are only waiting for the scholarship money to buy shoes. They no longer worry too much about working. A father who works is a strange thing to see, and the same goes for working children and mothers. You go to the towns and they are all at home. Before, they went to work in the peanut harvest; now they don't plant much anymore. Precisely because they have *Oportunidades*, they no longer want to work in the field.

(Carmen, 44 years old, Pahuatlán de Valle, August 2008)

Parallel to palliative poverty programs, the state redesigned a "new neoliberal rural subject" (Fitting, 2011) motivated by the aspiration of becoming a business owner (Lem, 2007). In the spirit of "entrepreneurship," the state launched the program *Pueblos Mágicos* (Magic Towns).[3] Practices, discourses and interventions from governmental, non-governmental and civil associations, often indistinguishable or overlapping, expressed the privatizing tendency of the state as they created "service providers" and "cultural promoters," trained in small business administration, charged with spreading the local food, crafts and "organic products." As a municipal authority, David enthusiastically defended this development path:

Here in Pahuatlán we must bet on tourism, not on agriculture, and we have to make people realize it. Here in Pahuatlán there is nothing else! We have the hanging bridges, we have the artisans! People are going to come eat the traditional food of Pahuatlán and see the really nice arches, the houses and the

17th century church. Many people in the communities and people from here embroider tablecloths and dresses. *Papel amate* crafts made in San Pablito are in high demand.

(David, Pahuatlán de Valle, April 2011)

Landscape and culture are made into commodities whose circulation feeds the transformation of rural spaces into tourist zones. In order to attract visitors from the capital of the country and its surroundings, government agencies and private operators promoted fairs and local ritual celebrations. The government supported Pahuatlán's transition to Pueblo Mágico by improving roads, sewers and the town square and installing underground wiring to create a "rustic" aesthetic. This investment was justified by the belief that the creation of jobs would mitigate the fall in remittances and discourage risky migration to the United States. As part of the landscape reconversion, street vendors and beggars were evicted, and the Sunday market was relocated away from the center of town to make space for tourism. Commerce based on local handicraft production took over the center. This over-exploitative work, highly feminized, sustained countless Otomí, Nahua and Mestizo households in the region. After a few years, the results of the *Pueblo Mágico* had not met the expectations of most people. Informality was widespread, and tourism did not produce the expected economic benefits. Instead, commercial rents went up and so did the cost of life in general.

Our observations of the general conditions in Pahuatlán are important to understanding the process of reintegration. "Knowing where returned migrants arrive is very important, since it has been found that the context [of arrival locations] may help or hinder the possibilities of incorporation to the labor market [and] access to education and health [...]" (Woo Morales & Flores Álvarez, 2015, p. 29). Based on the 2010 Population and Housing Census, these authors (2015, p. 29) find that, at the national level, most returned migrants (53.4 percent) go back to localities with fewer than 15,000 people. In that regard, the difficulties of reintegration into the areas of work, education and health forced some returnees to re-emigrate to the United States or move to other cities.

Mexico City, and the cities of Tulancingo and Pachuca in the neighboring state of Hidalgo (160.4, 40.5 and 88.4 km away from Pahuatlán, respectively), have been important attraction centers for Pahuatecos/as since the 1940s and continue to be so today. Migrants returning after the crisis, as well as their parents and grandparents in previous generations, think of those places as spaces where they could resolve what they did not find in their place of origin. In fact, a significant number of people in our sample of households, and returned migrants, began their working lives or went to school in some of those cities.

Return to Pahuatlán

Of the 51 returned people interviewed, 35 were men and 16 were women, a proportion similar to the national statistics of return in 2010: 72 percent men and 28 percent women (Woo Morales & Flores Álvarez, 2015, p. 30). For Pahuatlán, we distinguish those who returned alone, without dependents, and the return of the family group. Both types remained in the United States for 12 years on average. Men had more crossings in their trajectory, and none was older than 35 in their last return to Pahuatlán. The first group, comprised of two women and 19 men, single or married, went alone and came back alone, without dependents. They were not able to regularize their migratory situation during their time in the United States. The second group, smaller in size, was integrated by men and women who came back married and with very young children. They were also unable to legalize their migratory status after over a decade of living in the United States.

Other studies have highlighted the importance of distinguishing between returnees without dependents and the return of family groups. Moctezuma and Martínez (2016, p. 140) maintain that this variable has an important predictive weight regarding the likelihood of staying of those who return. The authors argue that migrants who return with their families tend to abandon the circular mobility pattern and re-establish themselves in Mexico. Based on following households and individuals for almost ten years, we were able to ascertain that the family return does not necessarily imply the reinstallation of the entire group in the parents' birthplace, nor does it entail the end of the migratory trajectory of these workers. This is due to the fact there are usually children born in the United States who are emigrating to Mexico in these households. Further, re-emigration of another family member, or even of the entire group, is frequent. Although unemployment and underemployment, combined with the greater restrictions and risks of clandestine border crossings, encouraged return to Pahuatlán, they did not cancel the migratory trajectories deployed in an accelerated manner in the 1990s.

Return migration without dependents

Those who returned alone—single, married or divorced—arrived at the paternal home, in whose construction or improvement they had contributed through the remittances sent to their family. The return to the paternal home involved the transition from living in North Carolina in "homes of single men"—where they took care of their own food preparation, laundry, house cleaning and healthcare—to living in their parents' home, once more, as adult children, whose social reproduction depended on the work of mothers and/or wives. An example of this is the case of Ramiro, 26 years old, who migrated in 2000 and returned in 2007 to the paternal home, where he lived with his parents and two adolescent sisters. Even though he contributed to the family expenses, he assumes that this is his father's obligation and that he will become independent when he gets married.

These young males are part of that cohort who managed to go beyond the basic educational level of the previous generation. In the 1980s, the *Tele Secundaria* (distance learning program for secondary school) coverage was extended in the municipality, and high school coverage was extended in 2000. The youngest left their paternal home with little work experience and "failed" educational trajectories, characterized by their underperformance. We registered a generalized opinion among high school teachers who felt that students' desire to migrate was related to low levels of academic achievement and abandonment of school trajectories. A high school teacher from the locality of Xolotla explained:

> It is the lack of awareness, because there is no other reason. The student graduates from secondary school thinking about going away to work, going to the United States or to other places in the country. About twenty percent of our high school graduates are in the United States.
> (Professor Diana, Xolotla, Pahuatlán, January 2008)

Another teacher with migratory experience in the United States, said that migration has not brought anything good to the young people nor to the population of the municipality: "only bad habits and inappropriate ways of dressing, like *cholos*."

Despite these negative opinions, those who migrated to North Carolina for the first time as single individuals, sent remittances home on a regular basis. An employee of the Microbank pointed out that single children sent the greatest amount of remittances from North Carolina. After the crisis, the households associated with single migrants, which during nearly a decade depended on the dollars sent by their children, saw their economic situation crumble. A significant portion of these resources was used in the education of younger siblings, thus contributing to the reproduction of the next cohort of cheap workers in places where commodity production did not support livelihoods. Almost everyone stated that since school "didn't please them, they preferred to go to Carolina;" however, paradoxically, they sponsored their younger siblings' education and, when interviewed in Pahuatlán, considered that "it's always best to finish school."

Almost none of the younger returnees had work experience before their first trip to the United States. Mothers and fathers were convinced that school would allow them to leave behind the despised jobs they had in the field, the factories, as porters in the big supply centers of the capital, or as domestics. This explains why they wanted their children to continue studying as a secure path to overcoming the poverty of their households. Upon returning to the town, these young people saw their hopes of working in the municipality or in the neighboring towns dashed. Their work experience was limited to construction work. The few who, upon their return, managed to insert themselves in that sector did so in the lowest positions, earning precarious salaries. Only two migrated to Mexico City, and another re-emigrated to North Carolina, once more "with no papers." After a few months, the latter returned to the city of Guadalajara. Some returnees from San Pablito, Pahuatlán, at least had the opportunity of temporarily inserting themselves in the fabrication of *amate* paper and *chaquira* jewelry, activities that used to belong exclusively to women. Others invested their few savings brought from the north in a vehicle to offer public transportation or set up a business—small grocery stores, bars, beer shops, small restaurants. These small businesses catered to the demands of foreign teachers and bureaucrats settled in the county seat and, in particular, of the tourists that were expected to visit the *Pueblo Mágico* that Pahuatlán became in March 2012. Taxis soon saturated the market and few enterprises remain in business.

The precariousness of employment in Mexico, the difficulty of maintaining their businesses and the lack of planning their return have affected the reinstatement of these returnees, who "do not return in favorable conditions that would allow them to reinstate as workers on their own, or as retirees" (Mestries, 2013, p. 183). In this scenario of generalized precariousness, these young migrant returnees went on to join the ranks of the surplus population. Once again, they started the cycle of employment-underemployment-unemployment that has marked their lives since their early childhood. These men wander around the streets of their towns, waiting for "something to come by, anything" that allows them to overcome their difficult situation. Some blame themselves for having wasted the savings they brought back on gifts for family and friends, on alcohol and women. They are convinced that things have not turned out well given their "bad head and bad acquaintances."

Almost all of them had a hard time talking about the real reasons for their return. Initially, they alluded to the desire of seeing their families and friends they had left in town, and to the monotony of their lives in the United States: "from home to work and from work to home, it was boring." During a long interview or in successive talks, they admitted that the reasons that forced them to come home were the lack of work or the decrease in wages, the tiredness and physical discomfort caused by the long and heavy working hours, the loneliness, the failure, the persecution of immigration authorities and racism. Their elusive answers are tainted by shame in the face of the failure of their migratory enterprise, having wasted the best years of their lives, abandoning their parents and school, which could have been, as teachers believe, a reliable way to overcome the chronic poverty that has taken hold of their households. The young migrant returnee is an ambiguous subject: on the one hand, problematic, but on the other, someone who, at some point, contributed to the revitalization not only of his home, but also of the municipality.

Family return migration

Under the family return migration modality we include, on the one hand, those instances in which parents and children settled in Pahuatlán upon their return and who have medium-term plans to reinsert themselves after achieving a given goal, usually that of building their own house. This goal will pave the way towards adulthood as fathers and mothers capable of supporting and providing education for their children. A second modality is the "segmented" family return, which is a compensatory strategy adopted by these young returnee couples with very young children. In this modality, these parents failed to meet the goal of becoming independent from their parents and settling in Durham or Pahuatlán with their own means due to the unforeseen effects of the crisis. To an extent, their return represents for them and the community an economic failure, but also an unstable scenario. We observed that in this group of families settled in Pahuatlán in a segmented manner, one of the spouses re-emigrated to North Carolina shortly after their return or a few years after. The purpose of this re-emigration was to recover their jobs, trying to maximize their saving capacity in a few years by reducing the number of mouths to feed, rent payments, and other daily expenses. These families also believed that in Mexico the reproduction of the workforce is less expensive because costs are transferred to the extended family who receives no payment for these tasks, which compensates the low state investment in public services. Thus, Cravey's assertion that "the value of the peculiar commodity that is a human worker is highly contingent on historical and geographical context" is confirmed (2003, p. 618).

Unified family return

Only two interviewees and their partners resettled in Pahuatlán with their children born in the United States and remained there during the years in which we followed their trajectories. Soon after, they had additional children, consolidating family networks and ties with schools and health services that make raising children easier for these couples that already had their own house upon their return, built with savings and remittances sent to their parents.

Raúl built his house with dollars and great determination. Building a house in a plot prone to flooding and near a spring was not an easy task. Despite this, he was able to do it after his first four years in Durham, working from company to company, from subcontractor to subcontractor, building houses for others, sleeping badly and eating worse. In 2000, he had already built the first floor, thus securing a safe home for his widowed mother, Celsa. This fulfilled a dream she had for many years after the accumulated miseries of working as a laborer paid with corn or starvation wages as a domestic in Mexico City. The remittances sent by Raúl also financed his younger sister's computer studies in the neighboring city of Tulancingo.

In 2008, after 12 years and many crossings between both countries, he returned to the town with his young wife from southern Mexico and a young son with a Viking name. His wife, Sofia, had stopped working in a restaurant when she "became" pregnant because Raúl did not want her to go back to work. Upon their return, they left behind the payment of rents and bills from a "nice" apartment in Durham to settle in Raúl's house. By then the building had a second floor to accommodate them comfortably. Raúl crossed the border back to Mexico in a van, carrying his family, home appliances and a few cherished household items. Celsa, Raúl's mother, had managed her absent son's savings well and continued to sell homemade sweets to cover the daily expenses, even though Raúl's remittances "never ceased." Mother, son, daughter-in-law and grandson made up the new household, provisioned by Raúl, who became the sole provider of a home that continued to grow with the birth of a granddaughter in Pahuatlán. Despite longing for his income in Durham, the city's beautiful wooded landscapes, the cleanliness of its streets and freeways and the orderly life, Raúl decided to invest his savings in a business in Pahuatlán. He tried to offer inflatable games, tables and chairs to rent for parties, but the fragile economy of most households did not allow for those luxury expenses. Instead, he bet on a short-lived small cleaning supplies store whose profits were meager due to the payment of the rent of a commercial space in the downtown area of a reconverted *Pueblo Mágico*, something that neither Raúl nor Sofia had foreseen upon their return. In addition, Sofia began her studies at a cosmetology school in Tulancingo. Her bus tickets and monthly payments depleted the family budget. Raúl did not give up and changed course. He bought a Suburban and in 2014 he was still driving people from a nearby town to the county seat. He did not dismiss the possibility of going back north, but he would make sure to leave his family safe in the town to avoid exposing them to extortions, kidnappings and detentions when attempting a new crossing.

Segmented family return

This arrangement, adopted by households who returned in the first years of their demographic cycle, entails even more unpredictable circumstances. Like the return modalities described above, the return migrant may be a foreigner in his/her own land, in the sense that a process of readjustment-adjustment and resocialization becomes necessary in certain relational codes, according to the family's vital cycle and the reference groups (Rivera Sánchez, 2015, p. 246). With the segmented family return, relationships and positions in the family constellation become drastically disrupted, as well as the access to the group's resources that often trigger conflicts and irreparable ruptures. The segmented return, conceived as a family savings strategy and protection of the most "vulnerable," is premised on the complementarity of female labor and the ideal of the perfect worker (Binford, 2013). In this modality, the migrant worker in the destination country is released from the burden of his dependents, a situation that reduces his reproduction costs by transferring them to the countries of origin. In many cases, however, women have actually been co-providers in these households in the United States.

Under a first arrangement, women with their children lead the return to the town, waiting with uncertainty for the father's return sometime after. Often, this is the beginning of a marital separation and, in the end, of abandonment. In 2011, we interviewed Laurita in Pahuatlán de Valle. After her return from the United States, she resided in her mother-in-law's home, with her young son who was born in the United States, while her husband, Alonso, remained in Durham. Upon her arrival in Virginia, Laurita, 23 years old, lived with her married siblings for a few years. After meeting and marrying Alonso, they began their life together in an apartment where they paid a US$500 rent. Laurita stopped cleaning houses soon after getting together with Alonso.

> The first few years, we lived by ourselves, just the two of us. In the end, we went to live in a house, with three other friends. Between all of us, we paid the bills. As you can recall, the crisis of 2009 was pretty awful. We had a van, just out of the car dealership. It was nice. My husband's salary was enough to pay for the truck, rent, food, phone bill, everything. And, all of a sudden, work started to slow down really fast, until we reached the point where we had to return the truck, because we couldn't make ends meet. The crisis was very hard, when people got together, they all complained about not having enough money. There was such a lack of work. In fact, right now work is still scarce, it has not picked up as before. That was one of the reasons I came back, to save money, "because if you go back home, we save money," Alonso told me.
>
> (Laurita, Pahuatlán de Valle, April 2011)

After a few months, Laurita went back to her father's house with her young son. Alonso remained in Durham. In the end, the relationship ended.

Unlike this "arrangement," in the returnee sample we found out that in most households made up by Pahuatecan parents and young children born in North Carolina, the husbands re-emigrated to Durham soon after settling in the town with their wives and children.

Elena, a 2004 returnee, with a Pahuatecan husband and two children born in Durham, states that job loss was no stranger to them. It was not the first time that they and their fellow migrants experienced a crisis. Since the time she and Mario arrived in North Carolina in 1999, "there, each year, life was shitty. The government puts more pressure on the undocumented to discourage them and make them return to Mexico," she asserted. She believes that those who returned in 2008 "got scared. They were those who had been there less time and didn't know how to endure."

> When December approached, [one had to] start saving and not send any money to Mexico, because we knew the cold was coming and it snowed a lot. Those who work outdoors don't have work. It was scarce in construction. Those who work indoors, there was more work in that season, for example, restaurants, cleaning and all that. So, some stop working in construction and start working indoors, although it pays very little, but it is safer. [Men] went without work for weeks. During those days one only had enough to eat.
>
> (Elena, Pahuatlán de Valle, March 2009)

Of course, life must go on when it is cold. Houses, schools and offices must be kept clean. Children need to get ready for school. Sick people need to be cared for. Food, prepared in homes or restaurants, must get to the table. Hospitals and hotels keep demanding cleaning services and supplies for their daily operation. We allude to reproductive processes carried out in homes, neighborhoods, informal networks, public and private institutions involved in social reproduction circuits

(Bhattacharya, 2017; Farris, 2019), where immigrant or racialized minority women have an important presence as cheap workers and/or as mothers and wives. Since their arrival, Pahuatecans filled these feminized labor niches.

Elena and her husband returned in 2004 before things got worse. What she earned at the laundry shop allowed her to pay the woman who cared for her daughter when she went back to work after the first months of childbirth. Her salary allowed her to help Mario out with the rent and the bills. In addition, she put money away for the project they both had in mind upon returning to the town. However, a second pregnancy came along to disrupt the fragile equilibrium between her laundry shop salary and the payment of the babysitter. This happened to a majority of women we interviewed who returned in the years before and during the 2007–2009 crisis.

Husbands say they re-emigrated because their projects were left unfinished. Mario, for example, convinced Elena that he should return to Durham by himself, arguing that he did not feel satisfied with the business they had set up upon returning to Pahuatlán with their savings. He also stated that the business would produce enough income for Elena and the two children's expenses, while he could save more earning in US$. Mario wanted to do other things such as build apartments in Tulancingo. "He had a big plot of land that he'd bought, and he'd always wanted to build commercial spaces and apartments for rent. That was his goal, really." When men emigrate after leaving their partners and children in Pahuatlán, it is like starting all over again, according to the women we interviewed. "They become like a person who has just arrived, without anything" (Luisa, San Pablito Pahuatlán, October 2008). They went back to single-men homes, a sort of voluntary degradation, almost at the minimum level of their needs and satisfaction of their livelihoods, with the sole purpose of exchanging their labor force with greater advantages over other more expensive workers. Mario's remittances started decreasing and becoming more sporadic, and a sentimental relationship pointed to the formation of a new family. Elena was left in charge of the business and its ups and downs. She kept it going with the help of her mother who stopped working at a local market stall.

> Now she helps me with the housework, to take care of the children, she cooks for them, because if she didn't, they'd have to wait until I came home at night. I told her "it's best if you stay home to take care of the children and I'll give you even a little money. I pay the expenses, the electricity, everything. I will pay for everything; just help me with the children."
> (Elena, Pahuatlán de Valle, March 2009)

Women also harbor re-emigration plans. The return was for Elena just a stop along the way:

> I'm still young [and] have thought a lot about going back [to the United States], because I returned and haven't achieved all I wanted. Because I do have my business and I can't complain, but here I earn enough just to get

by. I'd like to go for another four or five years to finish a house, because I have a house that's not finished, and I'd like to finish it properly. Also, save some money because when my children get older and go to the university, it is going to be harder for me.

Elena, just like two other returnees under that same modality, after almost a decade and after many ups and downs—marital problems, lengthy procedures with school and health institutions, permits and legalization of birth certificates in both countries—crossed the border again without documents. After a short time, she paid for her teenage children's return to Durham where they are currently studying (see Chapter 3). All these women returned to their condition as part-time, hypermobile workers and eager mothers looking for the social mobility of their children to rid them of the abuses and deprivations of life "as immigrants."

Finally, a modality of an extremely marginal segmented family return was the re-emigration of mothers or, even more exceptional, of both adults who left children born in North Carolina in the care of their grandparents. Long distance maternity—extended and normalized among Latin American and Philippine female immigrants in the United States and Europe (Hondagneu-Sotelo & Avila, 2003; Parreñas, 2001)—is a severely stigmatized strategy in Pahuatlán, adopted most often by the poorest women who are single mothers. Women with H2 work visas adopt this strategy to combine temporary work outside the country with their responsibilities as mothers of children born in Mexico. Marina and Miguel, who returned to Pahuatlán with two children born in the north, attempted this modality of return and re-emigration.

> We came back because I like it here, my town. When we came back, we were here with my mother-in-law. We started building a house here and decided to go back to Carolina again, but it was a bad attempt. The two of us planned to go for a while but without the children, so we did not have to worry, because sometimes we did not have a nanny to take care of them and it was a lot of pressure. We decided they would stay here with their grandparents and we left. We left in 2003, but I could not stand being without my children, because we had never left them alone, I could not stand leaving them alone. I was there for only three months and I told my husband: "You know what? I am going back to my children. You stay here to work and I'm going there to my children." After three months, I came to be here with them, and he stayed there to work.
> (Marina, Pahuatlán de Valle, September 2009)

Marina was the only interviewee who decided to continue her unfinished high school studies and enrolled in a university in Tulancingo. She said she wanted to mend the "bad decision" of going north and having children at a very young age. The last time we saw her, she and Miguel had finished building their house. Both drove the taxi they had bought with part of their savings, and she was looking for a job in "government programs."

Conclusions

In the municipality of Pahuatlán, first migration to the United States declined between 2007–2009. However, not everyone that left came back. Similar to the migratory flows to the United States, the return to Mexico was selective as well. More men than women returned and, as has been reported by other authors (Alarcón et al., 2009), those who had migrated in the last few years were more likely to return, presumably because they had less time to settle and were affected most frequently by unemployment and underemployment. Many of them, being relatively young, had their first children in North Carolina, a privileged destination of the most recent migratory cohorts in the area under study.

Drawing from the theory of social reproduction developed by Marxist feminists (Bhattacharya, 2019; Farris, 2019; Verschuur, 2013), we identify in the crisis of 2007–2009 and in the statistics of return migration in those years, the production of a relative surplus population. Social reproduction theory

> urges us to push the question of differentiation further and pitch it not just at the level of the labour market which expresses the price of labour-power, but at the level of production of the value of labour-power [...]. The value of labour-power as a commodity, like all commodities under capitalism, is determined by the value of the means of subsistence deployed in its reproduction.
>
> (Bhattacharya, 2019, p. 117)

The hardening of the border and the decrease in wages due to the difficulties of combining wage labor with the care for small children in the young double-provider households analyzed here shows the inextricable articulation between production and reproduction. This articulation contributes to the explanation of the socio-demographic profile of the so-called "new return" (Moctezuma & Martínez, 2016), and, therefore, the understanding of the selectivity of return. While male returnees complained about the decrease of work in the construction sector during and after the crisis, women asserted that there was work for them. However, the work was poorly paid, unstable, part-time and difficult to obtain because papers were required. As a result, domestic work in homes was a refuge for many women. Although they are largely invisible, these women are essential in deindustrialized economies that require massive female participation in the labor market, even if the sexual division of labor has undergone some modification in the double-provider households. Despite the fact that women were less exposed to the ups and downs of the construction sector, the lives of these essential female service workers and their changing relationship with reproductive work demonstrate how gender and class articulate perversely throughout their life cycle. As we have documented, those who were more prone to be sacrificed in the return arrangements adopted in these young households turned out to be the mothers with preschool children. Given their illegal condition, these women do not have access to the welfare subsidies that could ease the burden of their workloads at home. In addition, they temporarily lose hyper-flexibility compared to the women who undertake these activities with the support of social relations and institutions that extend between workplace, home and the different sites of reproduction circuits.

Notes

1 Between 2007 to 2010 the number of Mexican unauthorized immigrants in the United States declined from 6.9 to 6.2 million. The number of Mexican unauthorized immigrants declined because more left the US than arrived. Mexicans remain a much larger percentage of all unauthorized immigrants than those from any other birth country (Passel & Cohn, 2018).
2 In 1997, San Pablito Pahuatlán, an Otomí settlement, was one of the first localities with very high levels of marginalization incorporated into the Program for Education, Health and Nutrition (known as PROGRESA, its acronym in Spanish). Interpellated as "extreme poor," segments of the Mexican rural population, like the inhabitants of San Pablito, became legitimate objects of intervention and regulation from above (D'Aubeterre Buznego & Ayala Galí, 2011, p. 106). In 2002, during the presidency of Vicente Fox, this program changed its name to *Oportunidades*. In June 2012, 3,400 families in the municipality received extreme poverty subsidies.
3 In the context of tourism as a path for the development of the country, in 2001 the Mexican government launched the *Programa de Pueblos Mágicos* (Magic Town Program). The objectives were to structure complementary and diversified tourist products aimed at middle and low sectors, create touristic products taking advantage of local cultural expressions, generate tourist products defined by "adventure," foster tourist flows that produced greater income for the benefit of the receiving community and local businesses, fashion tourism as a tool of sustainable development and promote tourist activity as a work option and way of life for the populations involved (Secretaría de Turismo, 2014).

References

Alarcón, R., Cruz, R., Díaz-Bautista, A., González-König, G., Izquierdo, A., Yrizar, G., Zenteno, R. (2009). La crisis financiera en Estados Unidos y su impacto en la migración mexicana. *Migraciones Internacionales*, 5(1), 193–210.
Arroyo-Alejandre, J., Berumen-Sandoval, S., & Rodríguez-Álvarez, D. (2010). Nuevas tendencias de largo plazo de la emigración de mexicanos a Estados Unidos y sus remesas. *Papeles de Población*, 16(63), 9–48.
Bastia, T. (2011). Should I stay or should I go? Return migration in times of crises. *Journal of International Development*, 23(4), 583–595.
Bhattacharya, T. (2019). From the production of value to the valuing of reproduction. In P. Osborne, E. Alliez, & E. John (Eds), *Capitalism: Concept, idea, image. Aspects of Marx's capital today* (pp. 105–120). London: Centre for Research in Modern European Philosophy.
Bhattacharya, T. (2017). How not to skip class: Social reproduction of labor and the global working class. In T. Bhattacharya (Ed.), *Social reproduction theory. Remapping class, recentering oppression* (pp. 68–93). London: Pluto Press.
Binford, L. (2013). *Tomorrow we're all going to the harvest. Temporary foreign worker programs and neoliberal political economy*. Austin: University of Texas Press.

Canterbury, D. C. (2012). *Capital accumulation and migration*. Leiden: Koninklijke Brill NV.
Carbonella, A., & Kasmir, S. (2015). Dispossession, disorganization and the anthropology of labor. In J. G. Carrier & D. Kalb (Eds), *Anthropologies of class: Power, practice and inequality* (pp. 41–52). Cambridge: Cambridge University Press.
Cravey, A. J. (2003). Toque una ranchera, por favor. *Antipode, 35*(3), 603–621. https://doi.org/10.1111/1467-8330.00341
D'Aubeterre Buznego, M. E., & Ayala Galí, E. (2011). Migración, producción artesanal y subsidios a la pobreza. In M. E. D'Aubeterre Buznego & M. L. Rivermar (Eds), *Migraciones en la huasteca poblana. Actores y procesos* (pp. 51–71). Puebla: BUAP, ICSyH.
Farris, S. R. (2019). Social reproduction and racialized surplus populations. In P. Osborne, E. Alliez, & E. John (Eds), *Capitalism: Concept, idea, image. Aspects of Marx's capital today* (pp. 121–139). London: Centre for Research in Modern European Philosophy.
Fitting, E. (2011). *The struggle for maize: Campesinos, workers, and transgenic corn in the Mexican countryside*. Durham, NC: Duke University Press.
Fraser, N. (2017). Crises of care? On the social-reproductive contradictions of contemporary capitalism. In T. Bhattacharya (Ed.), *Social reproduction theory. Remapping class, recentering oppression* (pp. 19–36). London: Pluto Press.
Gill, H. (2010). *The Latino migration experience in North Carolina. New roots in the Old North State*. Chapel Hill, North Carolina: The University of North Carolina Press.
Griesbach, K. A. (2011). Local-federal immigration enforcement in North Carolina: Mapping the criminal immigration overlap. *Norteamérica. Revista Académica del CISAN-UNAM, 6*(número especial), 91–127.
Hahamovitch, C. (2003). Creating perfect immigrants: Guestworkers of the world in historical perspective. *Labor History, 44*(1), 69–94.
Harvey, D. (2004). *El Nuevo imperialismo. Acumulación por desposesión*. Madrid: Editorial Akal, S.A.
Hondagneu-Sotelo, P., & Avila, E. (2003). "I'm here but I'm there": The meanings of Latina transnational motherhood. In P. Hondagneu-Sotelo (Ed.), *Gender and US immigration: Contemporary trends* (pp. 317–340). Berkeley: University of California Press.
Kofman, E., & Raghuram, P. (2015). *Gendered migrations and global social reproduction*. New York: Palgrave Macmillan.
Lem, W. (2007). William Roseberry, class and inequality in the anthropology of migration. *Critique of Anthropology, 27*(4), 377–394.
Mestries, F. (2013). Los migrantes de retorno ante un futuro incierto. *Sociológica, 28*(78), 171–212.
Moctezuma Longoria, M., & Martínez, D. T. (2016). El retorno de migrantes mexicanos, con acento en Michoacán. In E. Levine & M. Verea (Eds), *Nuevas experiencias de la migración de retorno* (pp. 135–158). México D.F.: Universidad Nacional Autónoma de México.
Molyneux, M. (2006). Mothers at the service of the new poverty agenda: Progresa/Oportunidades, Mexico's conditional transfer program. *Social Policy & Administration, 40*(4), 425–449.
Parreñas, R. S. (2001). *Servants of globalization: Women, migration and domestic work* (p. 309). Stanford: Stanford University Press.
Pascual de Sans, Á. (1983). Connotaciones ideológicas en el concepto de retorno de migrantes. *Revista de Sociología, 20*, 61–71.

Passel, J. S., & Cohn, D. (2018). US unauthorized immigrant total dips to lowest level in a decade, number from Mexico continues to decline, while Central America is the only growing region. *Pew Research Center*. Available from https://www.pewresearch.org/hispanic/2018/11/27/u-s-unauthorized-immigrant-total-dips-to-lowest-level-in-a-decade/

Rivera Sánchez, L. (2015). Narrativas de retorno y movilidad. Entre prácticas de involucramiento y espacialidades múltiples en la ciudad. *Estudios Políticos*, *47*, Instituto de Estudios Políticos, Universidad de Antioquia, 243–264.

Secretaría de Turismo. (2014). Guía de incorporación y permanencia. Pueblos mágicos. Retrieved from http://sectur.gob.mx/wp-content/uploads/2014/10/GUIA-FINAL.pdf

Verschuur, C. (2013). Reproduction sociale et care comme échange économico-affectif. L'articulation des rapports sociaux dans l'économie domestique et globalisée. In C. Verschuur & C. Catarino (Eds), *Genre, migrations et globalisation de la reproduction sociale* (pp. 23–38). Geneve: Graduate Institute Publications, L'Harmattan.

Williams, F. (2014). Making connection across the transnational political economy of care. In B. Andersen & I. Shutes (Eds), *Migration and care labour. Theory, policy and politics* (pp. 11–31). New York: Palgrave Macmillan.

Woo Morales, O., & Flores Álvarez, A. L. (2015). La migración de retorno de migrantes mexicanos en el siglo XXI. *Revista población y desarrollo: Argonautas y caminantes*, *11*, 23–36.

6 "In Zapotitlán, we won't have to pay for so many things"

The Great Recession, return migration and social reproduction

Introduction

> [The United States] broke everything up and ruined us. There are many abandoned families, women left by themselves. I have a house, but not a spouse. What's the point of having a house if the family has split up?
> (Karina, 50 years old, Zapotitlán Salinas, February 2012)

> For me, the United States has taken away half of my family ... but I think it has given me more than it has taken.
> (Juana, 34 years old, Zapotitlán Salinas, June 2016)

This chapter explores how the Great Recession and new rounds of border militarization beginning in the mid-2000s shaped return migration to Zapotitlán. In Chapter 2, we presented household survey data demonstrating that, after 2007, fewer Zapotitecos/as migrated to the United States for the first time and more individuals returned to the village. These significant changes in mobility patterns raise a number of questions about the experiences of people along the transnational migrant circuit. Given the dismantling of rural economies in neoliberal Mexico (see Chapters 2, 3 and 4), why did some migrants return to Zapotitlán? Into what context did return migrants in the late 2000s and early 2010s reinsert socially and economically? Which migrants re-migrated to the United States and why? How did migrants and others make sense of these changes?

The economic and social context of Zapotitlán into which migrants returned can be conceptualized as a "remnant place;" anthropologist Gerald Sider's reference to rural communities devastated by unfavorable terms of trade for commodities (Sider, 2006). Without commodity production or adequate subsistence production, such places are forced to export labor. Although migration may provide remittances and maintain a portion of the population in place, the social reproduction of the community becomes more uncertain. For the American and Canadian communities he analyzes, Sider argues that social reproduction becomes more dependent upon the state. In what follows, we explore how the state intervened in social reproduction and local development through a tourism project and how these processes played out in Zapotitecos/as' lives. Credit from

DOI: 10.4324/9780429454196-6

different types of financial institutions mediated productive and reproductive relations in Zapotitlán, often in the form of microloans to stimulate women's "empowerment." Finally, we analyze if and how remittances played a role in social reproduction.

Focusing on *return* migration can be problematic because it invokes methodological nationalism. Analytical concerns switch from immigrants in destination countries to return migrants in places of origin. This simply reverses the direction of mobility and emphasizes the social and cultural differences among places. Methodological nationalism can reify dichotomous thinking: there/here, non-citizen/citizen, away from "home"/"home" (Schiller & Salazar, 2013). Thinking in terms of "remnant places," however, maintains a holistic gaze on capitalism as a heterogeneous global system. Remnant places are not outside of capitalism. In fact, they are created through the uneven development processes inherent to it. Instead of dichotomies related to space and identity, we can think in terms of migrants—differentiated by class, gender, ethnicity, "illegality"—inserted into different assemblages of capitalist relations. In Chapter 4, we explained how economic and social relations in Zapotitlán were dismantled during successive waves of neoliberal policies. For migrants returning to the village after 2007, inserting themselves economically and socially into a remnant place like Zapotitlán was sometimes experienced as a refuge from "illegality" and the economic burdens associated with the high cost of living in a global city such as New York. However, insertion was shaped by a dearth of productive activities and fewer supports for social reproduction.

Maintaining a holistic gaze on capitalism as a heterogeneous global system can be extended to our conceptualizations of the relationships among production and social reproduction. As discussed in the introduction, social reproductive labor produces and reproduces labor-power, making it key to understanding the global economy. The multiple links among productive and social reproductive labor are important to keep in mind when considering migrants' complex decision-making processes about mobility. These are rarely only about work, but involve important considerations related to social reproduction, such as where children should be educated and what family members need to be cared for and where. Gender traverses decisions about mobility because of how most social reproductive tasks are assigned to women in rural Mexico and female migrants in the United States.

The views posed by Karina and Juana at the beginning of the chapter hint at the immense cost of social reproduction for transnational families, often registered in the conflicts and tensions that traversed relationships among family members. After many years of separation from her spouse and children, Karina poses a powerful critique of the association of "progress" with migration. In Juana's case, we want to understand under what circumstances losing half of one's family could be compensated through migration. These considerations of migration provide glimpses into the difficulties of social reproduction for a mobile working class formed from the devastation of rural economies. By situating trajectories of migration and return within the frameworks of class and

The return of hard-working immigrants: carefully navigating the perils of "fracaso"

Our interviews with 31 return migrants revealed complex trajectories of migration and return. We identified two men incarcerated and deported after being apprehended in the border area. Another man could not cross after multiple attempts within a month-long period. After his savings ran out, he returned to Zapotitlán. These cases allude to the increasing criminalization of immigration, which spawned a more violent and deadly border environment. Reduced migrant circularity was closely tied to the increased danger and expense of clandestine crossings (see Chapter 2 and Lee, 2018). Five men returned due to health problems that impeded their ability to work. One woman returned because of her partner's mental health crisis (see below). Four men had their hours cut or were unemployed because of the crisis. One woman returned because her husband lost his job during the crisis (see below). The remaining respondents returned to reunite with their families and/or because they had accomplished their goals. In this chapter, we focus on women's experience with return in order to highlight the relationships among crisis, social reproduction and gender.

In Chapter 4 we discussed how the powerful trope of the "hard-working immigrant" establishes normative behavior for successful migrants. Those who have sent regular remittances to cover their family's needs, financed the building of houses, and—for a select few—opened a store or other small business are esteemed by villagers. In these cases, the sacrifice of migration paid off.[1] But, in the absence of material proof of hard work, migrants can be shamed for "not doing anything" or "being lost;" the shaming punishes by calling into question migrants' moral worth as providers for their family members.

Within this discursive and normative context, admitting to family, friends and researchers that one has "failed" can be an uncomfortable, painful and shameful experience. This was even the case with researchers with more than a decade of experience in the community, in the course of which they developed strong rapport with villagers.[2] Many individuals did, in fact, open up to us about painful feelings stemming from unmet expectations of migration, abandonment, conflicts with family members, discrimination in the United States and other difficult situations. However, when we asked return migrants if they had lost their job or had their hours cut back during the Great Recession, most assured us that they had not become unemployed or underemployed due to the economic crisis. Many knew other immigrants in New York who lost their job and some remarked that there was an increase in the number of unemployed arriving at workplaces asking for work during the Great Recession, but few included themselves among the affected.

Only four of 31 return migrants we interviewed stated that they came back to Zapotitlán because they lost their jobs or had their hours cut during the crisis.[3]

Three worked in construction and one in a restaurant.[4] A fifth person, based in Los Angeles, had his hours reduced and moved to New York where he worked two restaurant jobs for a couple of years before returning to Zapotitlán. These individuals were considered successful migrants because they had sent regular remittances to their families, built houses and invested in businesses in Zapotitlán with earnings from their jobs in the United States. It is possible that this represents an undercount of the number of people actually affected by labor market contraction because of the sensitive nature of disclosing job loss.

Carla: economic crisis and competition among low-waged workers

In 2002, Carla left Zapotitlán with her husband and one-and-a-half-year-old son. They settled into an apartment in the Bronx which they shared with her husband's extended family. With the certification of a completed beauty course from an esthetician school in Tehuacán, Carla found work in a nail salon in Manhattan where she made about US$280 per week, including tips, a salary far below minimum wage.[5] Her husband, who had been to New York a few times previously, worked in a pizzeria earning US$500 weekly. While this salary may have been above minimum wage, their combined salaries did not cover their basic expenses. They did not represent a living wage for New York City.[6] Until their son was old enough to go to school, they paid a babysitter US$20 per day to care for him. When he was older, either his dad would pick him up from school and take him home to the apartment or, more frequently, he would sit in the salon until his mother finished work.

In early 2007, the couple decided to have another child. They moved into a larger apartment paying considerably more—US$750 per month for rent. Their growing family needed more space and privacy. In late 2007, Carla's hours were cut back because fewer clients came into the salon in the fall and winter months. After she had the baby in early 2008, she stayed home to care for the infant. A few months later, her husband quit his job at the pizzeria when his employer reduced his salary to equal that of a Guatemalan co-worker. Carla described her husband's frustration:

> So [my husband] said, "Well, if [the Guatemalan worker] can do it [for 400 dollars per week], let him do it!" So my husband left the job. But I told him, "Look, you didn't have work for a month, so maybe ... (she doesn't finish the thought)." But it wasn't fair for him! He said: "Look, if they now give me 400 dollars [per week], how am I going to say "yes" for 400 dollars if I work from 5 am to 3 pm?"
>
> (Carla, 29 years old, Zapotitlán Salinas, June 2011)

Indignant, and unwilling to work for less pay, her husband searched for another job for several months but without success. The couple soon felt the pressures of mounting debt. Carla explained: "So, we said, 'Well, in Zapotitlán, we won't have much of an income, but we won't have to pay rent. We won't have to pay for so many things.'"

Carla's husband's inability to find another job was most likely related to the contraction of the economy during the Great Recession. The unemployment rate in New York City rose sharply from 5.6 percent in 2008 to 9.3 percent in 2009, and it remained elevated through 2010 (9.5 percent) and 2011 (9.1 percent).[7,8]

The jobs held by Zapotitecos/as in New York's service industry did not meet living wage standards, relegating the majority of them to a position at or near the poverty threshold. Without work and with an infant and young child to care for, Carla and her husband returned to the village hoping to relieve themselves of debts they would not be able to pay. Although they had not saved money to build a house in the village, they had managed to save enough to buy a bus to shuttle townspeople back and forth between Zapotitlán and Tehuacán. Carla's husband drove the bus virtually every day to pay for food, health care and education costs back in Zapotitlán where they lived with Carla's family. She lamented the high costs of health care in Mexico, especially with respect to treating her son's asthma and the cost of her third child's birth in Zapotitlán.[9] These costs had been covered by the public health insurance plan in New York City.

Given her husband's low income, the couple would take a long time to construct a house in Zapotitlán, but on the upside, Carla felt relatively settled there. Eventually, her eldest son adjusted to school and improved his Spanish, and his coordination and physical strength improved because he was able to play outside more. Did she want to go back to the United States? "I think we have adjusted to living here. I would like to go back, but just thinking about not being able to take my children, or that I would have to go alone, I lose interest."

Only one of Carla's three children was a US citizen. Despite her interest in returning to work, she did not want to subject her non-US citizen children to a dangerous clandestine border crossing. She also did not want to be in New York without them. The ability to stay with her children in Mexico was supported by her husband's steady employment as a bus driver. Carla and her husband were among the very small number of migrants who managed to live from self-employment in the village. Ursula and Beatriz's experiences, discussed below, were more typical of the difficulties associated with productive investments and self-employment for return migrants in Zapotitlán.

The "flexibility" of deteriorated bodies: return migration, illness and injury

Hit by cars while delivering food on bicycles, venous ulcers in legs caused by standing too much during shifts, and the accumulation of stress from fast-paced restaurant work were some of the ways that Zapotitecos/as' bodies and psyches were damaged during the flexible work regimes common to undocumented Mexican immigrants in New York.[10] Five of 31 migrants returned because their poor health did not allow them to keep working. Return migration as a result of stress symptoms among restaurant workers may have increased during the crisis as restaurant managers reduced the number of personnel and increased the workload of remaining workers in an effort to cut operation costs. "Illegality" complicated work-related injuries because undocumented workers did not receive sick or vacation days during which they might have recuperated. Furthermore, they generally lacked access to state-sponsored health services except for emergency care. This made it difficult for workers to be treated for chronic health conditions (mental or physical) resulting from workplace conditions.

Ursula: "I didn't want to go back. I had nothing to go back to"

After finishing middle school, Ursula worked in a garment factory in Zapotitlán. Four years later, when she turned 20, she married a Zapotiteco and left for New York with him, a few months before the September 11th attacks. They lived with her husband's brother, his wife and their two small children on the Upper West Side of Manhattan. She found work in a Dominican restaurant busing tables and remained there for six months until she became pregnant with her first child. A year after that child's birth, she became pregnant again. After their second child was born, the couple was in need of additional space to accommodate their growing family. They moved into an apartment a few blocks away. Ursula's sister arrived from Mexico to take care of the children and Ursula went to work at the same restaurant-bar as her husband to help make ends meet. Together, they began their shift after the establishment closed at 3:00 am, cleaning and stocking until noon when it opened again for business. With both of them working, they were able to afford the apartment, childcare and basic necessities. They sent money to her husband's parents in Zapotitlán who supervised the construction of a house and storefront on the main highway through town and another house and storefront near the town's baseball field. Her husband's goal was to return to Zapotitlán and start a restaurant and convenience store. These businesses, he believed, would support their family in the town and he would not have to migrate in the future.

Unlike her husband who saw the family's future in Zapotitlán, Ursula was happy in New York where she was able to count on her sister's help with childcare and the children were enrolled in preschool at no charge and had access to health care at virtually no cost. This was especially important because her second child developed asthma and required constant medical treatment.[11] Like many immigrant women with children in the United States, Ursula promoted her family's settlement through the utilization of public assistance and development of community ties (Hondagneu-Sotelo & Avila, 1997).

> My husband had his parents in Zapotitlán and he wanted to come back to see them. I thought, no, I didn't want to go back, I had nothing to go back to. Over there [in New York] I had my children and my siblings. I would talk with them and visit them. I had my sister there, too. We spent lots of time together. We were always together. I felt complete there.
> (Ursula, 30 years old, Zapotitlán Salinas, June 2011)

When Ursula became pregnant with her third child, she stopped working. Her husband, who worked every day to cover household expenses in New York and save to build houses and start a business back in Zapotitlán, experienced high levels of stress. He felt the stress more acutely when Ursula stopped working and they were forced to make do with a single salary. Ursula tried to convince him to take a few days off work to recuperate. However, like most undocumented migrants, his employer offered no paid vacation or sick days.[12]

> I told him many times: "take a week off so you can recuperate" or "take two days off." He said: "we are not going to stay here. I do not want to be here. I want to leave. If I stop work, I will earn less." He didn't want to rest because he said that the more he worked, the faster we would be able to return [to Zapotitlán].
> (Ursula, 30 years old, Zapotitlán Salinas, June 2011)

Ursula was unable to convince her husband to take time off. The grueling work routine took its toll. Sick from stress, Ursula's husband returned with Ursula and the children to Zapotitlán in 2007. The family's return was not precipitated by the Great Recession but draws attention to a "crisis" of a different sort: the unwillingness of a society to provide adequate health care for workers, especially "illegal," racialized minorities. "Illegality," a crucial element in the construction of a transnational working class, conditioned both the work-induced stress and the limited options for treatment of illness.

Upon arrival, the couple opened a restaurant in the village with savings and loans from family members. However, after a few months, they closed it because they did not have enough clientele. In a town of under 3,000 people, the local market was quickly saturated with restaurants and convenience stores, the most common family businesses. These tended to fail in the first year.

Six months after returning to Zapotitlán, Ursula's husband re-migrated to New York to pay the debt the couple acquired opening the restaurant and to send remittances to pay for the day-to-day expenses of their family. Her husband believed it would be less stressful for him to maintain the family in Mexico. Ursula resigned herself to this decision, knowing that while her children could move freely back and forth across the border, she and her husband would not be able to securely settle long-term in the United States because of their "illegal" status. The prospect of having to cross and return again was daunting. She explained: "I brought them back [to Zapotitlán]. They adapted. After, they would have to adapt again [to New York] and then return and begin again here? It's a lot. I feel a little more settled here. I don't want to go [to New York] again."

Although she felt settled in Zapotitlán, Ursula was not convinced that the family was better off in the village. By switching from a family migration pattern to a military-style, male sojourner pattern, the family had fewer expenses in New York. However, Ursula's partner's remittances and the small earnings she received from the convenience store barely covered medical costs, school fees, food and clothing for their three young boys.[13]

Beatriz: "I came home because my mom couldn't take care of my son anymore"

While Carla and Ursula migrated with their spouses soon after they married, other women left Mexico unaccompanied as single mothers. Beatriz, introduced in Chapter 4, migrated to New York in 2002 to be able to provide a better life for her son. She was strongly motivated to migrate to overcome the stigma of *fracaso*, "failure," for having a child as an unwed woman. She placed her son in her mother's care for six years while she worked in restaurants and in retail in New York. After three years of living in the United States, she gave birth to a daughter.

Beatriz returned to Mexico in 2009 when her mother complained that she was no longer able to provide adequate care for her grandson because she was increasingly debilitated by her diabetes.

> I came home because my mom couldn't take care of my son anymore. He was in primary school, and he had more homework. "I need you to come home," she said. I told her that I still wanted to build a house. And she asks me, "And your son?" She says, "You have already bought the land [for the house]. Little by little you can build the house." "Just give me another year," I asked her. "No *hija*," she told me. "Because if your son doesn't get a good start in school, he isn't going to learn. They will fail him." And so I said, "Well, if that's the case, I would rather be with my son."
>
> (Beatriz, 29 years old, Zapotitlán Salinas, June 2011)

Beatriz's return to Zapotitlán meant the end of the remittances her mother needed to pay for insulin. If Beatriz found a job locally, she knew the best wage she could expect would be enough only to support her children. Despite the loss of support via remittances, Beatriz's mother agreed to these changes, knowing her health would not allow her to be the sole caregiver of the boy. She did not want to fail Beatriz as a caretaker.

Beatriz returned to the village with her three-year-old daughter in 2009. Her seven-year-old son, who Beatriz left at the tender age of eight months, had to confront the difficult process of getting to know his mother and little sister. After several months, Beatriz's relationship with her son improved, particularly after they played basketball together and she cheered him on as he played games in the local league. Beatriz encouraged her daughter to speak Spanish so that the girl would be able to communicate with her family and others in the village. Eventually, Beatriz's daughter stopped asking her mom to call a taxi to take them back to New York and her son became accustomed to his mother's daily presence.

Beatriz gave up the house she wanted to build in Zapotitlán and regular economic support for her mother to assume the affective and emotional work necessary to ensure that her son had a good start in school. Her mother's deteriorating health weighed heavily in Beatriz's decision to return. Ironically, Beatriz's return placed her mother's health in greater jeopardy because there would be fewer economic resources for the diabetes medication. However, Beatriz's presence alleviated her mother's workload as her grandson's sole caregiver. The contradictions among social reproductive goals were impossible to resolve.

Upon arrival in Zapotitlán, Beatriz worked in a garment factory for a year, a job she performed before migrating to New York. The several garment factories in town remained open throughout the 2000s and 2010s. Not only did they continue to employ local women, they also brought in adolescent men and women from smaller towns and ranchos on buses each day. The resilience of the factories was most likely due to the continued access to a low-cost workforce disciplined to accept extremely low wages with no benefits. Despite her low wages, Beatriz was excluded from public assistance programs because, she believed, her parents were originally from another town. Although they had resided in Zapotitlán for many years, the distribution of public assistance was generally reserved for families with long-standing ties to the community.[14]

During this time, her brother returned from New York and used his savings to purchase several motorcycle taxis or *mototaxis*. When we conducted a third interview with Beatriz, we learned that the father of her daughter—a Zapotiteco who remained working in New York—sent her money to help with the purchase of the mototaxis. Beatriz left her job at the garment factory to drive the mototaxi full-time, earning slightly more than sewing clothes. She relied on regular remittances from her New York-based partner to cover many household expenses in Zapotitlán.

At first, we were puzzled why she had not shared with us the important role her partner played in maintaining her household. We learned that she had good reasons for withholding this information from us until she could trust us. Her partner's family in Zapotitlán made every effort to draw his attention to Beatriz's unacceptable reputation in an attempt to persuade him to cut off his support for her and the daughter. They did not recognize their son's daughter as a member of their family. We observed this type of behavior with different families a number of times in our research as parents competed with daughters-in-law and grandchildren for remittances. Because Beatriz had her son as a single mother—even before she met her current partner—his family drew on the gendered trope of Beatriz as a "failed woman" with morally questionable behavior. There was no expiration date for the stigma of a woman's fall from grace. In an effort to contain tensions and conflicts with his family, she was cautious in sharing information about her partner's support.

From our first interview with Beatriz, she told us she was interested in returning to New York. She acknowledged that local wages could not cover her family's expenses, but her mother's health and her son's fear kept her in Zapotitlán. Beatriz worried that her mother could suffer a *susto*, a sudden fright sometimes leading to shock, and worsen her delicate condition. In fact, it was widely believed that *susto* was the cause of diabetes and cancer. Beatriz's trepidation was particularly understandable because clandestine border crossings had become more dangerous and violent in the previous few years (Lee, 2018). Her son, aware of these dangers from popular movies about human trafficking across the US-Mexico border, was terrified that he and his mother wouldn't survive the desert crossing. His sister, a US citizen, would be able to fly from Mexico City to New York. It was hard for the children to understand why their crossing circumstances would be so different. A painful outcome of "illegality" is that children in the same family had different migratory statuses. This becomes a source of inequality, reaching deep into the intimate spaces of the household (Dreby, 2015). US immigration policy initiates and maintains a caste-like system of social difference based on migration status among spouses and children (Boehm, 2012).

In 2012, the state government eliminated Beatriz's most important source of income when it banned mototaxis because they did not meet safety standards. The state offered a 2-for-1 program, whereby two mototaxis could be exchanged for a regular taxi concession and the equivalent of US$1,000 toward the purchase of a car to be used as a taxi. However, the credit terms to finance the remaining cost of the car were too expensive, according to Beatriz. She and others speculated that the prohibition of mototaxis was a ruse to disguise the imposition of predatory financial relationships between the state officials, their banking partners and working classes.

We did not have a fourth interview with Beatriz in Zapotitlán because she left for the United States. During an interview with her in New York, we learned that she and her son were detained by the Border Patrol at the border checkpoint. However, for some reason none of us understood, she was allowed to enter and continue on to New York.[15] Without a source of income and facing high entry costs to breaking into the taxi market, Beatriz decided that she and her children would have better opportunities in the United States. She would have higher wages, the children could go to school in New York and Beatriz would have more help with parenting by reuniting with her partner. Once in the United States, she could offer her mother regular remittances to help pay her expenses, including those incurred to treat her diabetes. She would also be able to avoid the negative gossip spread by her partner's family in Zapotitlán. Beatriz hoped that when her daughter turned 19, she would be able to initiate the process by which her brother and Beatriz might regularize their immigration status. Beatriz alleviated her son's fear about a clandestine desert border crossing by paying more than US$10,000 for the use of other individuals' documents so that he could cross at a border checkpoint. This was an option which was physically safer than crossing through the desert. However, it put Beatriz at risk for felony fraud charges and time in prison, a punishment meted out to at least one other villager. The debt she incurred to use others' documents would take several years to pay off.

Gilda: "there were times when grief would flow out of me"

In the late 1990s, Gilda—introduced in Chapter 4—left her two children in her father's care and migrated to New York hoping to provide a better life for her them.[16] Most importantly, she hoped that her income in New York would help her children study for university degrees. That way, she explained, they could avoid ending up as menial laborers like her. She spent a total of 12 years in New York, frequently working seven days a week. During this time, she labored as a domestic, an elderly woman's caretaker, a dishwasher, cook and kitchen supervisor before assuming the care of a small child. Gilda's "fast hands" and "doing the work of two people"—the colloquial ways that she proudly described her exploitative work routine in New York—permitted her to pay for her expenses in New York and her children's education, health care, clothing and other everyday expenses in Zapotitlán. Over time, she also managed to build a house in Zapotitlán, purchase a small house to rent out, and acquire two other house lots as investments. However, as with many migrants, including Ursula's husband discussed above, the intensive work routine took a toll on Gilda's health. Her last job in New York, caring for the small child, was one Gilda needed to avoid exacerbating the aches and pains that plagued her worn-out body.

In 2010, her father passed away and she returned to Zapotitlán a few days later. She initially planned to stay for two months and then go back to New York to continue working. However, nearing 50 and with knee problems, Gilda would have had a difficult time crossing the increasingly militarized border on foot—a trip that sometimes took days—and running from *la migra*, if it was required. In the event that she needed medical treatment while in New York, the out-of-pocket cost would be virtually impossible to pay. Because of these considerations, she called her employers to tell them she wouldn't return to care for the child.

In addition to her health problems, Gilda was bitterly disappointed that her children had not obtained university degrees, despite having steady economic support. Against Gilda's wishes, her son migrated to New York after he finished secondary school. Her daughter Irene had completed a few years of university but had not finished her degree. Gilda lamented the difficulties she faced as a transnational mother:

> [Migration] isn't so nice because you go to NY with the illusion that you don't want your child to suffer like you did, but my daughter was influenced by bad people who told her, "your mother doesn't love you, she loves your brother more. If she loved you she would have taken you with her to NY." So my daughter started to drink ... and then found a boyfriend.
> (Gilda, 50 years old, Zapotitlán Salinas, January 2012)

Although Irene and her partner had three children together, he did not financially support either her or the children. This represented a glaring example of the gender inequalities among poor and working-class Mexicans, particularly in rural towns, where religious ideas underpin the notion that having children is a woman's "cross to bear" whether or not they have the support of biological fathers. Although she conceded that Irene was vulnerable to others' manipulative behavior in her absence, Gilda was upset because Irene failed to take advantage of the sacrifices Gilda had made for her. For her part, Irene constantly complained that her mother left her alone for many years, and that the loneliness and feelings of abandonment were too much to bear.

Throughout the time we interviewed her (2012 and 2013), Gilda was no longer able to work. She could no longer see well, her eyes worn out from the years of sewing clothing at piece rate. Further, her knees ached, preventing her from standing for long periods. She received some money from renting a house she owned. Gilda's son, who remained in New York, sent remittances to cover basic expenses for Gilda, Irene and her children. Although Gilda was grateful for her son's support, she deeply regretted that he did not study for a professional degree. She felt that her experience with migration had not been worthwhile; her son was condemned to be a manual laborer and her daughter had failed to finish her education and became a single mother in Gilda's absence.

> There were times when grief would flow out of me, because of the sorrow my daughter left in me. She did not know how to take responsibility for herself like she should have. I tell her, if she had just finished her degree, she would have a different life.

Gilda worried that migration planted unrealistic expectations in children's minds:

> Here you see pretty houses. One day they will fall down, because [their owner] does not have a good job. One has to always be there [in the US] and then the family can enjoy the house here. One has to be successful there for years so that one's daughter can be well dressed here. But, what do you want? A parent who is giving all of their life there for some good clothes? Or to have the loving affection of your parent?
>
> Now that I have come back, I have been analyzing life. We are causing big problems by migrating and not thinking about why we are giving our children everything and not knowing how to say "no" and put them in their place. Our children are living fantasies; they are in the clouds with their brand clothing that even their parents don't wear [in the US]. Their parents wear used clothing donated to migrants so they can save money. I am one of them! ... In Mexico in ten years, there is going to be a lot of human garbage. We are at fault, because we do not guide ourselves, and we do not guide our children.[17]
>
> (Gilda, 50 years old, Zapotitlán Salinas, January 2012)

Gilda's disillusionment with migration was mixed with self-blame for the structural conditions that overdetermined her subject position as a mother-migrant. The restructuring of US labor markets with high demands for women of reproductive age in service sector jobs along with the criminalization of migration reconfigured domestic groups into transnational families living across borders (Boehm, 2012). In Zapotitlán, the feminization of migration along with reduced circularity across the militarized border created large numbers of "transnational mothers" who continued to feel responsible for—and to be viewed as responsible for—the affective and material care of their children, much as Hondagneu-Sotelo and Avila found among domestic workers in Los Angeles (Hondagneu-Sotelo & Avila, 1997). Similar to Dreby's findings among Mexican migrants in New Jersey (Dreby, 2010), mothering-from-a-distance in Zapotitlán involved regular remittances, consistent communication and maintaining good relationships with children's caregivers. However, there was a widely shared belief in the town that a mother could never be fully replaced by others, and that children would suffer in their absence. One could live without one's father, but not one's mother.

Although Gilda embodied the highly valued *mujer abnegada*, or self-effacing woman, who sacrificed everything for her children, and the hard-working immigrant (see Chapter 4), things had still gone wrong from her point of view.[18] The notion that migration was about progress (see Chapter 4), meant that life should get better, especially for the next generation. Beyond the inability to improve her children's precarious social and economic positions, Gilda was dependent upon her son's remittances to cover household expenses. Despite having a house and some modest investments, Gilda faced the last decades of her life in poverty.

Her daughter received 800 pesos (US$60) every other month from *Oportunidades*, a conditional cash transfer program that provided money to mothers or female guardians with children enrolled in school. The program required the beneficiaries to take their children to medical checkups and attend talks by nutritionists and psychologists all of which took place during working hours. Gilda explained "If Irene lived alone, it would never be enough for her. It is a very small amount for so many requirements."

Gilda's predicament illustrated the basic contradictions of migration for Zapotitecos/as. Migrants were forced to leave to take care of their families. As long as a migrant works in the United States, the family in Mexico will be able to avoid some of the worst effects of poverty in Mexico. However, migrants generally had to live *in* poverty in the United States to accomplish this goal.[19]

Unlikely to migrate again because of her age, the physical toll that work had taken on her body and the dangers of the militarized border, Gilda struggled with the idea that the "sacrifices" she made had not led to more permanent social mobility for them. Despite her productivity, "doing the work of two people" for her employers, the end of her productive life was replete with laments for her perceived personal shortcomings in her social reproductive labor as a transnational mother. In her own estimation, she had failed in her work as a mother, one who would provide guidance and care to ensure a better life for her children. Moreover, her children had failed to take advantage of the small, but important, advantages that came with the steady remittance income from their mother. In particular, they failed to complete their education. Gilda could take some consolation in the idea that her son was a hard-working migrant, although his undocumented status condemned him to a marginal and precarious place in US society. If deported, he would likely be an un- or underemployed worker in Mexico. In her own mind, the structural conditions that underpinned Gilda's limitations as a transnational mother receded from view and were replaced with self-blame.

Transnational mothering and "illegality"

Gilda and Beatriz's struggles to meet the material and emotional needs of their families as transnational mothers represent some of the human costs of the feminization of migration (Donato, Gabaccia, Holdaway, Manalansan, & Pessar, 2006; Ehrenreich & Hochschild, 2003; Parreñas, 2001) and the construction of "illegality" through militarized immigration enforcement which restricts migrants' mobility (De Genova, 2002). As Boehm (2012) argues, despite the fact that "illegality" criminalizes individuals, in practice it "targets groupings of people—families and communities—and young people within these networks" (p. 131). Undocumented transnational mothers' efforts to ensure a better life for their children are often sidelined due to "illegality." Gilda's daughter, Irene, and Beatriz's son—both of whom were placed in the care of their grandparents in Zapotitlán—expressed the difficulties of growing up for years without the affective and emotional support of their mother.

This is not to suggest that we believe that there is an objective "care deficit" if children are cared for by "other mothers." Yarris (2017) has shown that, in Nicaragua, grandmothers who assume care of grandchildren after the mothers' migration represent an essential resource for transnational families and reconfigure gendered cultural expectations about motherhood across generations. We agree with Yarris that the popular and academic discussions about the "care deficits" associated with "absent migrant mothers" are harmful for transnational families with alternative caregiving arrangements. However, the assigning of dependent care to biological mothers continued to be a relatively intractable feature of the gender regime that we encountered in Zapotitlán.[20] As a result, it was not uncommon for female migrants to feel guilty because they did not live up to the ideals of motherhood, despite the fact that they fulfilled other vital tasks associated with reproducing the family, such as providing economic support.

The experiences of women's migration and return that we have considered up to this point illustrate the complexity of decision-making processes surrounding mobility. Within this complexity, the household demographic cycle emerges as an important factor in mobility. With the responsibility to care for school-aged children and infants—the latter of which removed the women from the workforce— and the difficult circumstances their husbands faced with unemployment and mental health issues, Carla and Ursula's families' burdens were relieved by returning to Mexico. Beatriz, on the other hand, saw her family's future in New York. She believed she would be able to leverage the best opportunities for her US-born daughter and her Mexican-born son in New York. While he was condemned to undocumented status, he would be able to attend better schools and receive better health care in New York than in Zapotitlán. This echoes Carolina's reasons for remaining in New York with her US-born children (see Chapter 4). Carolina's children's inheritance would be the education they received in the US, not land or houses in Mexico. On the other hand, with two grown children, Gilda had fewer social reproductive responsibilities than Beatriz, and therefore, was under less pressure to re-migrate to New York.

Remittances and non-migrant households

Up to this point, we have discussed the complex intersection of gender, family and migration. As return migrants, Beatriz, Gilda and Ursula (once her partner re-migrated back to New York) counted on steady remittances from partners or sons to cover the costs of household expenses. Carla's family lived from the investment they made in Zapotitlán when they arrived from New York: a bus for local transportation between Zapotitlán and Tehuacán driven by her husband. However, what was life like for someone who lived without access to remittances during and after the Great Recession?

The answer to that question was initially the reason that the research design included a "control group" consisting of households with no active migrants within the domestic group during the last five years. However, after several rounds of interviews with these households, we discovered that three of them depended, to a greater or lesser extent, on relatives who remitted money to them on an irregular basis. A fourth household had no access at all to remittances from extended family. It was in the most precarious position in the sample. By drawing on some details from one of the households from this group, we gain insight into some of the impacts of migration and return for non-migrant households as well as how remittances partially sustained social reproduction for non-migrant households.

Juana: employment in the local tourist service economy

Juana and her partner had two toddler daughters when he left for New York in the late 1990s. In his absence, she lived with her in-laws. Her mother-in-law appreciated Juana's company and assistance in caring for her five sons. Juana's partner rarely sent any money home, and it took her many years to build a separate house on her in-laws' land. When her daughters were in primary school, she learned that her partner had started his own family in New York and was not coming back to Zapotitlán. The news devastated Juana and her daughters. In the immediate aftermath, she wanted to move back in with her parents. However, in an unusual display of solidarity, her in-laws begged her and the girls to stay. They would continue to help Juana raise the girls. They took her side in the matter, disappointed that their son had reneged on his responsibilities. This surprised Juana's partner who had expected his parents to follow his lead and cut their ties with Juana. She decided to stay with her in-laws, who took care of her daughters during the day when she worked as a domestic in Tehuacán to cover household expenses.

By the time her daughters reached adolescence, Juana had taken up full-time work in a restaurant opened by her sister's husband, a migrant who returned to Zapotitlán in 2006 due to a nervous breakdown after working as a kitchen manager/chef/cook in a New York City restaurant. Situated next to the highway, the establishment attracted truck drivers shuttling goods across the Mixteca and billed itself as a welcoming spot for tourists coming to experience the desert. For decades, researchers and visitors had been drawn to the dramatic desert landscape surrounding the town, an interest that grew after the institutionalization of the area as part of the Tehuacán-Cuicatlán Biosphere Reserve in the late 1990s. Throughout the 2000s, state funding for tourism projects increased in an effort to boost local development and ecological conservation (Lee, 2014). The incorporation of the desert into a natural protected area and the transformation of Zapotitlán into a tourism destination is part of the development of the "nature industry" that links the region to similar developments in Mexico and elsewhere (Martínez-Reyes, 2016; see also Macip & Zamora, 2012).

The menu at the restaurant featured dishes with ingredients from local cacti and other desert plants. Producing a culinary experience that involved consuming—materially and symbolically—the landscape, emerged from state-led efforts to fashion a service economy based on tourism from the remnants of the dismantled rural economy in Zapotitlán. The framed diplomas on the walls of the restaurant announcing the completion of courses in tourist services and hygiene interpellated the owner and other restaurant workers as certified service providers in the emerging tertiary economy. However, despite its symbolic ubiquity, the tourist economy was not capable of absorbing the majority of unemployed workers as had the onyx industry in the 1970s and 1980s.

Although working in the restaurant provided Juana with a steady wage— roughly equivalent to the highest salaries in the local garment factories and the wages she had earned as a domestic in Tehuacán—it was not enough to cover all her household expenses. Despite several attempts, Juana failed to gain acceptance into *Oportunidades*. Her daughters left secondary school because of the mental stress occasioned by the experience of being abandoned by their father and the resultant precarious economic situation. They found jobs in the village: the oldest cared for a teacher's infant during the day while the youngest worked cleaning rooms and attending the front desk at a local hotel. Juana pooled resources with her daughters in order to pay for food and other household expenses.

Juana participated in an informal rotating credit association savings group with other women from her extended family.[21] By saving just 20 pesos a week, she could expect a payout equivalent to about two weeks of salary at the end of the year. During the period we interviewed her, she used these savings to pay for part of her daughters' *quinceañera* celebration and for a family emergency. She admitted that she sometimes fell behind in her payments. Given that her group was comprised of family members, she was not penalized with a late payment fee, as was the case with many government-sponsored savings groups. However, it was clear to us that despite their regular employment, Juana and her daughters struggled to cover all basic household expenses.

Despite the fact that Juana was in the control group, a group without regular access to remittances, she still benefited—sometimes indirectly—from the fact that she had four brothers working in New York restaurants. Three of them had their hours reduced during the Great Recession, but they still managed to send remittances occasionally to their extended family in Zapotitlán. One sent regular remittances to Juana's parents, thereby alleviating the burden of care on Juana and her other siblings, who were able to channel more resources to their nuclear families. Furthermore, when her mother became ill and required full-time care, her brothers convinced Juana to quit her job for a time and paid her the same amount as her salary to care for the elderly woman. Finally, Juana's brothers contributed to her daughters' *quinceañera* celebrations as well as some other ceremonial expenses.

It may be that this connection to remittances in the form of an extended family safety net rather than a regular contribution to household income gave Juana some piece of mind. If she were ever *really* in a bind, she would be able to count on her brothers' help. She maintained friendly relations with all of them, periodically speaking to them on the phone. She also visited her mother regularly and was very attentive to her health needs. This potential safety net gave Juana more of a positive take on migration, since there were many ways that remittances partially financed her household's social reproduction.

> For me, the United States has taken away half my family. We have had rifts among siblings and sisters-in-law. But, it has also given me a lot. My brothers helped me when I most needed them. And now my job exists thanks to [the restaurant owner] who came back, started his business and gave work to various people. Yes, [the United States] has taken many things from me, but I think it has given me more than it has taken.
>
> (Juana, 34 years old, Zapotitlán Salinas, June 2016)

Conclusions: gender, social reproduction and return

Immigrant labor markets in the United States contracted during the Great Recession. However, this seems to have affected Mexican immigrant men more than women. Several men we interviewed returned to Zapotitlán after being let go or having their hours severely reduced in construction or having their hours or pay reduced in restaurants and supermarkets. Carla and Ursula came back because their partners made the decision to return after having their pay reduced or suffering from stress, respectively. Gilda and Beatriz also returned to Zapotitlán, the former due to her father's death and the latter to resume care for her dependent children. In sum, while men lost jobs or experienced severe cutbacks in hours and pay, the women we interviewed did not. One way to understand this is to consider that men's wages were generally greater than women's "complementary" wages, and, therefore, could be reduced. Women's wages, on the other hand, were already below the legal minimum (Carla's salary at the nail salon, for example) and could not be reduced without calling too much attention to the violation of labor law and/or alienating the already pauperized, feminized workforce. One section of the reserve army of labor could be exploited further (men) while the other probably could not be exploited much more without seriously jeopardizing the façade of "free" labor (women).

Another way of viewing the gendered impacts of the Great Recession may be related to the key role Mexican immigrant women occupy in social reproductive work. As Farris has argued for Europe, the neoliberal economic restructuring which sent "native" women into the labor market created the need for a "regular" army of care and domestic workers. Immigrant, racialized and Muslim women filled in the slots of this "regular" army which could not be easily replaced by another group of workers (Farris, 2019). In the case of Zapotitecas in New York, Gilda worked as a nanny, a job directly tied to social reproductive work in private households. However, even Carla's work in the nail salon and Ursula's work in the restaurant are examples of commodified social reproductive work in the private for-profit sphere. The Great Recession had little impact on the cheapened, feminized workforce tied to social reproduction in New York.

In the area of production, return migrants tended to emphasize their positive contributions to the firm's productivity. However, their experiences of social reproductive labor revealed ambivalence, confusion, remorse and sometimes anger. These expressions were striking, particularly when many of them could be considered "successful" migrants. They had built more durable houses for their families out of cement block, purchased lots for additional houses or businesses, invested in their children's education, covered medical expenses for their nuclear and extended families and contributed to community projects, such as remodeling the church.

Despite these public successes that were the result of sacrifices made through migration, through multiple follow-up interviews we learned of more than a few unmet expectations which continued to be painful experiences for return migrants. These struggles tell us something of the difficulties that migrants, return migrants and other family members face in their efforts to reproduce lives which they consider "good" lives, ones lived with dignity. Uncovering these frustrations and other negative emotions illustrates some of the wounds and trauma caused by migration, separation, feelings of abandonment, the experience of violence along the migrant route, the stress of "deportability" and other conditions which traverse the daily lives of migrants and their family members.

Carla, Ursula, Beatriz and Gilda's stories illustrate a range of complex situations that precipitate return migration: seeking to avoid indebtedness during unemployment, mental health crises, re-assuming care for dependent children placed in the care of relatives in Mexico and the death of a family member. Carla and Ursula reluctantly returned with their partners who thought that, once back in Zapotitlán, they would experience some relief from the stress of debt and grinding work routines. Although the women had worked in New York's service economy, they were caring for their infant children full-time when their husbands made the decision to return. Carla and Ursula's husbands' place in the lowest rungs of the service labor market as "illegal," disposable labor subjected them to significant wage reduction during the crisis and an exhausting, stress-inducing work routine. Without paid maternity leave or subsidized childcare, it would have been difficult for Carla and Ursula to find a job that covered the expense of infant care and their husbands' lost wages. Dependent upon their partners' income, especially at this point in the household demographic cycle, both women were subject to their partners' decisions to return.

Beatriz's mother insisted she return to Zapotitlán and re-assume care for her son. Her mother, who cared for the boy for six years in Beatriz's absence, argued that he needed his mother to take care of him now that he was school-age and required attention to his progress in school. When Gilda learned of her father's death, she returned hastily to pay her final respects during the week-long funeral rituals. Although she planned to re-migrate shortly after, her deteriorating health, along with the prospect of a difficult clandestine crossing, influenced her decision to stay in Zapotitlán.

Return migrants face a much more complex set of realities and conundrums in which they make decisions about their mobility and their children's mobility than rational actor frameworks can account for. Physical dangers in clandestine crossings, leveraging best educational and social opportunities for children, caring for sick family members, maintaining relationships with intimate partners, establishing and maintaining a sense of belonging, and so on—in short, attempts to optimize social reproduction under very difficult circumstances—inform decisions about crossing international borders.

Ursula, Beatriz and Carla's attempts to create productive opportunities in Zapotitlán from remittances illustrate the problems of transferring human and economic capital to a remnant place (Sider, 2006). Although Ursula and her husband could draw on their restaurant experience in New York to open their own establishment in the village, they competed with other families who also opened restaurants. Yet, in a town of less than 3,000, the food service market was quickly saturated, and most restaurants were destined to fail. Beatriz's mototaxi business—which only covered a portion of her household expenses—was subsidized by remittances from her partner in New York. While Carla and her husband lived on his earnings from the bus they bought with savings from their jobs in New York, they lived with family members because their income was not sufficient to finance the construction of a house for their nuclear family. Many migrants want to open a business in Mexico that would support their family and eliminate the need to be forced to migrate again to the United States, but this "Mexican dream" is very difficult to achieve. Economic and social capital may be transferred, but it may not sustain productive investments without help from additional support in the form of remittances.

Missing from the celebratory accounts of remittances and development in sending countries is how migration contributes to the loss of human and social capital in many remnant places in Central Mexico. Migrants transfer their energy, skills, creativity, knowledge, goodwill and many other talents along with their labor to the United States. While these losses are difficult to quantify, we can begin to see their dimension when Irene talks about how difficult it was to grow up without her mother or when Karina, a woman whose spouse and children have been in the United States for years, shares her frustration: "[The United States] broke everything up and ruined us. There are many abandoned families, women left by themselves. I have a house, but not a spouse. What's the point of having a house if the family has split up?"

If migration promised anything to people in Zapotitlán, it promised a better life. Gilda directly questions that premise, telling us that Mexico will be "full of human garbage" because "our children are living fantasies." Gilda's comments highlight how migration allows for distinction through consumption (Bourdieu, 1984), but it does not stimulate social mobility through education and productive investment.[22] It did not bring the "progress" she imagined when she decided to migrate. In the case of Beatriz, her responsibility to care for her mother could be met economically through regular remittances, or with Beatriz in Zapotitlán so that she could assume the reproductive care of her son and lessen her mother's reproductive role, but potentially jeopardize her mother's health because of her lack of resources to pay for medical treatment. As time went by, it made more sense to Beatriz to take her children with her and re-migrate to the United States. While she felt this would leverage the best opportunities for her family, she was also aware that her son, especially when he became an adult, would not escape the exclusion brought by "illegality." The specter of "deportability" hangs heavily on the mixed-status family; this is one way that immigration policy fractures the intimate relationships among family members. By bringing a class and gendered perspective to return migration, the irresolvable dilemmas of social reproduction come into view.

Notes

1 Leisy Abrego poignantly analyzes the sacrifices made by transnational Salvadoran families whose members endure years of separation in order to ensure the social reproduction of family members in El Salvador (Abrego, 2014).
2 Lee has conducted research in Zapotitlán since 1998. In 1998 and 1999, Lee visited the community monthly. She lived in the community in the summer of 2000, and from January 2003 to August 2004. Frequent visits from March 2005 to August 2005 were followed by a summer visit in 2007. Finally, research in the summers of 2011, 2012 and 2013 correspond to the data collection phase of the present chapter.
3 The total of 31 includes the 29 in-depth interviews with return migrants and two individuals who were identified during subsequent fieldwork as return migrants and incorporated into the third phase of the research.
4 Of the three who labored in construction, two worked in New York City and one in Florida. We interviewed the wife of the restaurant worker, who returned with her husband after he lost his job.
5 The wages of nail salon workers tend to be well below minimum wage, even when tips are included. Workers in the nail salon industry in New York City (and elsewhere) suffer multiple forms of abuse and discrimination (Nir, 2015).
6 The minimum wage had been far below the poverty threshold since the 1980s (New York State Assembly, 2004), and therefore, was not an accurate measure of the minimum needed to meet basic expenses. As an alternative to the minimum wage, labor-rights groups advocated for the so-called living wage, a level of compensation that met the basic needs of the working poor. The living wage, which varies across the country, is greater than the Federal Minimum Wage, and includes expenses for food, housing, childcare, health care, transportation and other necessities. (Living Wage Calculator: http://livingwage.mit.edu/articles).

152 *Recession, return and social reproduction*

7 Unemployment statistics for New York are available at: https://labor.ny.gov/stats/laus.asp.
8 According to a United States Department of Agriculture report, household food expenditures declined during the Great Recession and recovered slowly, only reaching pre-recession levels in 2015. Households significantly reduced restaurant spending. More of the food consumed away from home was purchased from limited-service establishments, i.e., fast food restaurants, than full-service restaurants (Cho, Todd, & Saksena, 2018). According to the Bureau of Labor Statistics, employment in full-service restaurants in the city fell by nine percent from the end of 2007 to 2009 (Perry, 2019). In New York City, consumption spending, including money spent on food and beverages in restaurants, fell by 11.4 percent in 2009. According to our interviews, in these difficult conditions, restaurants cut labor costs by reducing salaries, as in the case of Carla's husband, reducing employees' hours or firing workers.
9 It was not clear why Carla was not enrolled in *Seguro Popular*, the public health insurance program in Mexico.
10 Recent scholarship in critical medical anthropology analyzes how the accumulation of US firms rests not only on the ability to exploit a docile, "illegal" Latino workforce at the point of production, but also on avoiding paying the costs of medical care stemming from work-related injuries and illnesses (Holmes, 2013; Horton, 2016; Steusse, 2018).
11 High rates of asthma among Latino and African American children in New York City has been well documented (López, Chantarat, Bozack, Lopez & Weiss, 2015). Substandard housing, characterized by crowding, and unsanitary and deteriorated structures, is correlated to higher levels of cockroach allergens (Rauh, Chew & Garfinkel, 2002). Research shows that prenatal and childhood exposure to indoor allergens—particularly cockroach allergen—in children in New York City combined with mothers' exposure to air pollution during pregnancy can increase risk for children's development of cockroach allergy, one of the greatest risk factors for asthma in low-income communities (Perzanowski et al., 2013).
12 For further details, see Lee 2018.
13 Ursula was not enrolled in *Seguro Popular* when we interviewed her. The family paid out-of-pocket for doctor consultations and medications. Public school expenses included uniforms, books, school supplies, funds for special events and the accompanying decorations and fees for the maintenance of buildings and grounds. These expenses could total several hundred US$ per child per year and were often a significant source of debt for families.
14 The political clientelism associated with this public program is discussed in depth by Ayala Galí in her study of a rural town in the state of Puebla (Ayala Galí, 2016).
15 This interview in New York was not part of the original methodology. Instead, a member of the ethnographic team traveled to the area to interview Zapotitecos who had re-migrated to the United States and others who had remained there during the study period (2011–2014).
16 In our research, Gilda's children were the only ones we encountered who were placed in the care of a male relative, although it is clear from the interviews that they had frequent contact with Gilda's sisters who lived nearby during her long absences. Children were usually cared for by maternal grandmothers in Zapotitlán, a fairly common pattern of care in Mexico and elsewhere in Latin America (Dreby, 2010; Yarris, 2017).
17 Horton describes how "ideologies of childhood," that is, childhoods free from want, inform motivations to migrate among Mexican and Salvadoran women (Horton, 2008).
18 Shirlene Soto discusses models of maternal femininity (Soto, 1986).
19 Binford makes this same point for Mexican migrants who participate in the Seasonal Agricultural Worker Program in Canada (Binford, 2013, p. 144).
20 In Mexico, middle-class and upper-class women employers employ poor, working-class and/or indigenous women to provide domestic labor (Durin, 2017).

21 Carlos Vélez-Ibáñez has provided detailed analysis of the economic and social functions of rotating credit associations in Mexico and among Mexican Americans in the US (Vélez-Ibañez, 2010).
22 Binford challenges the idea that investments in education lead to transgenerational mobility in Mexico for rural youth supported by remittances from parent-migrants participating in the Canadian Seasonal Agricultural Worker Program (Binford, 2013, pp. 130–134). Even if higher levels of human capital are achieved through migrant remittances, it is difficult for the investment to be valorized because: a) the number of jobs created each year represents only a fraction of the growth of the economically active population; b) competition for jobs devalues educational qualifications; c) more years of schooling does not result in significantly higher wages, and d) rural youth must compete against urban youth who typically have more social capital and networks to connect them to the best jobs.

References

Abrego, L. (2014). *Sacrificing families: Navigating laws, labor and love across borders*. Stanford: Stanford University Press.
Ayala Galí, E. (2016). *Los retos de la politica social en México. Combate a la pobreza y equidad de género*. Puebla: ICSyH-Benemérita Universidad Autónoma de Puebla.
Binford, L. (2013). *Tomorrow we're all going to the harvest: Temporary foreign worker programs and neoliberal political economy*. Austin: University of Texas Press.
Boehm, D. A. (2012). *Intimate migrations: Gender, family, and illegality among transnational Mexicans*. New York: New York University Press.
Bourdieu, P. (1984). *Distinction: A social critique of the judgement of taste*. Cambridge, MA: Harvard University Press.
Cho, C., Todd, J. E. & Saksena, M. (2018). Food spending of middle-income households hardest hit by Great Recession. Retrieved 30 June 2019 from Amber Waves: Economic Research Service, United States Department of Agriculture website: www.ers.usda.gov/amber-waves/2018/september/food-spending-of-middle-income-households-hardest-hit-by-the-great-recession/.
De Genova, N. P. (2002). Migrant "illegality" and deportability in everyday life. *Annual Review of Anthropology*, *31*(1), 419–447. https://doi.org/10.1146/annurev.anthro.31.040402.085432
Donato, K. M., Gabaccia, D., Holdaway, J., Manalansan, M. & Pessar, P. R. (2006). A glass half full? Gender in migration studies. *International Migration Review*, *40*(1), 3–26. https://doi.org/10.1111/j.1747-7379.2006.00001.x.
Dreby, J. (2010). *Divided by borders: Mexican migrants and their children*. Berkeley: University of California Press.
Dreby, J. (2015). *Everyday illegal: When policies undermine immigrant families*. Oakland: University of California Press.
Durin, S. (2017). *Yo trabajo en casa: Trabajo del hogar de planta, género y etnicidad en Monterrey*. Ciudad de México: Centro de Investigaciones y Estudios Superiores en Antropología Social.
Ehrenreich, B., & Hochschild, A. R. (2003). *Global woman: Nannies, maids and sex workers in the new economy*. New York: Metropolitan Books.
Farris, S. (2019). Social reproduction and racialized surplus populations. In P. Osborne, É. Alliez & E.-J. Russell (Eds), *Capitalism: Concept, idea, image. Aspects of Marx's capital today* (pp. 121–131). London: CRMEP Books.

Holmes, S. M. (2013). *Fresh fruit, broken bodies: Migrant farmworkers in the United States.* Berkeley: University of California Press.

Hondagneu-Sotelo, P., & Avila, E. (1997). "I'm here, but I'm there": The meanings of Latina transnational motherhood. *Gender and Society, 11*(5), 548–571.

Horton, S. B. (2008). Consuming childhood: "Lost" and "ideal" childhoods as a motivation for migration. *Anthropological Quarterly, 81*(4), 925–943. https://doi.org/10.1353/anq.0.0034.

Horton, S. B. (2016). *They leave their kidneys in the fields: Illness, injury and illegality among US farmworkers.* Oakland: University of California Press.

Lee, A. (2014). Territorialisation, conservation, and neoliberalism in the Tehuacán-Cuicatlán Biosphere Reserve, Mexico. *Conservation and Society, 12*(2), 147–161. https://doi.org/10.4103/0972-4923.138413

Lee, A. (2018). US-Mexico border militarization and violence: Dispossession of undocumented laboring classes from Puebla, Mexico. *Migraciones Internacionales, 9*(35), 211–238. https://doi.org/10.17428/rmi.v9i35.444

López, R., Chantarat, T., Bozack, A., Lopez, A. & Weiss, L. (2015). Reducing childhood asthma triggers in public housing: Implementation and outcomes from an East Harlem community health worker program. *Environmental Justice, 8*(5), 185–191. https://doi.org/10.1089/env.2015.0017.

Macip, R. F., & Zamora, C. (2012). "If we work in conservation, money will flow our way": Hegemony and duplicity on the coast of Oaxaca, Mexico. *Dialectical Anthropology, 36*, 71–87.

Martínez-Reyes, J. E. (2016). *Moral ecology of a forest: The nature industry and Maya post-conservation.* Tucson: The University of Arizona Press.

New York State Assembly. (2004). Rewarding work: A fair minimum wage. Retrieved 19 September 2019 from https://nyassembly.gov/comm/WAM/2004MinWage/#toc5.

Nir, S. M. (2015). The price of nice nails. *New York Times.* Retrieved from www.nytimes.com/2015/05/10/nyregion/at-nail-salons-in-nyc-manicurists-are-underpaid-and-unprotected.html.

Parreñas, R. S. (2001). *Servants of globalization: Women, migration and domestic work* (p. 309). Stanford: Stanford University Press.

Perry, M. J. (2019). New York City restaurant recession? Retrieved 30 June 2019 from Carpe Diem: American Enterprise Institute website: www.aei.org/publication/new-york-city-restaurant-recession/.

Perzanowski, M. S., Chew, G. L., Divjan, A., Jung, K. H., Ridder, R., Tang, D. ... Miller, R. L. (2013). Early-life cockroach allergen and polycyclic aromatic hydrocarbon exposures predict cockroach sensitization among inner-city children. *Journal of Allergy and Clinical Immunology, 131*(3), 886–893. https://doi.org/10.1016/j.jaci.2012.12.666.

Rauh, V. A., Chew, G. L. & Garfinkel, R. S. (2002). Deteriorated housing contributes to high cockroach allergen levels in inner-city households. *Environmental Health Perspectives, 110*(SUPPL. 2), 323–327.

Schiller, N. G., & Salazar, N. B. (2013). Regimes of mobility across the globe. *Journal of Ethnic and Migration Studies, 39*(2). https://doi.org/10.1080/1369183X.2013.723253.

Sider, G. (2006). The production of race, locality, and state: An anthropology. *Antropologica, 48*(2), 247–263.

Soto, S. (1986). Tres modelos culturales: La virgen Guadalupe, la Malinche y la Llorona. *Fem, 10*(48), 13–16.

Steusse, A. (2018). When they're done with you: Legal violence and structural vulnerability among injured immigrant poultry workers. *Anthropology of Work Review*, *39*(2), 79–94. https://doi.org/10.1111/awr.12148.

Vélez-Ibañez, C. G. (2010). *An impossible living in a transborder world: Culture, confianza and economy of Mexican-origin populations.* Tucson: The University of Arizona Press.

Yarris, K. E. (2017). *Care across generations: Solidarity and sacrifice in transnational families.* Stanford: Stanford University Press.

7 Economic crisis and the social reproduction of Mexican transnational working classes

Introduction

Through the details of the daily lives of women and men from rural Central Mexico, this book analyzed the impacts of economic restructuring in Mexico and the United States in the 1980s and 1990s, and the financial and economic crisis of 2007–2009. By following people from Pahuatlán and Zapotitlán for more than a decade, we learned how individuals such as Aleida (Chapter 3) and Gilda (Chapter 4) experienced the erosion of their life conditions as poverty worsened in the 1980s. Lucía (Chapter 3) and Beatriz (Chapters 4 and 6) described their experiences as workers in the United States and what kind of life they expected to create for themselves and their children. Finally, Julia (Chapter 5), Carla (Chapter 6) and others explained why they stayed or returned to Mexico as the dark days of the Great Recession pressed down on the working classes.

In these conclusions, we will summarize our main findings by drawing together the experiences of Pahuatecos/as and Zapotitecos/as through whose lives we can detect broader economic and political transformations. We will also discuss the implications of our research for the study of migration-return, class and gender particularly through the lens of social reproduction. We believe our contributions have not only something to say about the Mexican migrant lives we analyze here, but also about the forces and tendencies that produce new classes of precarious migrant workers and how gender structures the selectivity of return and migration.

From migration-return to the social reproduction of working classes across spaces

Throughout this book we have situated migratory flows within broader historical processes of capital accumulation. From this perspective, "migration" or "return" do not capture the whole field to which we are referring. Rather, they invoke methodological nationalism (Glick Schiller & Salazar, 2013) and confine the analytic gaze to only one or another dimension of what we view as a complex, multidimensional process. Methodological nationalism runs the risk of reifying dichotomous thinking—here/there, us/them, citizen/"illegal"—that, in

DOI: 10.4324/9780429454196-7

turn, shores up xenophobic thinking and praxis. As Gupta and Ferguson (1992) argue, "[t]he enforced 'difference' of places becomes part and parcel of a global system of domination" (p. 17). They urge us to denaturalize cultural and spatial divisions by turning our attention to how these are "produced and maintained in a field of power relations in a world always already spatially interconnected" (1992, p. 17).

In order to heed Gupta and Ferguson's call, we have attempted to maintain a holistic gaze on capitalism as a heterogeneous global system (Wolf, 1982). We have sought to understand how Pahuatecos/as' and Zapotitecos/as' labor is included in productive processes, while they are simultaneously excluded and devalued socially and culturally (Heyman, 2012). Instead of dichotomies related to space and identity, we can think in terms of migrants—differentiated by class, gender, ethnicity, "illegality"—inserted into different assemblages of capitalist relations. This vision requires not only a focus on the productive sphere—the insertion in labor markets, wages, employer-employee relations, etc.—but also on social reproduction and the daily struggles beyond the workplace to secure a dignified life. This wide-angle lens in our research is an attempt to come to terms, ethnographically, with the notion that capitalism is a total system: one in which the labor to produce commodities and the labor to produce people are intimately connected (Bhattacharya, 2017b, p. 3). Therefore, our understanding of class takes into account both production and social reproduction.

By focusing on the formation of a transnational, mobile *working class*, our approach goes beyond methodological nationalism in order to bring into view the fundamental reshaping of migration-return flows between de-capitalized and disarticulated areas of Central Mexico and areas renewed/remade by recent capital investment on the East Coast of the United States. By using the term *working class*, we are not simply referring to a group of people who have jobs (Bhattacharya, 2017a, p. 68). Instead, we start from a broader notion, one outlined by Marx but more recently fleshed out by feminist thinkers like Bhattacharya and Fraser (Fraser, 2014). In their view, a fuller understanding of workers takes into account their lives beyond the tasks they perform while on the clock. "In thinking about the working class," Bhattacharya argues, "it is essential to recognize that workers have an existence beyond the workplace. The theoretical challenge therefore lies in understanding the relationship between this existence and that of their productive lives under the direct domination of the capitalist" (Bhattacharya, 2017a, p. 69).

Workers surplus to capital in Central Mexico were and are absorbed into labor markets on the East Coast as illegalized, racialized and therefore, cheapened labor. In this view the border is not the boundary between two self-contained socio-political spaces, with Mexico on one side and the United States on the other. Rather it is a "value-filtering" mechanism (De Genova, 2005; Heyman, 2001; Kearney, 2004) cheapening labor by activating the symbolic violence of the "illegal" racialized discourses and the immigration industrial complex (Golash-Boza, 2009) that over-determines the value of bodies out-of-place. Not only are we referring to the value of their labor performed for capitalism, but

158 *Crisis and transnational working classes*

also to Mexican immigrants' social value, of how they are judged to be deserving, or not, of belonging to society more generally.

Accelerated migration and US insertion: fragmented, heterogeneous class subjects

> In the 1980s, people didn't have the American Dream here. We didn't even think about it. When Luis [the first migrant from Zapotitlán] left and people began to talk about New York, then the worm got into us, and we started thinking about going to New York. Then the rock ran out, production stopped and the local economy went bad.
>
> (Pedro, Zapotitlán Salinas)

In the framework of the broad transition from Fordist to flexible accumulation since the 1980s, the Mexican state, under the pressure of the United States (Harvey, 2003), embraced neoliberal policies that dismantled life conditions in rural areas such as Pahuatlán and Zapotitlán (Binford, 2013, pp. 47–48). Surplus populations filled the ranks of the accelerated migratory flows from Central Mexico to the East Coast of the United States. These emerged in the last two decades of the twentieth century, contributing to unprecedented levels of Mexican migration to the United States. Migrants were absorbed into restructured zones of *Nuevo* New South and New York City, relaunched through foreign and domestic capital investments.

The flows after IRCA, the last amnesty, comprised a new migratory regime marked by "illegality" (De Genova, 2005), reclassifying undocumented immigrants and subordinating them to a lower-class position vis-a-vis other "unskilled" workers. Their condition of deportability cheapened the value of their labor-power, rendering them suitable for the low wages and precarious work conditions that characterized the offerings at the bottom of the labor markets in the United States. By using the notion of accelerated migration, we linked the relationship between the speed of transitions in migration dynamics and the changes in the pattern of accumulation that led to an increased demand for cheap, disciplined and disorganized workers.

The feminization of migration, that is, the growing presence and visibility of women in these migratory flows who took jobs in domestic work, cleaning services and alongside men in restaurants, was one dimension of the feminization of work more generally (Archer, 2013; Oso & Ribas-Mateos, 2013; Verschuur, 2013). These processes responded to deindustrialization and the growth of the service sector in the United States, a sector that required individuals—women and men—who could be molded into workers willing to accept the long-hours, always-available, invisibilized dimensions of feminized work (Hondagneu-Sotelo, 2007). The insertion of Pahuatecan and Zapotitecan women and men as flexible workers reflected the reorganization of the international division of labor in the current accumulation regime.

In our research, we documented the selectivity of migration from the 1980s up to the mid-2000s, identifying the overlap of several forms of mobility that characterized the new migratory regime. A Fordist, "military model of migration" that dispatched mostly married men, with or without papers, to the United States to work in agriculture and manufacturing, gave way to a mobility pattern under flexible accumulation of single women with or without dependents, a pattern that overlapped with the migration of young couples with or without children. The hardening of immigration policies prompted the loss of circularity of migration flows and longer periods of residence in the United States. Consequently, they acquired the profile of settlement migrations. Like Lucía (Chapter 3) and Ursula (Chapter 6), the mother-worker-undocumented subject emerged in this rapid transition from a circular migration to a temporary settlement migration, resulting in the formation of families integrated by couples at the beginning of their demographic cycle and binational households. As with men, capital covets women as a cheap, disciplined and disorganized labor force and, at the same time, an object of persecution and deportation due to their migratory status.

We considered how production and social reproduction articulated in the shaping of these subjects, in order to highlight tensions with which migrants constantly struggle. For example, in their attempt to make effective their children's citizenship rights, these female workers underscore their identities as mothers in their claims and "immediate struggles" (Narotzky & Smith, 2006) in different circuits of reproduction—schools, clinics, hospitals, churches and nonprofit organizations. These struggles can eventually become what Fraser calls "boundary struggles":

> Especially in periods of crises, social actors struggle over the boundaries delimiting economy from society, production from reproduction, and work from family—and sometimes succeed in redrawing them. Such boundary struggles ... are as central to capitalist societies as the class struggles analyzed by Marx.
>
> (Fraser, 2017, p. 25)

Although migrant mothers consider their claims for their children's recognition—their potential boundary struggles—as legitimate, they are forced to hide due to their condition of "unwanted foreigners" (Luibhéid, Andrade & Stevens, 2018; Oboler, 2014; Smith & Winders, 2007). The conceptualization of these mother-worker-immigrants as secondary contributors to the reproduction of their households compounds their official exclusion from US society. In this logic of hiding their condition as workers yet making visible their identities as mothers, we discover the effects of the hyper-masculinization of the category of class, on the one hand, and, on the other, the hyper-feminization of the category of gender (Bettie, 2003).

By following women like Gilda (Chapter 4)—single mother, industrial homeworker in Zapotitlán, elderly care worker and restaurant worker in New York—and Elena (Chapters 3 and 5)—who cobbled together part-time jobs caring for children, in manufacturing and in restaurants—we hope to have demonstrated that women, along with men, are class subjects (Bettie, 2003). While the women's labor and migration trajectories demonstrate the ways in which flexibility, precarity and disposability traverse their working lives on both sides of the border, they also show how they have moved through different class positions with respect to the wage relationship. Carolina's (Chapter 4) labor providing childcare in her home for other immigrant women "liberated" other mother-workers for New York's service economy (Colen, 1995). Lucía (Chapter 3) lost her job and separated from her violent partner during the worst years of the crisis. In exchange for food and a small stipend, she cleaned, cooked and cared for her sister's children. Few scholars have appreciated this work, veiled by kinship, friendship and shared nationality, as a significant contribution to production and reproduction, particularly when it is naturalized as simply an extension of a maternal instinct of care (for an exception see Fernández-Kelly & García, 1990). The heterogeneity of the working classes under flexible accumulation (Carbonella & Kasmir, 2014), therefore, was not only marked by gender and migratory status, but was also manifest in the micro-differentiations of women's variable position vis-a-vis the wage relationship and formal and informal work.

The analysis illuminated migrants' discourses about "deservingness" and the right to belong, closely linked to forms of self-exploitation. In Chapter 4, we discussed the forms of discipline that traverse gendered, "illegal" subjects laboring as restaurant workers, domestics and garment factory workers. Gilda (Chapter 4) and others extolled the virtues of their abilities to work hard and autonomously. The desire for autonomy forms part of the construction of a neoliberal, flexible worker who is continually working on herself to produce more, faster and better. We view this discourse as a way to make oneself visible through a moral claim of belonging and recognition that extolls pride in one's hard work, notwithstanding one's "illegal" status.

Likewise, the mother-worker-undocumented migrant (Chapter 3) claims her moral right to belong through the labor she performs for her US-born children. These women remind us that they are not "abusing the system" because their contribution to the reproduction of their children is "discounted" from their paychecks. This ambiguous discourse comes from their subject position as mothers of native-born children. These discourses protect undocumented Pahuatecos/as and Zapotitecos/as from the insults and injuries acquired from those who discredit them as cheap, racialized "others" through quotidian horizontal and vertical racism (Lefevbre, 2011, p. 259) they experience in the workplace and on the street. In a paradoxical manner, these subjects have internalized the idea that they are not deserving of citizenship or social protections. Rather, they deserve a meager salary and nothing more. The self-exploited being is "free" to improve, attempting to reach an always-receding finish line measuring greater levels of production. This represents a more efficient form of subjectification and subjugation, because the class struggle turns inward. The subject struggles against her/himself (Han, 2017). Collective class struggle is abandoned and replaced by a repressive individualism in which problems are internalized and can only be resolved by the individual working on him or herself. Women and men hope their work will advance their children's mobility. However, the undocumented men and women we interviewed consider themselves responsible, to some extent, for their "illegality." For these reasons, Pahuatecos/as and Zapotitecos/as, as fragmented, heterogeneous subjects, are hardly able to articulate a class identity and recognize themselves in the struggles of workers against capital. Job loss, cutbacks in working hours, growing deportation threats and detentions in the interior of the country further disciplined those who managed to stay during the crisis.

Economic crisis and the limits of the dual frame of reference

Many first-generation migrant workers put up with salary cutbacks and reductions in working hours, underemployment and unemployment in part because, as Binford (2009) claims, following Waldinger and Lichter (2003), migrants use a dual reference structure, to compare the salaries and working conditions in destination countries with the much lower income and poorer livelihood conditions of the majority of families in their origin countries. Canterbury (2012, p. 50) argues that "the tyranny of the exchange rate" operates in the capitalist system in these cases. With the relatively high exchange rate of the US dollar in peripheral countries, migrants from these countries can have a real or illusory feeling that they earn more than they would working in their own countries.[1]

Why does this "dual structure" continue to operate during periods of weak economic growth? In reference to our case study, what happens when the US economy experiences a recession, accompanied by layoffs, reduced working hours and cutbacks in pensions and welfare programs? Canterbury's analysis (2012) of migration to the United States from 2000 to 2009, and particularly during the Great Recession (2007–2009), offers insights to debate the reach of neoclassical and neoliberal theories in migration and return. They allow us to explain why, despite the last crisis, an important proportion of the immigrants that we studied stayed in the United States.

Under these circumstances, politics and political factors tend to take a predominant role in the reduction of migration in countries with a high level of concentration of capital. On the one hand, the intervention of elites of the dominant classes argue for restrictive measures and the contention of migration, while another sector of capitalists—linked to the construction sector, services and agribusiness—employ immigrant labor, offering low salaries to reduce the costs of production in order to stimulate the economy and lift it out of crisis. The characteristics of the US economy, Canterbury argues, reveal that the crisis is embedded in the deep structure of US capitalism. It is not a cyclical, exceptional or temporary phenomenon, subject to a dynamic that can be reversed and restore lost jobs, impoverished homes, livelihoods and former working conditions.

We subscribe to Canterbury's central argument that it is the level of capital accumulation in a country and not the economic growth in the previous period that is important to people when they make decisions about migrating, staying there or returning to their countries of origin, even when the destination country suffers an economic crisis. With a high level of capital accumulation, a country can sustain an elevated standard of living with respect to other countries, independently of being in an economic and financial crisis (2012, p. 47). Although the economic crisis can be severe, in countries that expel labor and those that absorb it, the high level of capital accumulation in the latter countries continues to provide more opportunities to poor immigrants. Canterbury points out that workers can lose their jobs in both places, but compared with origin countries, the net social security can be much more solid and better buffer unemployment in destination countries. In our study, we verified the relevance of this explanation when analyzing the selectivity of return migration.

The selectivity of staying (in the US)/returning (to Mexico), gender and social reproduction

The analysis of the selectivity of return takes into account those who returned as well as those who stayed in the United States. We argue that gender shaped the experience of the formation of these new classes of workers, both in terms of their oscillating relation to capital as well as their reinsertion in Mexico. Return, in most cases, involved a destabilization of reproductive conditions for these workers and their families.

The economic crisis had far-reaching effects for different sectors of the native and immigrant working classes, including Mexican migrants in the United States, their transnational households and the communities in Mexico from which they came. Recall Adriana (Chapter 5) who observed that "we were all affected by the crisis." She noted that neither citizens, residents nor undocumented migrants in Durham escaped hardship. During the crisis, however, return was selective; only some Pahuatecos/as and Zapotitecos/as returned to Mexico. The rate of staying for Pahuatecos/as was 73 percent (27 percent returned) and for Zapotitecos/as 64 percent (36 percent returned) (see Table 2.3). We attribute these community-level differences to the substantially higher cost of living in New York compared with North Carolina (see Chapter 2). From these figures, we can see that there was no "massive" return of migrants.

Within each community, the rates at which men and women returned varied. A greater percentage of Pahuatecan women returned than men. This can be explained with reference to the conditions of social reproduction for a particular group of women: young mothers with preschool age children. These women, who returned at a higher rate than other women, had comparatively shorter periods of residence in the United States. Burdened with heavy workloads in the home, these women lost their hyper-flexibility. Women with older children had a comparatively easier time balancing productive and reproductive labor because they had the support of social relations and institutions (particularly schools) that extended between workplace and home and into the different sites of reproduction. Mothers of preschool-aged children tended to return with their partners and children, accounting for the cases in the category of "family returns." The majority of men who returned to Pahuatlán did so alone, without other family members.

In contrast, a greater percentage of men from Zapotitlán returned to Mexico than women. While men lost jobs or experienced severe cutbacks in hours and pay (Carla's husband, Chapter 6), the women from Zapotitlán did not (Gilda and Beatriz, Chapter 6).[2] When compared with Pahuatlán, Zapotitlán's migration flow started about a decade earlier (Chapter 2). Many women who had migrated as young, unmarried women in the 1990s, had school-age and adolescent children by the time the crisis hit, and therefore, they were less likely to return to Mexico. Carolina (Chapter 4), for example, had three US-born children in school, and was firmly oriented toward raising her family in the United States where she felt they had the best educational and economic prospects.

Our longitudinal study allowed us to follow families during many years and we found different patterns of return among them, partly accounted for by having US-born family members. Some migrants had invested in building a home in Pahuatlán and Zapotitlán and used their savings to establish a business. Once they returned to their villages, these families were mostly likely to stay long-term. Not all who returned, however, settled permanently in Mexico. Elena (Chapter 5) and Ursula (Chapter 6) returned with their partners and children. Yet, in less than a year, their partners re-migrated to the United States alone in order to continue working toward their goal. By re-migrating alone, these men reconfigured themselves as "the perfect immigrant" (Hahamovitch, 2003), a worker without dependents that places a burden on the destination country. This process of self-cheapening one's labor transfers the costs of social reproduction to the family and origin communities. These men believed that by shedding the costs of maintaining their families in the United States, they could "start from scratch," that is, work toward their goals but now with fewer costs and more possibilities to save money.

Women with preschool-aged children who returned to Mexico shortly before, during, or shortly after the crisis re-migrated to the United States when their children were of at least primary school-age. Elena (Chapter 5) and Beatriz (Chapter 6) and other women in this position, waited until they could insert their children in school in the United States so that they could regain their hyper-flexibility and resume the working lives that were suspended because of their caretaking responsibilities for young children. These women's trajectories highlight the demise of the male breadwinner among these working classes; in this case, these women's return to Mexico represents a period of latency in the labor force, another example of how these classes experience an oscillating relationship with capital. These are not the full-time workers formed in the image of Manchester's industrial working class. Rather, these are workers whose habitus is shaped by a constant cycling among employment, underemployment and unemployment. The formation of class is not linear; it is uneven and full of ruptures (Carrier, 2015; Kalb, 2015; Smith, 2015).

A variation on this last pattern of family return occurs when the father and mother re-migrate together to the United States leaving their children with grandparents. Their objective is to accumulate savings more quickly working at the same time, without the burden of caring for children. This modality is particularly stigmatized by the community not only because of the mother's abandonment of her children, but also because of its potential to dissolve the ties that maintain the social fabric.

An uneven crisis: The Great Recession and the service sector

To further understand the selectivity of return it is important to examine the impacts of the crisis on particular sectors in which Mexican immigrants were inserted (Levine, 2015; Villarreal, 2014). While the greatest number of Mexican immigrant jobs were lost in the construction sector—a finding that explains job loss among men from Pahuatlán—low-wage jobs in the service industry were less vulnerable, a finding that accords with Rothstein's analysis of immigrant workers in New Jersey from Tlaxcala—a state adjacent to Puebla in Central Mexico (Rothstein, 2016). For example, in New York, some service industries experienced declines during the first part of the Great Recession (August 2008–March 2009) but recovered significantly in the months that followed (March 2009–September 2009). For example, restaurants, health care, social assistance (a category that includes home health care or elderly care) and other services (a category that includes dry cleaning, laundry services and personal care) made significant gains in the second period, a demonstration of the resilience of the low-wage service sector tied closely to social reproduction. These sectors employed Mexican immigrants like the Zapotitecos/as described in this book. On the contrary, construction, manufacturing and the banking and finance sector experienced significant declines in both periods (Fiscal Policy Institute, 2009).

Why was the low-wage service sector relatively unaffected by the economic crisis? The neoliberal restructuring of the economy changed the organization of social reproduction for native workers. As more native women entered the workforce, reproductive tasks were commodified and performed by immigrant women in the home (domestics, nannies, elderly care) or through men and women's labor in commercial services (restaurants, laundry services, etc.) (Kofman & Raghuram, 2015; Parreñas, 2001). This process further accelerated because the provision of social reproduction by public institutions declined and there was no change in the gendered division of labor within the household. As Farris argues (2019), social reproductive tasks cannot be fully mechanized nor outsourced, and must be performed by living labor in close proximity to consumers. During the crisis, the industries performing social reproductive tasks did not experience the major cutbacks observed in construction and manufacturing, a finding scholars corroborate for Europe (Bastia, 2011; Farris, 2019). Similar to what Farris observed in Europe with racialized surplus populations (2019), the reserve army culled from disarticulated places like Pahuatlán and Zapotitlán was transformed into the "regular" army of care, domestic and service workers. Pahuatecan women who left manufacturing switched to janitorial services and food preparation in their homes, selling food to other workers. This confirms the resilience of the service sector linked to social reproduction during the crisis. Immigrant workers in low-wage service industries, like the Pahuatecans and Zapotitecans described in this book, cannot be easily replaced by another group of workers at this time. In sum, the Great Recession had little impact on employment in the cheapened, feminized workforce tied to social reproduction in New York and North Carolina. When the crisis hit the construction and manufacturing sectors, on the other hand, workers in these industries, like Pahuatecan men, were more likely to face reduced hours and unemployment.

While examining how the crisis of social reproduction in the United States has been temporarily resolved with immigrant labor from Mexico was one objective for this study, we also attempted to shine a light on the changing conditions of the reproduction of Mexican migrants' labor-power (Bhattacharya, 2017b). As discussed in Chapter 5, we agree with Fraser (2017) that while social reproduction is essential for capitalist accumulation, accumulation tends to destabilize social reproduction processes. For example, native women's incorporation into the labor market beginning in the 1970s left unattended the social reproductive work formerly carried out in the home. This problem was "resolved" by the large-scale importation of Mexican immigrant labor channeled into social reproductive work in private homes and commercialized services.

Likewise, the cheapening and disciplining of "illegal" labor through the reclassification of Mexican immigrant labor as "illegal" (De Genova, 2005) and the disciplining power of the ever-present interior surveillance apparatus (Goldstein & Alonso-Bejarano, 2017) fortify accumulation, yet weigh like a nightmare on the immigrant population. They increase the number and intensity of challenges workers face to regenerate and replenish themselves in order to work the next day. Furthermore, these assaults on wellbeing are felt not only by those without documents, but also Mexican-origin US residents and citizens, who, while not the "official" target of surveillance and raids, feel as though they could be (Sabo & Lee, 2015). The struggle to maintain not only basic, biological needs, but to also maintain social life and develop human potentialities grows ever more difficult, particularly for illegalized and racialized Mexican immigrants. In mixed-status families, class differences created along the lines of migratory status fragment the very intimate spaces of family relationships (Boehm, 2012). We witness the inhumanity of the processes that produce differences and fragmentation among working classes and their impact on social reproduction. Pahuatecos/as who could not obtain driver's licenses to transit freely and without fear on their way to work and school (Chapter 5), the pain of family separations across borders (Chapter 6) and the pain of realizing that the "sacrifices" of migration were not worthwhile because economic or educational aspirations were not attained despite years in the United States (Chapters 5 and 6) are only a few of the ways that "illegality" is lived by undocumented Mexican immigrants.

Reinsertion and social reproduction in Mexico

The continuing need for remittances and the financialization of rural life

> Without changing US trade policy and ending structural adjustment programs and neoliberal economic reforms, millions of displaced people will be forced to migrate, no matter how many walls are built on the border.
>
> (Bacon, 2013, p. 276)

Despite the pronouncements of the "end of the Great Migration," or the somewhat misleading description of Mexican migration to the United States as "below net zero," people from Pahuatlán and Zapotitlán and hundreds of other communities continue to cross the border. Migration is still fundamental to the economies of such towns evidenced by the record US$35.5 billion sent back to Mexico in 2019 (BBVA Bancomer & CONAPO, 2019). What role do remittances play in daily life in Pahuatlán and Zapotitlán?

An important finding is that remittances, by and large, are channeled into the costs of basic subsistence. As discussed in Chapter 4, providing for families' basic needs appeared to be "progress" against the backdrop of worsening conditions of social reproduction in Mexico, forming a central motivation for migration. However, the failed attempts to create productive investments illustrate the problems of transferring human and economic capital to disarticulated, "remnant" places (Sider, 2006), such as Pahuatlán and Zapotitlán. For example, although Ursula and her husband (Chapter 6) could draw on their restaurant experience in New York to open their own establishment in the village, they competed with other families who also opened restaurants. Yet, in a town of less than 3,000, the food service market was quickly saturated, and most restaurants were destined to fail. Raúl (Chapter 5) decided to invest his savings in a business in Pahuatlán. He tried to offer inflatable games, tables and chairs to rent for parties, but the unstable and insufficient economy of most households did not allow for luxury expenses. Instead, he bet on a short-lived cleaning supply store whose profits were meager due to the high cost of rent for the downtown commercial space. Many migrants wanted to open a business in Mexico that would support their family and eliminate the need to migrate again to the United States, but this "Mexican dream" is very difficult to achieve. Economic and social capital may be transferred, but it may not sustain productive investments without additional future remittances.

Migrants from Pahuatlán and Zapotitlán who left in the early 1990s and remain in the United States continue to send remittances to their parents and siblings in Mexico to avoid their increasing impoverishment. Remittances and the poverty subsidies (see next section) mitigate the impact of the privatization of services (health, energy, electricity and education). A few migrants have been able to establish successful businesses (Juana's brother-in-law, Chapter 6). Some of these were established outside the town to avoid the market saturation common in small rural towns.

Missing from the celebratory accounts of remittances and development is the story of how migration contributes to the loss of human and social capital in rural Central Mexico. Migrants transfer their energy, skills, creativity, knowledge and many other talents along with their labor to the United States. While these losses are difficult to quantify, we have heard from women and men throughout this book about the costs of migration in terms of reduced wellbeing of their families. For example, Karina (Chapter 6), a woman whose spouse and children have been in the United States for years, shares her frustration: "[The United States] broke everything up and ruined us. There are many abandoned families, women left by themselves. I have a house, but not a spouse. What's the point of having a house if the family has split up?" If migration promised anything to people in Central Mexico, it promised a better life. Gilda (Chapter 6) directly questions that premise, telling us that Mexico will be "full of human garbage" because "our children are living fantasies." She, like many people we interviewed did not feel as though she or her family had benefited from migration in terms of social mobility or improved wellbeing.

The selective hegemony of poverty administration: the "poor" and "women"

The privatization of social resources in the neoliberal era resulted in the state's abandonment of broad segments of the Mexican population beginning 40 years ago. State withdrawal from social provisions was accompanied by successive selective intervention programs that configured new fragmented subjects, members of a varied sector of "extreme poor" worthy of assistance. In line with the logic of structural adjustment, programs transferred a substantial portion of their costs of operation to their beneficiaries. If eligible, individuals are co-responsible for their progress, but also their failures. These interventions have resulted in the criminalization of the dependent population for their "addiction" to social assistance and for the irrationality of their consumption habits. Program beneficiaries are accused of squandering social wealth that they played no part in generating. Despite these fundamental flaws, state subsidies, along with salaries and remittances, are essential for the reproduction of poor, rural households.

In 2007, the year in which return migration increased substantially, the student scholarships offered by the state program *Oportunidades* (later called *Prospera*), provided 945 pesos (US$87) for each primary and secondary student every other month. In 2013, *Programa 70 y Más* (Program 70 and More) now *Programa Pensión para Adultos Mayores* (Pension Program for Older Adults) began operation, providing a "compensatory pension" for Mexico's elderly population. According to the National Council of the Evaluation of Social Development Policy, this economic support is ten times less than a "regular pension" offered by the state institutions serving salaried employees. These programs reflect the fragmentation in the coverage of social protections (Enciso, 2018).

Taking into consideration the distinction Fraser (1997) makes between redistribution and recognition policies, we argue that the neoliberal programs of social assistance focalized and directed toward the relative surplus population displace the tension between capital and labor toward the division and hostility among employed and unemployed factions of the working class, fueling class fragmentation. In this perverse game, the population most marginalized—rural women specialized in transnationalized, stratified social reproduction and care—is marked as inherently abusive, deficient and insatiable; beneficiaries of an undeserved generosity. This discourse informs both nativist, anti-immigrant attitudes in the United States, and the affronts and insults that circulate in origin communities employed against those in need, turning them into targets of contempt.

There is no direct relation between the expulsion and incorporation of so-called cheap labor in deindustrialized economies. As we have demonstrated in this book, gender is one of the structures that mediates the selectivity of the relative surplus population. To understand how gender shapes a variety of practices, identities and institutions implicated in migratory regimes, it is necessary to overcome the limited analysis of gender at the individual level of the difference between men and women and the statistical register of their unequal participation in migratory flows. From this perspective, we consider gender not only as an individual status that shapes lived experience, but also as a structure that underpins social inequality. Conceiving gender as a structure and not only as an empirical individual attribute permits the recognition of its manifestation in the global restructuring of work and in the selectivity of migration and return.

The feminization of work in tertiary economies and the feminization of migration are processes that have gone hand in hand in many different parts of the world. The incorporation of the much sought-after labor of immigrants in destination countries mitigates the effects of the disarticulation of the Fordist gender assemblage: male-waged worker-provider-head of family/woman-housewife-dependent. Although undesirable for their procreative capacities and their claims on the state for recognition of their children, immigrants from neoliberalized zones, both in the Global North and South, constitute a key piece of the social reproductive circuits that sustain the labor force and that have suffered the onslaught of privatizing policies.

For these new classes of workers, migration and return during the years of the 2007–2009 crisis represent important milestones in migrant workers' oscillating relationship with capital. The experiences documented here through an ethnographic approach, although mediated by particular histories and geographies, account for the forces and tendencies underlying the formation of these new classes of precarious workers.

Notes

1 An earlier version of this argument appeared in D'Aubeterre and Rivermar Pérez (2015).
2 One possible explanation is that men's wages were generally greater than women's "complementary" wages, and, therefore, could be reduced. Women's wages, on the other hand, were, in some cases, already below the legal minimum (Carla's salary at

the nail salon, for example, Chapter 6) and could not be reduced without calling too much attention to the violation of labor law and/or alienating the already pauperized, feminized workforce. One section of the reserve army of labor could be exploited further (men) while the other probably could not be exploited much more without seriously jeopardizing the façade of "free" labor (women). In other words, there was potential for men to experience more net change in salary during the crisis than women.

References

Archer, S. (2013). Cambios de paradigma en el pensamiento feminista de EU. *Mundo Siglo XXI*, *9*(31), 11–26.
Bacon, D. (2013). *The right to stay home: How US policy drives Mexican migration*. Boston: Beacon Press.
Bastia, T. (2011). Should I stay or should I go? Return migration in times of crises. *Journal of International Development*, *23*, 583–595. https://doi.org/10.1002/jid.
BBVA Bancomer & CONAPO. (2019). *Yearbook of migration and remittances*. Retrieved from www.bbvaresearch.com/en/publicaciones/mexico-yearbook-of-migration-and-remittances-2019/.
Bettie, J. (2003). *Women without class: Girls, race, and identity*. Berkeley: University of California Press.
Bhattacharya, T. (2017a). How not to skip class: Social reproduction of labor and the global working class. In T. Bhattacharya (Ed.), *Social reproduction theory: Remapping class, recentering oppression* (pp. 68–93). London: Pluto Press.
Bhattacharya, T. (2017b). Introduction: Mapping social reproduction theory. In T. Bhattacharya (Ed.), *Social reproduction theory: Remapping class, recentering oppression* (pp. 1–20). London: Pluto Press.
Binford, L. (2009). From fields of power to fields of sweat: The dual process of constructing temporary migrant labour in Mexico and Canada. *Third World Quarterly*, *30*(3), 503–517. https://doi.org/10.1080/01436590902742297.
Binford, L. (2013). *Tomorrow we're all going to the harvest: Temporary foreign worker programs and neoliberal political economy*. Austin: University of Texas Press.
Boehm, D. A. (2012). *Intimate migrations: Gender, family, and illegality among transnational Mexicans*. New York: New York University Press.
Canterbury, D. C. (2012). *Capital accumulation and migration*. Leiden: Koninklijke Brill NV.
Carbonella, A., & Kasmir, S. (2014). Introduction: Toward a global anthropology of labor. In A. Carbonella & S. Kasmir (Eds), *Blood and fire: Toward a global anthropology of labor* (pp. 1–29). New York: Berghahn Books.
Carrier, J. G. (2015). The concept of class. In J. G. Carrier & D. Kalb (Eds), *Anthropologies of class: Power, practice and inequality* (pp. 28–40). Cambridge: Cambridge University Press.
Colen, S. (1995). Like a mother to them: Stratified reproduction and West Indian childcare workers and employers in New York. In F. Ginsberg & P. Rapp (Eds), *Conceiving the New World Order: The global politics of reproduction*. Berkeley: University of California Press.
D'Aubeterre, M. E., & Rivermar Pérez, M. L. (2015). *Lo que dejamos atrás, lo que venimos a encontrar. Trabajo precario, nuevos patrones de asentamiento en Estados Unidos y retorno a México*. Puebla: Instituto de Ciencias Sociales y Humanidades, Benemérita Universidad Autónoma de Puebla.

De Genova, N. (2005). *Working the boundaries: Race, space, and "illegality" in Mexican Chicago*. Durham, NC: Duke University Press.

Enciso, A. (2018). Carece de pensión o apoyo económico, 26% de ancianos en el país. Quien cotizó en IMSS o ISSTE recibe $5,564 en promedio al mes; usuarios de programas sociales, sólo $580. *La Jornada*. Retrieved from https://jornada.com.mx/2018/10/15/sociedad/035n2soc

Farris, S. (2019). Social reproduction and racialized surplus populations. In P. Osborne, É. Alliez & E.-J. Russell (Eds), *Capitalism: Concept, idea, image. Aspects of Marx's capital today* (pp. 121–131). London: CRMEP Books.

Fernández-Kelly, M. P., & García, A. (1990). Power surrendered, power restored: The politics of work and family among Hispanic garment workers in California and Florida. In L. Tilly & P. Gurin (Eds), *Women, politics and change* (pp. 130–149). New York: Russell Sage Foundation.

Fiscal Policy Institute. (2009). New York City: A tale of two recessions. Retrieved 15 June 2019 from www.fiscalpolicy.org/FPI_NewYorkCitysTwoRecessions_20091119.pdf.

Fraser, N. (1997). *Justice interruptus. Critical reflections on the "postsocialist" condition*. London: Routledge.

Fraser, N. (2014). Behind Marx's hidden abode: For an expanded conception of capitalism. *New Left Review*, *86*, 55–72.

Fraser, N. (2017). Crises of care? On the social-reproductive contradictions of contemporary capitalism. In T. Bhattacharya (Ed.), *Social reproduction theory, remapping class, recentering oppression* (pp. 19–36). London: Pluto Press.

Glick Schiller, N., & Salazar, N. B. (2013). Regimes of mobility across the globe. *Journal of Ethnic and Migration Studies*, *39*(2). https://doi.org/10.1080/1369183X.2013.723253.

Golash-Boza, T. M. (2009). The immigration industrial complex: Why we enforce immigration policies destined to fail. *Sociology Compass*, *3*(2), 295–309. https://doi.org/10.1111/j.1751-9020.2008.00193.

Goldstein, D., & Alonso-Bejarano, C. (2017). E-terrify: Securitized immigration and biometric surveillance in the workplace. *Human Organization*, *76*(1), 1–14.

Gupta, A., & Ferguson, J. (1992). Beyond "culture": Space, identity, and the politics of difference. *Cultural Anthropology*, *7*(1), 6–23.

Hahamovitch, C. (2003). Creating perfect immigrants: Guestworkers of the world in historical perspective. *Labor History*, *44*(1), 69–94.

Han, B.-C. (2017). *Psychopolitics: Neoliberalism and new technologies of power*. London: Verso.

Harvey, D. (2003). *The new imperialism*. Oxford: Oxford University Press.

Heyman, J. (2001). Class and classification at the U.S.–Mexico border. *Human Organization*, *60*(2), 128–140.

Heyman, J. (2012). Capitalism and US policy at the Mexican border. *Dialectical Anthropology*, *36*(3–4), 263–277. https://doi.org/10.1007/s10624-012-9274-x.

Hondagneu-Sotelo, P. (2007). *Doméstica: Immigrant workers cleaning and caring in the shadows of affluence*. Berkeley: University of California Press.

Kalb, D. (2015). Introduction: Class and the new anthropological holism. In *Anthropologies of class: Power, practice and inequality* (pp. 1–27). Cambridge: Cambridge University Press.

Kearney, M. (2004). The classifying and value filtering missions of borders. *Anthropological Theory*, *4*(2), 131–156.

Kofman, E., & Raghuram, P. (2015). *Gendered migrations and global social reproduction*. https://doi.org/10.1057/9781137510143.
Lefevbre, R. (2011). Book review of Latino immigration to the US South. *Norteamérica*, 6(Num. Esp.), 257–264.
Levine, E. (2015). Why did Mexico United-States migration begin to decrease in 2008? *Problemas del Desarrollo*, 46(182), 1–15.
Luibhéid, E., Andrade, R., & Stevens, S. (2018). Intimate attachments and migrant deportability: Lessons from undocumented mothers seeking benefits for citizen children. *Ethnic and Racial Studies*, 41(1), 17–35.
Narotzky, S., & Smith, G. (2006). *Immediate struggles: People, power and place in rural Spain*. Berkeley: University of California Press.
Oboler, S. (2014). Extraños desechables: Raza e inmigración en la era de la globalización. *Interdisciplina*, 2(4), 75–96.
Oso, L., & Ribas-Mateos, N. (2013). An introduction to a global and development perspective: A focus on gender, migration and transnationalism. In L. Oso & N. Ribas-Mateos (Eds), *The international handbook on gender, migration and transnationalism* (pp. 1–35). https://doi.org/10.4337/9781781951477.
Parreñas, R. S. (2001). *Servants of globalization: Women, migration and domestic work* (p. 309). Stanford: Stanford University Press.
Rothstein, F. A. (2016). *Mexicans on the move: Migration and return in rural Mexico*. https://doi.org/10.1057/9781137559944.0001.
Sabo, S., & Lee, A. E. (2015). The spillover of US immigration policy on citizens and permanent residents of Mexican descent: How internalizing "illegality" impacts public health in the borderlands. *Frontiers in Public Health*, 3(June), 1–9. https://doi.org/10.3389/fpubh.2015.00155.
Sider, G. (2006). The production of race, locality, and state: An anthropology. *Antropologica*, 48(2), 247–263.
Smith, B. E., & Winders, J. (2007). We're here to stay: Economic restructuring, Latino migration and place-making in the South. *Transactions of the Institute of Brithish Geographers*, 33, 60–72.
Smith, G. (2015). Through a class darkly, but then face to face: Praxis through the lens of class. In J. Carrier & D. Kalb (Eds), *Anthropologies of class: Power, practice, and inequality* (pp. 72–88). Cambridge: Cambridge University Press.
Verschuur, C. (2013). Theoretical debates on social reproduction and care: The articulation between the domestic and the global economy. In L. Oso & N. Ribas-Mateos (Eds), *The international handbook on gender, migration and transnationalism: Global and development perspectives* (pp. 145–161). https://doi.org/10.4337/9781781951477.
Villarreal, A. (2014). Explaining the decline in Mexico-US migration: The effect of the Great Recession. *Demography*, 51(6), 2203–2228. https://doi.org/10.1007/s13524-014-0351-4.
Waldinger, R., & Lichter, M. (2003). *How the other half works: Immigration and the social organization of labor*. Berkeley: University of California Press.
Wolf, E. R. (1982). *Europe and the people without history*. Berkeley: University of California Press.

Index

Abrego, L. 93, 151
Adela 116
Adriana 67–8, 70, 111–12, 162
agriculture: agribusiness 27, 161; cash crops 29; disarticulation of 60; intensive areas of 31; small scale 26; subsistence 27, 60, 84
Alarcón, R. 62, 63, 128
Aleida 71–3, 156
Alonso-Bejarano, C. 45, 104, 165
Amanda 76–8
Amorós, C. 10, 13, 88
AMUCSS Mexican Association of Credit Unions for the Social Sector 62
Andrade, R. 159
Andreas P. 44
Appendini, K. 26
Archer, S. 9, 13, 158
Arias, P. 13
Arizpe, L. 30
Arroyo, J. 3, 26, 41, 45, 108
Assusa, G. 75
Avila, E. 65, 99, 127, 137, 143–4
Ayala, E. 152
Aysa, M. 43
Azúcar S.A. Sugar Co. 26

Bacon, D. 86
BANRURAL 26
Barrios, M. 6, 7
Basch, L. 6–7
Bastia, T. 12, 116, 164
BBVA Bancomer 2, 3, 26, 166
Beatriz 40, 98–100, 101–2, 139–41, 145–6, 148–51, 156, 163
Berumen, S. 3, 26, 108
Bettie, J.R. 11, 61, 97, 159, 160
Bhattacharya, T. 5, 112, 113, 114, 115, 126, 130, 157, 165, 170

Bickman, J. 80
Binford, L. 3, 7, 21, 27, 52–3, 63, 74, 80, 89, 92, 105, 124, 152, 158
Blanc-Szanton, C. 7
Boehm, D.A. 6, 45, 141, 143, 145, 165
Bolter, J. 45
border: Border Patrol 4, 44, 90, 141; clandestine crossings 4, 44, 134, 150; enforcement 3, 35, 44, 54, 102, 128; militarization 1, 3, 22, 44, 53, 56, 58, 90, 102, 106, 132, 154; porosity 4, 44; risks and costs of clandestine crossing 1, 44, 63, 65, 68, 98–9, 115, 120, 140–1; *see also* immigration policies
Bourdieu, P. 88, 151
Bourgois, P. 2, 39, 40, 41
Bracero Program (1942–1964) 3, 11, 15, 52, 63, 65, 103; agriculture of the U.S. Southwest 36, 63; *Braceros* 86
Bustamante, J. 19n2

Cachón, L. 43
Calavita, K. 43
Calderón, G. 26
Caldwell, B.C. 6, 45
California: agricultural fields in 32; pahuatecos workers in 64
Canterbury, D.C. 6, 7, 37, 62, 80, 113, 14, 116, 130, 161, 162
Cantor, G. 90
capital: financial 101–2; financial capital and migration 62; hyper-mobility 8
capital accumulation: by dispossession 7, 28, 60, 66, 112; flexible 7, 35, 71, 99, 158–9; Fordist 7, 61, 158; level of 116, 162; and migration 6, 156; new schemes 78; and reclassification of the population 7, 11, 165
Capoferro, C. 35, 53

Carbonella, A. 8, 9, 10, 11, 97, 105, 112, 160
care *see* social reproduction
Carla 135, 136–9, 145–50, 152–6
Carolina 87–8, 96–8, 100–2, 163
Carton, H. 27
Cassarino, J. 5, 6
Castañeda, X. 5, 69
Castellón, B.R. 32
Central America: immigrant labor from 2, 17
Central Mexico 1, 29; international migrants from 2, 25; rural 25
Chavez, L. 4, 45
Chew, G.L. 152
Chin, M. 39, 103
Chishti, M. 45
Cilluffo, A. 42
citizenship 18, 45, 46, 63, 159: illegibility 10; and recognition of noncitizen children 168; and recognition of U.S.-born children 71, 74, 76, 79, 115, 127, 159
class: as analytical category 9; androcentric bias of 11; classes of owners 31; confrontations of 74–5, 161; contradictory experiences of 10, 60, 160; contradictory mobility of 10; and cultural turn 9; de-classed 9; differentiated life standard and habits by 114; diffuse profiles of 9; disappearance of 9; disorganized class formation 9, 10; and gender 1, 3, 6, 8, 18, 61, 97, 112, 128, 162; and gender, sexuality, race, ethnicity 7, 11, 61, 157; formation 2, 7; hyper-masculinization of category 11, 159; inequalities of 111; instability of 61; make, unmake and remake of 37; malleability of 10, 61; new working classes 36, 88, 162; segmentation of working 11, 41, 79, 110, 112, 158, 165; subaltern sectors 31; upward mobility of 75, 116, 121, 161, 167; working 5, 18, 156; *see also* proletariat
Cobo, R. 67, 13
coffee: commercialization of 30; and family labor 30; as force that retains populations 65; and international migration 60, 62, 64; and loss of viability 60, 62, 64; and Pahuatlán economy 29–30, 64; and price oscillation of 64; and specialization 30; and state-subsidized production 26, 30, 64; and vulnerability of production 30, 64; *see also* INMECAFE Mexican National Coffee Institute
Cohn, D. 1, 41, 113
Coleman, M. 51
Comaroff, J. 8
Comaroff, J.L. 8
Comas, D. 77
CONAPO Consejo Nacional de Población 2, 3, 26
Connell, R.W. 13
Cook, S. 7
construction 161; and loss of jobs 108, 110, 128, 164; and mobility within U.S. South 78; Pahuatecan workers in 46, 65, 77, 117; as seasonal work 125; subcontracting in 110, 123; Zapotitecan workers in 91, 135, 148
CoreLogic 42
Cordero, B.L. 93
Cornelius, W.A. 4, 44
Council for Community and Economic Research 50
Cravey, A.J. 13, 37, 38, 68, 69, 74, 113
crisis: economic and financial (2007–2009) 26, 42, 77, 112, 117, 126, 128, 156, 168; devaluation of the mexican peso (1994) 17, 64, 90; Mexican oil crisis (1982) 86; and shadow banking system 42; and toxic financial instruments 42; *see also* Great Recession
Cruz, R. 128

D'Aubeterre, M.E. 68
Dávila, A. 103
David 117–19
Davids, T. 19n4
Davis, A. 88
Deeb-Sossa, N. 70
debt: external 25; personal 35, 67, 73, 111, 136, 147, 152n13
De Genova, N.P. 4, 43, 61–3, 102, 145, 157–8, 165
De León, J. 29, 44
Delgado, R. 6
deindustrialization: of the US economy 25, 36, 158; *see also* New York; North Carolina
Department of Homeland Security 51
deportability 4, 158
deportation 1, 44, 116, 159; apprehensions 4; exclusion 51n8; and fear 10; removals 44; and uncertainty 10; *see also* immigration policies; return migration

development 6; *see also* remittances
Diana 121
Dilts, A. 101
disposability: of migrant workers 4, 7, 17, 100, 160; *see* Great Recession
Divjan, A. 152
domestic work *see* reproductive work
domestic workers 87–8, 93, 94, 96, 142
Dow, J. 32
Dreby, J. 141, 144
Dunn, T.J. 44
Durand, J. 3, 35, 63
Durham County 37, 109, 117; Hispanic migrants in 37
Durin, S. 88, 152

Echeverri, M.M. 61
Ehrenreich, B. 14, 94, 145
El Informador & Interdenominational Newspaper 51
Elena 73–5, 117, 125–7, 159, 162–3
Enciso, A. 167
Ernesto 1
Escobar, M. 86
Espenshade, T. 4, 44
esquinero (day laborer) 94
ethnographic research 2, 14, 163; fieldwork in Mexico 14–15, 119–20; fieldwork in United States 15–16, 110, 115; historical ethnography 10
Eva 91–3
Ewald, U. 32

family: binational 70, 111, 117, 159, 165; conflicts and violence 12, 72, 75, 125, 140, 143, 148; f. formation 66, 79; mixed-status 136, 139–40, 151; reunification of (in US) 13, 65–6, 72, 74; separation of 92, 143–4, 145, 165, 167; *see also* household; return migration
Farris, S.R. 109, 112, 114, 126, 128, 149, 164
Federal Reserve Bank of St. Louis 42
Federici, S. 7, 11, 41
feminisms: African-American 11; Critical Feminist Theory 12; Structural theories 12
feminization: of craft production 119; of labor 86–7, 128; of migration 13, 90, 158, 144; of service economy 91, 99–100, 126; of work 13, 158; *see also* migration; social reproduction
Ferguson, J. 157

FIRE Finance, Insurance, Real Estate 36, 39, 41
Fernández-Kelly, M.P. 86, 92, 104, 160
Fiscal Policy Institute 164
Fitting, E. 25, 26, 27, 118
Flippen, C.A. 37, 38, 69, 72
Flores, A.L. 77, 86
Flores, J. 63
Flores, M.L. 108, 119, 120
Foner, N. 39
Foucault, M. 101
Fraser, N. 5, 7, 12, 13, 76, 79, 157, 159
Friedman, J. 36
Fuentes, A. 27
Furuseth, O.J. 37, 38, 66

Gabaccia, D. 145
Galinier, J. 29, 32
Gálvez, A. 103
Gandini, L. 6, 42
García, A. 160
García, B. 29
Garfinkel, R.S. 152
garment factories 17; gendered norms 86–7; industrial homeworkers 87, 91; in New York 39, 92; in Tehuacán 86; in Zapotitlán 86–7, 98, 137
GATT General Agreement on Tariffs and Trade 26
gender: and first migration 46–8; hyper-feminization of the category of 11, 159; as individual attribute 12–13, 108; intersectionality 12; and labor markets 13; and migration 12, 46; relations 5; and return migration 48, 148–9, 164–5; as structural element of migration 156; as structure 12; violence 12, 41; *see also* class; feminization; household
Gil, S. 61
Gilda 89, 93–5, 100–2, 141–6, 149–51, 156, 159, 160, 163, 167
Gill, H. 110
Gjokaj, L. 12
Glaeser, E.L. 39
Glenn, E.N. 39
Glick-Schiller, N. 6, 7, 156
globalization: process 61; and state support 8
Golash-Boza, T.M. 44, 45, 157
Goldring, L. 17
Goldstein, D. 45, 104, 165
Gonzales, R.G. 45
González, E. 40
Gonzalez-Barrera, A. 1, 41, 42, 44

González-König, G. 128
Goode, J. 97, 103, 104
Great Recession 18, 132, 136, 138, 147, 156, 161, 164–5; and anti-immigrant hostility 1; and decrease in wages 128; and decrease of Latino employment 43; and inequality between segments of class 42; and loss of jobs 42, 108, 111, 125, 134–5, 136; reduction of state expenses 116; uneven impacts on labor markets 108, 148–9, 164–5; *see also* return migration
Green, L. 60
Griesbach, K.A. 36, 64, 110
Griffith, D. 26, 35
Guilhem, O. 29
Gupta, A. 157

Hahamovitch, C. 43, 63, 114, 163
Hamann, E.T. 6
Han, B.-C. 101, 160
Harvey, D. 25, 26, 36
hegemony: expansive 27; selective 27, 35, 118, 167
Hernández Navarro, L. 25, 30
Hernández-León, R. 3
Herrera, F. 63
Heyman, J. 4, 44–5, 157
Hidalgo: Hidalguense Plateau 29; Pachuca 29; Tulancingo, regional market 29
Hirsch, J.S. 16
Hirschman, C. 35
Historical realism 2
Hochschild, A.R. 14, 87, 94, 145
Holdaway, J. 145
Holmes, S.M. 152
Hondagneu-Sotelo, P. 11–13, 61, 65, 99, 127, 137, 143–4, 158
Horton, S.B. 152
household: binational domestic arrangement 17, 62, 65–6, 99, 112, 139, 141, 162; complementary incomes 35, 86–7, 88; composition 66, 72, 76; demographic cycle 5, 13, 70, 77, 124, 128, 145, 149–50; diversifying economic activities 27, 62, 87–8; and division of labor 14, 128, 164; double-provider 76, 128; instability and uncertainty 65; long distance maternity 127, 144; males-only 38, 61, 69, 113, 120; of Pahuatecans in Durham 115, 125; with school-age children 115; single-family 38; transnational 162; undocumented children in US 62, 66, 70

Iglesias, N. 86
illegal: "aliens" 4, 44, 91; as criminalized category 45, 157, 159; subjects 102; workers 14, 91, 160, 165
illegality 4, 45, 95, 100–2, 128, 138, 141, 145, 151, 158, 165
illegalization 116
IMF International Monetary Fund 86; *see also* debt
immigrant analogy 95–6
immigration policies: Guestworker Programs 37, 63; H2 visas 127; heightened interior enforcement 3, 35, 44–5, 51n6, 90, 161; Immigration and Naturalization Act (1965) 39, 44; IRCA (Immigration Reform and Control Act 1986) 4, 43–5, 90, 158; IIRIRA (Illegal Immigration Reform and Individual Responsibility Act 1996) 44; Johnson-Reed Immigration Act (1924) (quota system) 39; and racism 76; and reproduction of cheap labor 45, 101–2, 110; securitization of immigration 44; selectivity of immigration 43, 287 (g) Program 51n6
indigenous populations: Nahuas 29; in North Carolina 76; Otomíes 29
INEGI Instituto Nacional de Geografía y Estadística 31, 34
Informador, E., & Interdenominational Newspaper 51
INMECAFE Mexican National Coffee Institute 26, 30, 64
International Coffee Organization Agreement 30
International Monetary Fund 25
ixtle (agave fibers) 32, 84
Izcara, S.P. 38
Izquierdo, A. 128

Jiménez, C. 75
Johnson, J.H. 37
Juana 132–3, 146–8
Julia 111, 116, 156
Juliano, D. 69, 73
Jung, K.H. 152
Jusionyte, I. 44

Kalb, D. 9, 10, 61, 163
Kalleberg, A. L 42
Karina 132, 133, 150, 167
Kasmir, S. 8, 9, 11, 97, 112, 160
Kasarda, J.D. 37
Kearney, M. 157

Kim, D.Y. 104
Kofman, E. 5, 7, 8, 10, 12–14, 37, 61, 109, 164
Kochhar, R. 42, 46

labor: affective 94, 100; as commodity 123; female wage 71; feminization of 76, 163, 165; global division 9; and kinship 160; liberalization of rural 2, 26; neoliberal organization of 71; part-time 14, 73, 75, 126, 159; peons 29, 30; precarious 67, 71–2, 158; rights 151n6; sexual division of 14; supply from Central Mexico 60, 62; supply to US economy 25, 63, 117; surplus 25–7; waged and unwaged 5, 96–7, 100–1, 160; *see also* illegality; mobility
labor markets: competition between workers 135; deregulated 14, 61; in North Carolina 37; of refuge 73; in the US East Coast 2, 157; *see also* feminization
Lara Flores, S. 27
Lara, G. 35
Laurita 124–5
Leach, B. 8, 9, 11, 60
LeBaron, A. 26, 36, 37, 60, 64
LeCompte, M.D. 15
Lee, A.E. 1, 14, 15, 29, 33, 34, 44, 62, 85, 90, 108, 134, 140, 147, 151, 152, 165
Lee-Treweek, G. 14
Lefevbre, R. 160
Lem, W. 118
Levine, E. 1, 26, 36, 77, 42–3, 50, 60, 64, 164
Lichter, M. 92, 161
Livestock, and Zapotitlán economy 32–3, 84
López, G. 19
López, R. 152
Lozano-Ascencio, F. 6, 42
Lucía 68–70, 75–6, 156, 159–60
Luibhéid, E. 159
Luisa 126
Lydgate, J. 44

Macías, S. 63
Macip, R.F. 30, 34, 64, 147
male: as independent migrant 63, 124, 138; as masculinized class subject 61; as worker/producer/breadwinner/head of household 9, 61, 63; *see also* household
Malone, N. 3
Manalansan, M. 145

manufacturing and industry (Mexico) 32, 34
maquiladoras: Border Industrial Program 86; expansion beyond border region 86
Marchand, M.H. 14
Marco Antonio 1
Marcus, G.E. 14
María 87, 93
Marina 127
Marroni, M.G. 63
Martínez C., L.A. 86
Martínez, D.E. 29
Martínez, D.T
Martínez-Reyes, J.E. 34, 147
Martínez-Schuldt, R. 44
Márquez, H. 6
Marx, K. 61
Massey, D. 3, 35, 63
Maskovsky, J. 97, 103, 104
Medicare *see* public assistance
Mestries, F. 6, 122
Mexican Migration Project 15, 46
Mexico City 29; internal migration to 88
Mezzadra, S. 8, 14, 37, 60–2
migration: and abandonment of school trajectories 95; accelerated 1–4, 25, 46, 60–4, 70, 79, 89, 158; and accumulation pattern 2, 4; below zero 41, 166; and changing socio-demographic profile 3, 4, 90; circuits Sierra Norte de Puebla-South of Texas-North Carolina 32, 68; class and gender 156; criminalization of 4, 43–5, 95, 134, 143; deceleration of migration 108–9; decline of circular m. Mexico-US 62, 65, 90, 134, 159; decline of first 41, 46–8; and deindustrialization of US economy 16, 42, 128; family 115, 138; first international migration 46, 90; as "gendered process" 12; habitus of 15; interethnic networks 67, 70; massive 64; migrant as "perfect worker" 79, 124; net zero 1; new geography of Mexican 35, 61; peak of first 46; otomí 32; post-IRCA 45; sacrifice and upward mobility 77, 89, 93, 98, 111, 123, 142–4, 151, 165; selectivity of m. by class and gender 12–13, 30, 63, 156, 159, 168; short-cycle 26, 60; unaccompanied single women or with dependents 61, 96, 139, 141, 159; under-registration of women 11; undocumented 2, 4, 64; to US East Coast 35; and US migratory policies 42; young couples with or without children 159; women's moral

redemption 68, 98, 139; *see also* Central Mexico; family; mobility; New York; *Nuevo* New South; social reproduction
migration perspectives: feminist geography 13; historical-structural 4, 7; human and social capital 6, 150; methodological nationalism 133, 156; neoclassical 4–5, 150; social network 4–5; transnationalism 6
migratory order, new global 7, 8, 159
migratory patterns 1, 4, 13; circular 4, 19, 44, 61; military model 17, 61, 65, 69–71, 79, 115, 138; seasonal 30, 63; settlement 45, 61, 159
Miller, P. 100
Minchin, T.J. 36, 66
Mintz, S. 29
mobility: and driver's license 78, 110, 165; and English language ability 78; unequal 13
Moctezuma, M. 120, 128
Mohl, R.A. 36–7, 60, 64
Mollona, M. 61, 79
Molyneux, M. 118
mothers *see* migration, women
Mouat, A.C. 32
mules: agricultural goods transported by 29; *arrieros* 32
Mummert, G. 13, 19, 65
Myhre, D. 26

NAFTA North American Free Trade Agreement 4, 25–7
Narotzky, S. 8, 10, 61, 159
National Council of the Evaluation of Social Development Policy 167
Nawyn, S.J. 12, 13
Neilson, B. 8, 14, 37, 60, 62
Nevins, J. 44
neoliberalism: and multiculturalism 12; and structural adjustment policies 3, 8, 16, 25–7, 30, 34, 65, 78, 118, 156, 158, 166–7; *see also* GATT; labor; NAFTA
neoliberalization 164
New York City 17, 165; deindustrialization in 39; ethnic diversity in 39; expansion of industry in 39; FIRE economy in 39; as a global center of trade, finance and services 38–9; and historical flows of immigrants 39; and interethnic conflicts 40–1; Korean employers 99–100, 103n7, 104n14; Mexicans migrants in 25, 40, 164; *see also* garment factories
Ngai, M. 39, 43

Nir, S.M. 151
Noferi, M. 90
Nolasco, M. 30
North American Free Trade Agreement (NAFTA) 4, 25–7
North Carolina 17, 67, 110, 117, 165; Durham-Raleigh-Charlotte corridor 25, 36, 113, 162; Hispanic populations in 37; Mexican migrants in 65–6; Orange County 38, 72, 109; Raleigh County 71; Wilmington 116
Nuevo New South 17, 108; deindustrialization of the 36–7; formerly the Old South 37; internal migration in 62; Mexican and Central Americans migrants in 36; New Latino South 38, 78

Oboler, S. 159
onyx (travertine): decline of industry 33, 85, 158; electricity subsidies 33, 85; and international migration 85, 89–90; quarries 85; and remittances 33; social differentiation 85; workshops 33, 85; and Zapotitlán economy 33, 85
Ong, A. 104
Ordóñez, J.T. 103
Oso, L. 7, 10, 11, 13, 61, 158
Otero, G. 26, 27

Pahuatlán 26, 67, 110, 156, 163, 164, 166; Atla 29, 116; craft production in 31, 61, 119, 121; Municipality of Pahuatlán 29–30, 62–3, 109, 128; Pahuatlán de Valle 29; San Pablito Pahuatlán 15, 29, 32, 38, 67–8, 71–2, 77, 119, 121, 126; Xolotla 29, 121; *see also* coffee; migration; peanuts; piloncillo; return migration; sugar cane
Pardo, S. 19
Parrado, E.A. 37, 38, 69, 72
Parreñas, R. 127, 145, 164
Pascual de Sans, Á. 6, 109
Passel, J.S. 1, 41, 43, 66, 113
peanuts: production in Pahuatlán 118
Peasant 25; families 27; subsistence producers 26; *see also* agriculture
Pedone, C. 61
Perry, M.J. 152
Perzanowski, M.S. 152
Pessar, P. 14, 145
Peutz, N. 62, 63
Pew Hispanic Center 4, 66
Pierce, S. 45

piloncillo (brown sugar) 64; hoarders and intermediaries 30; labor conditions 29–30; and Pahuatlán economy 29, 30; price oscillation of 30; specialization 30; vulnerability of 30
Pini, B. 8, 9, 60
Popke, J. 36, 37, 64
poverty: and living wage (U.S.) 135; subsidies (Mexico) 140, 144, 147, 167–8
Preibisch, K. 27
primary sector: in Pahuatlán 31; in Zapotitlán 34
privatization 25, 28; of the provision of care 14; services 166; social resources 167; water 27
production: decentralization of the productive processes 71; *see also* agriculture
production chains 13; relocalization of 7
PROGRESA Program for Education, Health and Nutrition (later Oportunidades) 167
proletariat: heterogeneous 9, 158, 160; new global p. 2, 8, 32, 78
PRONASOL National Program of Solidarity 26
public assistance (US): and dismantling of welfare state 97; public health care (Medicare) 116, 136–7; WIC Women, Infant and Children 116
Puebla (state): Atlixco 63; Mixteca 32, 63; Northern Sierra of Puebla 2, 17, 29–30, 60, 108–9; Tecali de Herrera 33; Xicotepec de Juárez (Villa Juárez) 31
Pujadas J.J. 77

race 8–11, 112, 114; hierarchies of 66
racism: conflicts 40–1; horizontal 161
recognition: versus redistribution 12; struggles 12
Raghuram, P. 5, 7, 8, 10, 12, 13, 37, 61, 109, 164
Ramírez-Velázquez, B.R. 26
Ramiro 120
Rauh, V.A. 152
Raúl 123–4, 166
Reichert, J. 89
remittances 62, 110, 137, 146; as basic subsistence 140, 166; and consumption 33, 35, 117; decrease of 1, 117; and development 167; and education 96, 121, 123; and financialization of rural life 166; and the Great Recession 111; and poverty 166; and productive investments 122, 166; as savings for retirement 75, 163; and social reproduction 132; as symptom of dependency 89, 144, 147–8, 149–51; and women 73, 75
Reosti, A. 12
reproduction *see* social reproduction
reproductive work: commodification of (paid domestic work) 66, 149, 164; unpaid domestic work 67
return migration 1, 18, 46, 133; criminalization of return migrants 121; and crises in social reproduction 110, 156; and the cycle of reproduction of capital 5; and destabilization of reproductive conditions 109, 162; and dual frame of reference 91, 114, 161; and financial crisis (2007–2009) 5, 17, 26, 112, 122, 125, 134–5, 148–9, 156, 164–5; and health 134, 136–8; increase of 1, 4, 41; of independent migrant 18, 120, 122; of family group 18, 115, 120, 122, 136, 138, 149, 163, 164; and net social security rate 113, 116, 150–1, 162; and oscillating relationship between work and capital 6, 17, 163; in Pahuatlán 48–50; as personal economic failure 93, 123, 134; rate of staying in US by gender 50; rate of staying in US by region 50; re-emigration to U.S. 119–21, 123–7, 141, 163, 164; and reinsertion 3, 6, 123–4, 136, 138, 140–4; reinsertion 119, 136, 138, 166; and reinsertion in handicraft production 121–2; reinstatement in a new social space 119, 122; and relocation in social space 109, 119; and reunification of family in Mexico 134; of segmented family 122, 124; selectivity of staying-return 5, 18, 50, 70, 108, 111–15, 117, 128, 148, 162, 164; and surplus population 122; and social reproduction crisis 18; and tyranny of the exchange rate 114, 161; of unified family 122–3; and US immigration policies 5, 18; in Zapotitlán 48–50; *see also* household; Great Recession
Ribas-Mateos, N. 7, 10, 11, 13, 61, 158
Ridder, R. 152
Rivera, L. 3, 103, 109, 124
Rivera-Batiz, F. 104
Rivera-Salgado, G. 6, 42
Rivermar, M.L. 68, 77
Roberto 110

Rodríguez, H. 6
Rodríguez-Álvarez, D. 3, 26, 52, 108
Rose, N. 100
Roseberry, W. 31
Rothstein, F.A. 6, 43, 86, 108, 164
Rubio, B. 26, 27
Runyan, A.S. 14
rural populations: in Central Mexico 2, 156; and disarticulation of social reproduction 8, 60; as extreme poor 167; new liberal rural subject 118; as surplus labor 60, 61
Rus, J. 30
Ruvalcaba Mercado, J. 29

Sabo, S. 165
Saksena, M. 152
Salazar, N.B. 133, 156
salt 32, 33, 84
Samuel 64, 114–15
Sánchez Korrol, V. 39
Sandoval, R. 3, 4, 5, 26, 108
Santiago, R. 86
Sassen, S. 10, 13, 36, 39, 40, 61
Schiller, N.G. 6, 7, 133, 156
Schonberg, J. 2
Schensul, J.J. 15
Secondary sector: in Pahuatlán 31; in Zapotitlán 34
Secretaría de Economía 51, 57
Secretaría de Turismo 129, 131
SEDESOL Secretaría de Desarrollo Social 29
Semple, K. 106
Sennett, R. 9
service economy 14, 78, 161, 164; expansion of 14, 158; loss of jobs in 108, 164; and Pahuatecan women in North Carolina 46, 65, 71, 128; in Pahuatlán 31; transition to s.e. in rural Mexico 27, 31, 33, 34, 60, 118, 146–7; and Zapotiteco/as in New York 19, 46, 91, 99, 137, 142; in Zapotitlán 34, 146–7; *see also* feminization; labor
Sider, G. 29, 79, 132, 150, 166
Silver, B. 37
Silvey, R. 12
Skeggs, B. 40, 69
Slack, J.. 29, 44, 90
Smith, B.E. 13, 37, 72, 79, 159
Smith, G.A. 2, 6, 8, 9, 10, 27, 35, 61, 75, 159, 163
Smith, H.A. 37, 8, 66
Smith, R.C. 3, 19, 40, 63, 95, 103, 104

social reproduction: and capital accumulation 5, 108; circuits of 159, 163; conditions of 111, 165; and crisis tendency 108, 165; destabilization of 5, 17; and gender, race and migratory status 114, 162; global reorganization of 94, 108–9, 149; and governmental support 18, 74, 76, 114; of immigrants families 101; of labor-power 112–13, 123, 125, 133, 156; and market 114; and production 100, 112, 128, 159; re-localized 62; of rural populations 166; stratified 62, 66–7, 71, 160, 165; theory 128; transfer of costs of 73; of workers and their families 5, 61, 101, 126, 156, 165
Soto, S. 152
Stephen, L. 71
Steusse, A. 152
Stevens, S. 159
Stresser-Peán, G. 29
Suárez-Orozco, M.M. 35
sugar cane 64; commercialization of 30; loss of viability 30, 60; and Pahuatlán economy 29–30; vulnerability of 30
super-exploitation 14, 74, 160
surplus population 8, 66; and economic crisis 112; from Central Mexico 157; industrial reserve army 148, 164, 169n2; racialized 164; as subsidy to capital 113

TABAMEX 26
Tang, D. 152
Tehuacán: regional market 32–3; *see also* garment factories
Tehuacán-Cuicatlán Biosphere Reserve 34, 147
tertiary sector: in Pahuatlán 31; in Zapotitlán 34
Tett, G. 42
Texas: agro-business area 32; Pahuatecan migrants in 38, 65; poultry and dairy ranches 32, 68, 72
Thompson, E.P. 10
tobacco: in North Carolina 68; Pahuatecos and Otomíes workers in 68
Todd, J.E. 152
Torres-Mazuera, G. 27
tourism 18, 147; cultural tourism 34; and decrease of remittances 119; landscape and culture as commodities 119, 147; *Pueblos Mágicos* in Pahuatlán 118, 122
transnationalism *see* migration perspectives

Trouillot, M.R. 29
Truong, T.D. 94

Ursula 136–9, 146, 148–50, 152, 159, 163, 166
US Bureau of Labor Statistics 42
US Census Bureau 42
US Department of Labor 42
US East Coast: economic restructuring of 15, 35, 64, 158
US South 66–7

van der Linden, M. 9
van Houte, M. 19
Velasco, P. 27
Velásquez, L.I. 31, 58
Vélez-Ibañez, C.G. 35
Veracruz 64
Verschuur, C. 12, 13, 48, 108, 109, 128, 158
Vertovec, S. 6
Villarreal, A. 1, 43, 164
Von Wachter, T.M. 42

wages: low 97, 101, 111, 116, 140, 158, 164; piece rate 30, 73, 85, 143
Waldinger, R. 92, 161
welfare state 61, 108, 116; dismantling of 61
Whiteford, S. 29, 44, 90
Wiest, R.E. 89
Wilson, T.D. 45
Williams, F. 109
Winders, J. 13, 37, 72, 79, 159
Wolf, E.R. 5, 9, 29, 30, 157
women: as administrator of remittances and resources 12, 126; as breadwinners 72, 67, 79, 96, 115, 127; as bridgehead 67–8; and daily struggles 79, 115, 145, 149, 157, 159; empowerment of 18; and experience of class 11; as good and sacrificing mothers 71, 75–6, 99; as head of household 78; as hyper mobile workers 72–3, 127, 157; as hyper-visible migrant workers 79; as illegal subjects 17; as migrant subject 11, 12, 68, 70; migration and deindustrialization of US 7, 61; as mothers of US citizens 160; mothers with older children 48, 74, 111, 127, 145; mothers with preschool children 48, 100, 117, 126, 136, 139, 149, 162, 163; as mother-worker-undocumented subject 17, 62, 71, 79, 159–60; as object of persecution and deportations 79; Otomí workers in Texas 68; Pahuatecas in Mexico City 67, 76; as precarious workers 70, 74, 79; as reproducer and dependent 12, 61, 63, 146; respectable 40, 69; as reunified wives 11; salaries as complementary income 14, 86–7, 124, 163; single 4, 67, 69; as single and free workers 73; single mothers 98; as surplus population of Global South 36; as suspicious migrants 69; as transnational mothers 99, 143; as uterus/containers of citizens 71; as working class 11; "working like a man" 94, 97, 101
Woo, O. 108, 119, 120
workers: affirming moral worth as 95–6; and disciplinary power 101–2; and English skills 99–100; flexible 8, 14, 73, 87–8, 100, 158, 159–60, 163; global 9; "hard-working" as disciplinary trope 93, 96, 97, 101–2; informal 64; self-exploitation 95, 97, 101–2, 142, 144; self-optimization 96, 99, 101–2; skilled 36–7; and struggles against capital 102, 160–1; unskilled workers 11, 36, 43, 95, 104n13, 104n14, 158–9; unwaged workers 9, 76, 96–7; waged workers 9; *see also* labor
World Bank 34
World Coffee Organization 30
Wright, M.W. 7, 13, 92–3

Yarris, K.E. 145, 152
Yeates, N. 94
Yrizar, G. 128

Zamora, C. 34
Zapotitlán Salinas 17, 26, 32, 156, 158, 163–4, 166
Zavella, P. 14, 69
Zenteno, R. 128
Zúñiga, V. 3, 4, 5, 6